GREAT CENTRAL SIGNALMAN

P. J. Wortley grew up in the Fens, but an interest in the Great Central followed a move to Rugby in 1964. A further move to Yorkshire allowed a model of Rugby Central to be considered, and research led to the receipt of signal box diagrams for the station from Iain Mackenzie, a former signalman. Subsequently Mr Mackenzie's signalling memoirs of Rugby and Braunston & Willoughby came to hand, which, together with his diagrams and explanations, provided the catalyst for this book.

Great Central Signalman

One man's passion for signalling in the 1940s and '50s

Iain Mackenzie
compiled by P. J. Wortley

• RAILWAY HERITAGE •
from
The NOSTALGIA Collection

First published in 2005

British Library Cataloguing in Publication Data

A catalogue record for this book is available from the British Library.

ISBN 1 85794 234 5

Silver Link Publishing Ltd
The Trundle
Ringstead Road
Great Addington
Kettering
Northants NN14 4BW

Tel/Fax: 01536 330588
email: sales@nostalgiacollection.com
Website: www.nostalgiacollection.com

Printed and bound in Great Britain

ACKNOWLEDGEMENTS

I would like to thank Iain Mackenzie for drawing all the signal box diagrams, his photographs, memories, notes, and explanations, and the help received from M. Back over many years; the Main Line Steam Trust and GCR Plc, Loughborough; B. Stephens for his help and encouragement; A. Franklin, M. Mitchell, D. Bullock and D. Caplan for their help with photographs, and also those unknown people whose photographs have entered collections over the years; the members of the Willoughby Society; Will Adams, editor, Silver Link Publishing Ltd, for all his help; and a big thank you to the railways as they once were, and the people who made them work.

FURTHER INFORMATION

For further information and explanations of the GCR and railway signalling the following websites are well worth accessing:

www.railwayarchive.org.uk – 'The Last Main Line' (The Record Office for Leicestershire, Leicester & Rutland)

www.signalbox.org.uk – a large site on signalling and signal boxes in this country

Publications:

Lewis *Railway Signal Engineering (Mechanical)* (1935, reprinted by P. Kay): a fascinating in-depth and well-illustrated book that every enthusiast should have

Nock, O. S. *Fifty Years of Railway Signalling* (ISRE 1962, reprinted by P. Kay): details of A. F. Bounds's papers and involvement in the Institution of Railway Signal Engineers

Both books can be purchased from Camden Miniature Steam Services, Barrow Farm, Rode, Nr Frome, Somerset BA11 6PS. Tel 01373 830151

Contents

Glossary

Back 'un	Distant signal
Board	Signal arm
Bobby	Signalman, from the original policeman of early railways
Box	Signal box
Cabin	Signal box
Cess	The lineside between the top of an embankment, or the bottom of a cutting, and the running line
Crow	A sequence of five locomotive whistle blasts similar to a cock's crow
Clanger wagon	Breakdown train
Dolly	LNER ground signal
Dummy	LMS and SR ground signal
Four-foot	The gauge or distance between the rails
Hard hat	An Inspector or other official, as they mostly wore bowler hats
On the dirt	Derailed
On Mother England	Derailed
Ord	GCR stopping passenger train
Running line	Tracks for through train movements, as opposed to sidings, refuge sidings, loops, etc
Stick	Signal arm
Six-foot	The distance between adjacent running lines

Railway companies

LNWR	London & North Western Railway (pre-Grouping)
MR	Midland Railway (pre-Grouping)
LMS	London Midland & Scottish Railway
GCR	Great central Railway (pre-Grouping)
LNER	London & North Eastern Railway
SR	Southern Railway
GWR	Great Western Railway

Introduction

To fully understand these memoirs it helps to place them in context. After all, 1930, 1940, 1950 and 1960 are a long time ago to many – in fact it's History! This period does in reality cover the development of major changes in Britain. Electricity became readily available in the 1950s – it was oil or gas lighting before – and lorries were de-regulated to be able to travel at more than 20 miles per hour! In the 1930s and '40s the horse and cart was the order of the day. Motorways began in the 1960s with the M1. Travel by car developed in the 1950s and '60s, but the average speed was about 40 miles per hour for comfort over any distance, the roads were definitely not wide, lit, or well marked or maintained! Headlamps on cars were more akin to candle-power.

Railways on the other hand were well developed. They were at the forefront of the technology of the day. Trains could travel at 60 or 70 miles per hour over long distances. Trains were the way we travelled. We travelled 'up' to London, should we ever go to the capital, and 'down our way' was common parlance. Both come from railway practice: 'up' to London and 'down' away from London, although it may have seemed like a contradiction regarding 'up north', and 'down south' for some of us, depending on where you lived.

The railway was a 'common carrier' and by law had to transport anything that anyone took to them, to anywhere in the country. Most stations, even small village ones, had sidings for coal delivery – after all, most of us heated our homes with coal. There was often a goods shed, and farmers would take their harvested crops to the goods yard to be loaded into trucks, which would be taken all over the country to cities so that people could have potatoes, fruit, etc. Most goods yards would have a cattle dock so that beasts could be loaded into cattle trucks for transport to the cities or local markets. When we had fishing fleets, fish trains were an express working from the ports to the cities. Newspaper trains were another speciality of the railways; there was no other way of distributing papers from London to all over the country for breakfast time. It was of course similar for the post. The Royal Mail had to use the railways – there was no other transport network or system that could do the job. Therefore railways seemed to be everywhere, and thundering passenger trains, express goods and newspaper trains, and mail trains, and rattling and clanking trucks, and drawn-out whistles, would punctuate the day, and even come through the still of the night. That eerie whistle at night was something else, the distant roar of a fast train or the rumble of a slow, the smoke and steam against the night sky and perhaps the moving red glow from the firebox silhouetting the cab side as the fireman shovelled coal into the firebox – and I must mention the stations at night.

As there was no electric light then, the station was lit by oil or paraffin lamps; these had a flame that burned on the outside of a mantle and made a quiet hissing sound in the quietness of the night, giving a dim yellow light to everything. Voices would echo through the station as a Postman arrived with mail sacks, slammed and locked his van door and asked about the next train. The clear 'dinging' sounds of bells and the noise of levers being pulled might be heard from the signal box, sounds drifting through the night if the box was close to the platform, then the quiet singing of the rails as a train approached. Suddenly the night time quiet would be rent by the loud creaking and hissing as the train drew in, and a reverberating squeal and graunching sound as the brakes brought the train to a stand. Immediately the click of door handles being worked, a hiss or roar of steam from the locomotive, the bang of carriage doors opening onto the stops, the rumble of trolleys being moved to the guard's van and the thud of mail sacks and whatever being transferred. The peculiar sound of voices at night, the bang of doors closing and the click of handles being closed, an echoing call of 'Right away!', the shrill of the guard's whistle, the waving of a lamp, a blast of steam and a loud shriek of a whistle from the locomotive, and the night would be split once again with the loudness of sound until the train was away and the clickety-clack of the carriage wheels and the red lamp of the last coach disappeared into the darkness at the end of the platform, and the upper-quadrant starter signal arm, or 'board', was heard bouncing, thumping and clanging back on to its stop to show 'on'. The red lamp from the signal would glow in the dark, the station lamps would hiss, a door would be shut and the quiet of the night would descend, awaiting the next train. Such was a station at night, unlike today.

Railways ran to a clock. It was the railways that standardised time across the country. Most people didn't have a wrist-watch in those days, so a man in a railway uniform with a pocket watch in his waistcoat pocket was someone special. You didn't just ask a policeman for the time! To be asked by relatives or at school if you wanted to be an engine driver when you grew up was recognition of a very good job with responsibility. A station master was revered even more – after all, he *ran* your local railway, and in a village he was looked on the same as the local vicar, the policeman and anyone else of high importance.

Although the job of engine driver was the epitome of the railway, anyone who worked on the network was important – even the porter in our village was an important man. After all, it was he who gave the guard the 'Right away' for the train to leave, it was he who helped you understand the complexities of train travel. On big stations 'Mind your backs!' was a common call as barrows of mail sacks from the guard's van of a passenger train were hastily moved to another train or to the waiting Royal Mail vans to be taken to the local Post Office for sorting for delivery. All very important and fundamental to a developing way of life, and all dependant on the railway.

So that was the railway in the days that we now see as History, although some of us can still actually remember them. All this activity – mechanical monsters worked by men, keeping the developing country and countryside working and in touch – was controlled by men who were not in the limelight, so to speak, men who worked often alone, away from the public who unknowingly depended on them. I refer of course to the signalman.

Everyone saw signal boxes, everywhere had a signal box. It was usually a tall building with lots of windows looking down on the railway, and of course no train moved without the signal for the off. This was where the signalman worked, we knew that, but only had a sketchy idea of what he actually did. Signal boxes were special places, and that is another value of these memoirs, allowing us to find out what signalling was about.

Of late I have been lucky enough to actually visit a working signal box, and it is a totally different experience from being on the footplate of a steam locomotive. A working locomotive cab can be dark, it is very hot, unbelievably noisy and windy, and it is bucking about with rumbling, crashing and clashing sounds. The fireman will be shovelling coal from the coal door in a tender lurching and dancing one way through the fire door of a locomotive that is lurching and dancing the other way. In contrast, the interior of a signal box is totally different. It is quiet for a start, although it can get noisy when levers are being moved in a hurry. You look out on the world, trains rumble by quite quietly and get a glance from the signalman. The world in a signal box is the movement of trains over the track controlled by that particular box, which is known as a 'block'. Some miles away on each side is another signal box. Communication is by bell, and there is a code to describe each train so that our signalman knows what train is coming; he can then set his levers and send his acceptance of the train on the 'block instrument' on the shelf. A bell signal must then be sent to the next box and a reply awaited before our signalman can set his levers for the train to continue onward. There is much more to it than just this, but that is the purpose of these memoirs. It is almost an abstract world in a signal box – movement and actions take place without any apparent effect on the world unless you understand the diagram above the signal frame. If it is illuminated, then you can see lights come on or go out relative to the progress of the trains, which helps one to understand that things are happening somewhere in the world outside the signal box windows. It took a while for me to come to terms with the way a signalman does his job.

Signalling may be just another job, but its importance comes out in these following pages, and it is good to read about something from a human point of view, something that has been superseded by the march of progress made as a result of men like the signalman.

So, back to the 1940s and 1950s, and Iain Mackenzie's memoirs.

P. J. Wortley

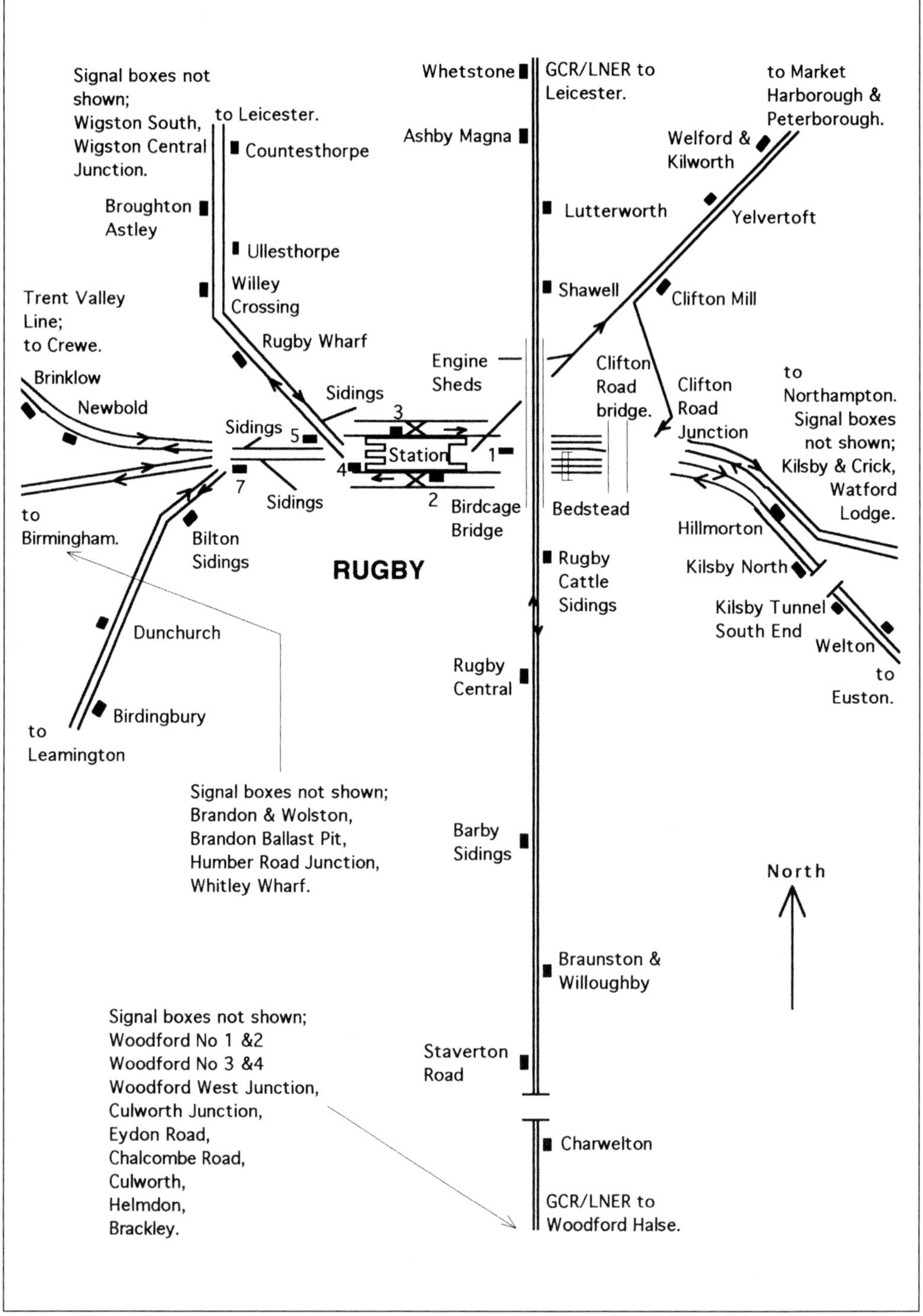

A schematic diagram of the railway network around Rugby. *PJW*

1
'ONE ON THE TOP'

In this day and age, when there are so many 'isms' – racism, sexism, ageism and so forth – there is one that has gone largely unnoticed, which I shall call 'hobbyism'. Those whose interests are horses, or cars, or fishing, or DIY, are described as 'enthusiasts', whereas, according to the media, those interested in railways are fanatics! It all fits in with 'the wrong kind of snow', and the 'anorak'. So for 70 or more years I have been a railway fanatic and have loved every minute of it, although the scenario of more recent times has caused a slight cooling off!

An interest in railways provides so many facets upon which one can concentrate for study, and signalling has fascinated me from a very early age. I remember my father nailing a narrow length of wood to the washing-line post to represent a signal and I would run up and down the garden path, arms pistoning, playing at trains. My home was in Rugby, so I didn't have far to go to see the real thing and, as my grandfather was a driver on the LMS, there was sufficient encouragement within the family. My grandparents' house was in South Street and backed upon the erstwhile Great Central, while the LMS was a stone's throw away, where the two lines crossed.

In those halcyon days pre-Beeching Rugby was at the centre of a fairly extensive network of railways. The lines from Crewe, Birmingham, Leamington and Leicester converged from the north, with those from Euston, Northampton and Market Harborough coming in from the south. To add interest, the LNER crossed by means of a girder bridge to the south of the LMS station. The embankment at the 'Birdcage' (the girder bridge) was a Mecca for trainspotters as there was always something moving: engines on or off the shed (2A) and trains arriving and departing on the main lines. With the LNER crossing on its elevated perch, a fierce rivalry was fired among the spotters. There were the LMS-ites and the LNER-ites, according to which line allegiance was bestowed. Naturally I was an LNER-ite.

Down trains on the LNER would simply appear with very little warning of their approach, whereas the Up trains could be seen far off across Clifton fields when a plume of white smoke would set up the cry 'One on the top!'.

The year 1939 saw the start of a World War and also saw the demise of a piece of signalling history, the enormous 44-arm signal gantry that was the biggest of its kind in the world. Resignalling of the main lines through Rugby with colour lights was undertaken in June 1939 and the 'Bedstead', by which nickname the huge beast was known, succumbed, being replaced by three four-aspect colour light signals with route indicators.

The 'Bedstead' was built at the expense of the Great Central Railway in 1899 as part of the agreement to allow that company's line to cross the LNWR at that point. The sighting of the original 22-arm gantry was impaired by the new bridge behind it, and the height of the structure was doubled in order to provide

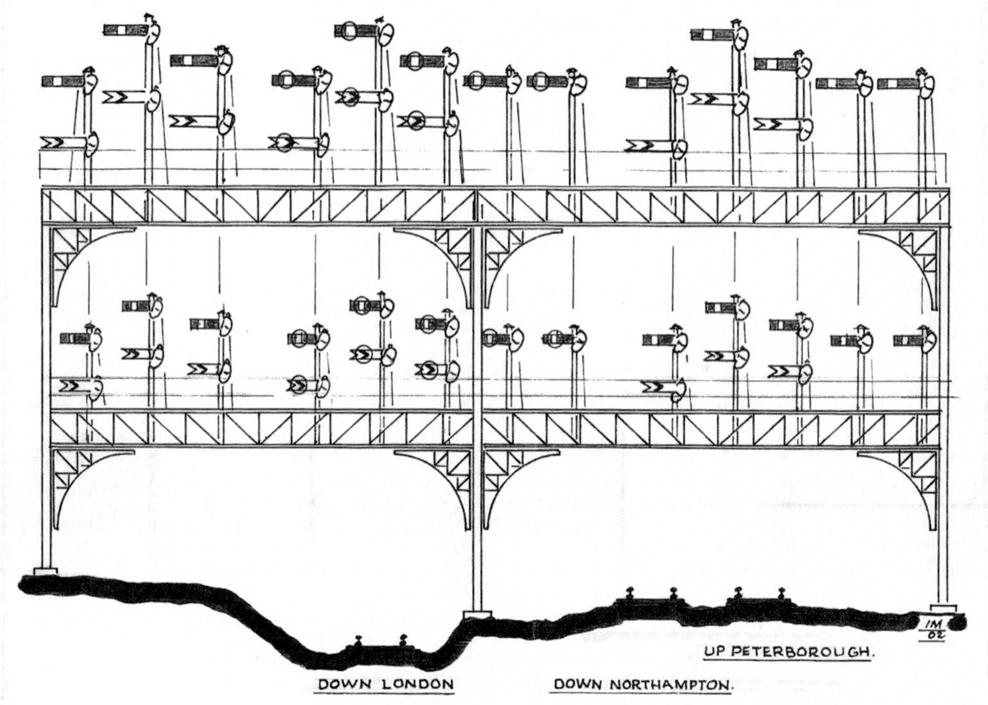

Above The 'Bedstead'. Reading from left to right, the routes it controlled were:

Down London to:
- Goods Loop, with fixed Distant
- Through line, with Rugby No 2 Distant/Rugby No 4 Outer Distant
- Platform 1, with Rugby No 2 Distant

Down Northampton to:
- Goods Loop, with fixed Distant
- Through line, with Rugby No 2 Distant/Rugby No 4 Outer Distant
- Platform 1, with Rugby No 2 Distant
- Bay 7
- Bay 8

Up Peterborough to:
- Goods Loop, with fixed Distant
- Through line, with fixed Distant
- Platform 1, with Rugby No 2 Distant/Rugby No 4 Outer Distant
- Bay 7
- Bay 8

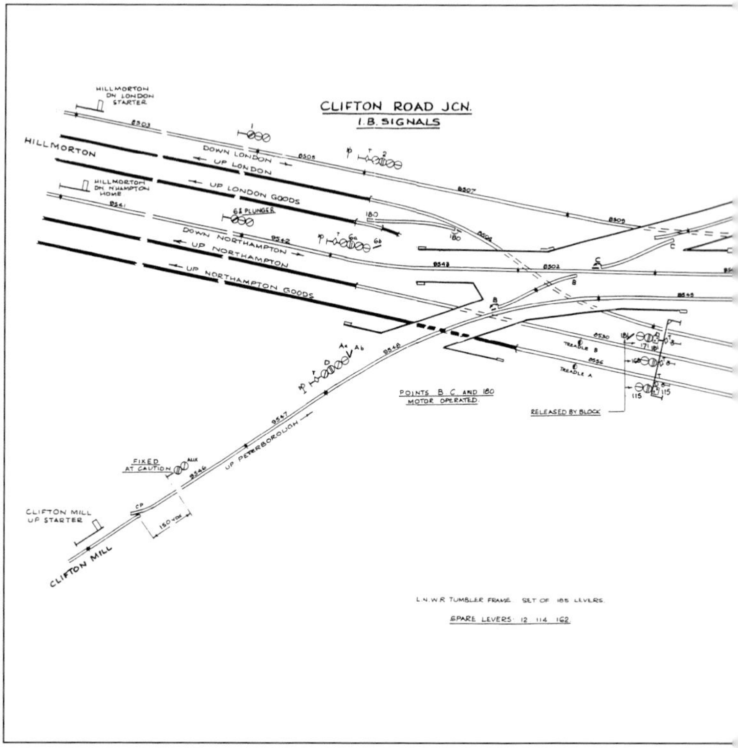

Above The 'Birdcage' bridge over the former LMS main line, with evidence of electrification. *I. Mackenzie.*

Below Rugby No 1 signal box diagram in 1948, showing the three four-aspect colour light signals (centre) with route indicators that replaced the 'Bedstead'.

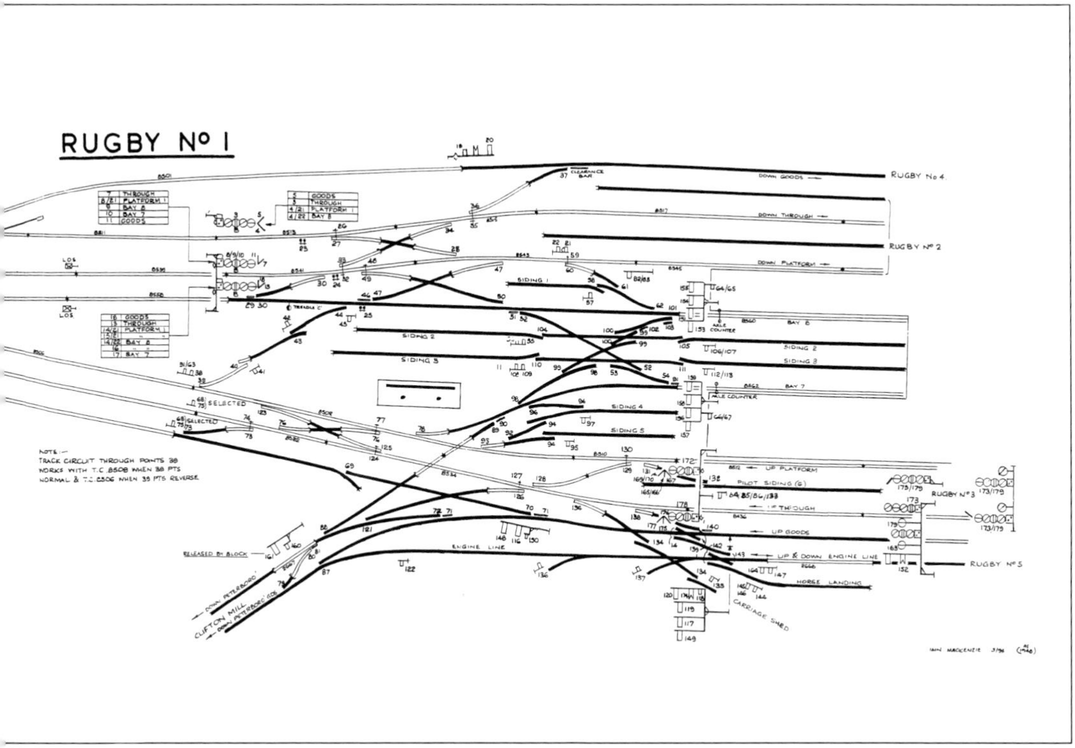

A classic shot of 'one on the top', albeit from a slightly later time. *I. Mackenzie*

a sky backing for the upper arms. The cost of maintaining it was borne by the GCR and LNER throughout its existence. As a small boy I remember seeing swarms of men reducing the 'Bedstead' to so much scrap iron, almost all of it going to the junk yard, although a quarter survived to replace an ageing gantry at Newbold on the Trent Valley line. That portion survived until 1964 when electrification sealed its fate.

This then was the largest signal gantry in the world. The LNWR also boasted many tall signals. My grandfather used to tell of sending his fireman up the post in foggy weather to see if the board was 'off', or clear. He didn't mention what would have happened if the hapless fellow suffered from a fear of heights. As a complete contrast, there was a diminutive signal in the cutting at the end of the Down platform at Rugby Central station. It carried two arms, a Stop and a Distant, and was a typical Great Central lower-quadrant signal. I was able to admire it on my daily walk to Eastlands School via the Black Pad, a footpath that led from Hillmorton Road to Lower Hillmorton Road along the top of the railway cutting. I claimed this as my favourite signal, but it too was replaced by a colour light in the late 1940s.

Above right **My favourite signal, with a 'K3' at Rugby Central in 1947.** *I. Mackenzie*

Right **The view looking north from the Hillmorton Road bridge at Rugby Central showing the colour light replacement (extreme left) of my favourite signal.** *I. Mackenzie*

2
An introduction to signal boxes

So, before we get our bikes out for you to accompany me on some visits to signal boxes, I feel it would be a good idea to explain a few basic facts to those whose knowledge of signalling is rather scant.

The signalman is the traffic policeman on the railway; indeed, originally signalling was the responsibility of the Railway Police, and when signal cabins and signalmen were introduced to control the trains, the nickname 'bobby' continued.

The Railway Policeman was stationed at regular intervals along the line controlling the safe movement of trains by time intervals. To

The LNWR 'stirrup' lever frame at Bilton Sidings. The 'stirrup' on the lever had to be pressed down to release the lever and pulled up to lock it after the movement had been made. The stirrup was linked to the interlocking and could not be pressed down if the lever was not free to be moved. The diagram is attached to the block shelf. *I. Mackenzie*

Above The LMS frame in Rugby No 7. Here the lever frame is set against the back wall. The handles are shorter and the frame is raised above the floor; this is because the lever interlocking mechanism is above the floor instead of in the locking room below, as was the practice of most other railways. The diagram can be seen on the Block Shelf, flanked by the many Block Instruments in this busy box. *I. Mackenzie*

Right One of the GCR signal boxes at Woodford, containing a Railway Signal Company frame. The long levers and catch handles are noticeable, as is the lower position of the catch handle. The diagram would have been above the Block Shelf supported from the roof, allowing the Block Instruments to be positioned on the shelf below it. *I. Mackenzie collection*

convey instructions he initially used hand/arm signals, then flags and later boards. Obstructions to free running such as road crossings, junctions or stopping places also had a Railway Policeman to ensure safety, and he worked within the station limits.

Signalmen operating levers to move signals and points from signal boxes came later, as did Block working. The signalman controls the points and signals within the station or junction limits, and therefore protects any obstructions. He also controls entry into and exit from the Block Section using Fixed Signals.

The Stop signal, in its normal On position, is and always has been a direct instruction to a driver to stop at that place. He must proceed no further until the signal shows Clear to Proceed, unless special instruction is given. British Railways, in its Rule Books, officially uses the words 'at danger' or 'showing danger', or just 'danger', with Stop in brackets. So in the days of this narrative, the Stop signal was, and showed, 'Stop', not 'danger' as in modern parlance.

The signalman is provided with what are known as Fixed Signals by which he conveys his instructions to drivers, and Block Instruments, by which communication, and visual reminders of that communication, is effected with signalmen in adjoining boxes for the safe working of the trains. Fixed Signals are so called because of their permanent locations at the trackside. Hand signals with flags/lamps are used at other times. Explanations of the tools of the trade are given in Appendix 2, which will provide greater understanding of the terms mentioned in the narrative.

On the bicycle rides we will visit many of the signal boxes around Rugby, and it may be helpful to show the different interiors of the various railway company signal boxes: the LNWR, Midland (later LMS) and the GCR (later LNER). The levers in the frame can be seen, together with the Block Shelf carrying the block instruments and the diagram.

The first thing you see when going into a signal box are the levers in the frame. To distinguish the work performed by the levers they are painted in a series of standard colours:

Yellow	Distant signals
Red	Stop signals
Black	points
Blue	Facing Point Locks
Brown	gate locks, ground frame release
Green	mechanical gongs (eg in a goods yard)
Black/white	detonator placers

When levers are adapted to operate electrical apparatus (signals or points) the handles are shortened to indicate the fact. This also prevents the operator from mistakenly using too much effort in the operation of the lever. Shortened levers are also painted in dual colours in accordance with the work done:

Blue/black	motor points
Yellow/red	IB (Intermediate Block) signals

A white patch on a red lever indicates that the signal is released by 'Line Clear' from the signal box in advance. Receiving 'Line Clear' allows the lever to be operated once only, which prevents a second train being allowed to enter the section ahead without authority.

The Block Shelf above the levers holds the Block Instruments for the Up and Down lines, the Block Bells, Track Circuit Indicators, Signal Repeaters, and any other instruments required at that box. The shelf also carries a small but vital piece of equipment, the Block Switch.

The Train Register

The Train Register was, and still is, the diary of events as they occur each day – every move involving trains, together with incidents and other happenings, is faithfully recorded. The extracts illustrated on pages 20-25 were recorded almost 45 years ago, but they give a minute-by-minute account of Leo Rippin's work as signalman on duty at Rugby Station* on that particular Friday, 22 January 1960 –

* During its history the GCR station at Rugby has three names: the original GCR name was Rugby Station; 'Rugby Central' was displayed on the booking hall awning in British Railways days, and at another time is was named simply Rugby.

frozen for all time and showing just how important accurate book-keeping has always been. In the event of a serious mishap, the Train Register is sealed and taken away for scrutiny to assist in an ensuing enquiry.

Close examination of the fourth page shows that no time signal was received that day – something that should have happened but didn't, so its omission is duly noted. The 'Remarks' column contains the Reporting Numbers of the trains together with loadings for Down freights and their destinations. Note on the same page that Leo has used abbreviations in some instances: '3518 65 [wagons] KB [Kirkby Bentinck]', 3522 50 [wagons] Huck T [Hucknall Town]'. Note also the reported times of the passenger trains: '2544 10/41 WFD' indicates that that train passed Woodford at 10.41 that morning. It can also be noted that the 24-hour clock was not yet obligatory, as Station Master J. E. Potts visited the box at 4.0pm.

The full 24-hour record for that Friday in 1960 illustrates the intensity of the traffic: 61 Up trains and 62 Down trains, 123 in total, the majority of which were freight. Thanks to the negative thinking of *all* governments and to the interference of the bully-boy roads lobby in our political system, the line was closed in 1966 as a through route. This, no doubt, brought jubilation to the Road Haulage Association, but we are now reaping the unwanted benefits of this crazy thinking. Here ends the lesson.

It is with great good fortune that this volume was rescued from the demolition of Rugby box on the Great Central, as the Train Register is something fundamental to signal box working but is practically unknown to those outside. It is still used in signal boxes today, alongside the computer!

The pages shown here are as the book lies open. On the left is the Up Line and on the right is the Down Line, with the date. It bears very careful study for many reasons. The method of block working described in Appendix 2 can be followed in the headings and entries on each page. The bell codes appear in the first column, 'Description how Signalled' (there are some special codes not covered in the list in the Appendix). The train Reporting Numbers in the 'Remarks' column are referred to in Chapters 4 and 9 in part.

The importance of proper working

It is worth relating at this stage the consequences of improper working brought about by irregular activities. The date was Saturday 22 May 1915, the time a little after 7am. The location was Quintinshill, a signal box on the Caledonian Railway just north of Gretna on the border between England and Scotland. It was very busy that morning, with goods trains occupying the Up and Down Loop Lines and a Down local passenger train shunted to the Up Line to clear the Down road for a late-running Down, London to Glasgow/Edinburgh, express, for which the Down Line signals had already been cleared.

In the signal box there were several crew members of the various trains detained there. There were two signalmen, one of them concentrating on entering into the Train Register all of the details that had been noted on a piece of paper by Signalman Meakin who had been on nights and should have been relieved at 6am. He had an unauthorised arrangement with his mate, Signalman Tinsley, allowing him to commence his morning shift half an hour later, at 6.30am instead of 6am. In order to avoid discovery of this illegal system by anyone scrutinising the Train Register, the details for that half-hour period were added later so that the handwriting would correspond. During all the chatter and activity a lack of concentration allowed an Up troop train to be offered, accepted *and signalled* with the previously shunted Down local standing in its path on the Up Line.

The collision that ensued was horrendous, but more was to follow, as the late-running London to Glasgow express, steaming under clear signals, ran into the wreckage, adding to the already dreadful carnage in which at least 227 persons lost their lives. The true number of fatalities will never be known as the Military Records of the personnel on the troop train were destroyed in the ensuing fire, which engulfed all five trains. The inferno did not subside for at least 24 hours.

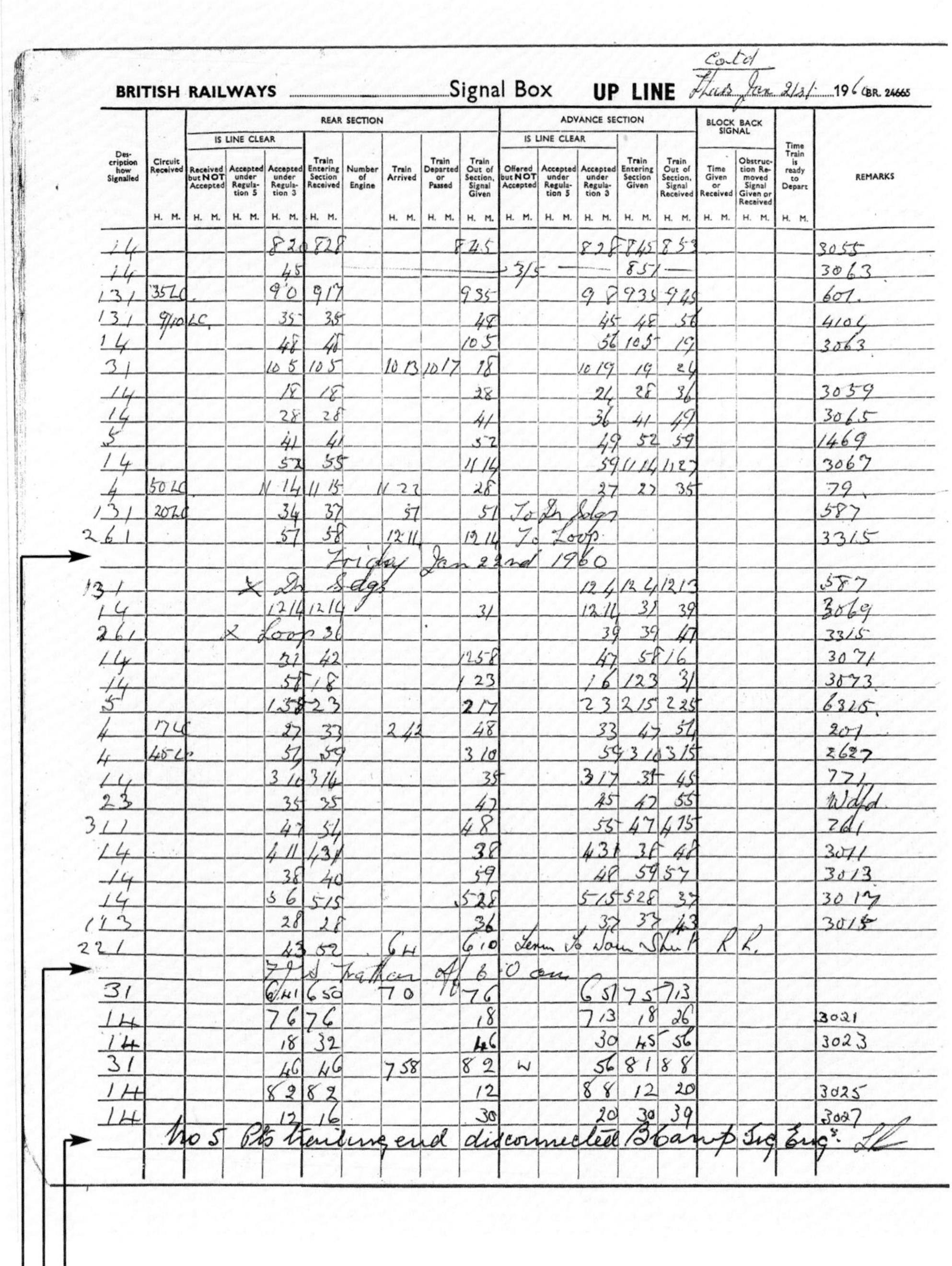

Contd

BRITISH RAILWAYS .... Signal Box UP LINE Thurs Jan 21st 1960 BR. 24665

Description how Signalled	Circuit Received H. M.	REAR SECTION – IS LINE CLEAR – Received but NOT Accepted H. M.	Accepted under Regulation 5 H. M.	Accepted under Regulation 3 H. M.	Train Entering Section Received H. M.	Number of Engine	Train Arrived H. M.	Train Departed or Passed H. M.	Train Out of Section, Signal Given H. M.	ADVANCE SECTION – IS LINE CLEAR – Offered but NOT Accepted H. M.	Accepted under Regulation 5 H. M.	Accepted under Regulation 3 H. M.	Train Entering Section Given H. M.	Train Out of Section, Signal Received H. M.	BLOCK BACK SIGNAL – Time Given or Received H. M.	Obstruction Removed Signal Given or Received H. M.	Time Train is ready to Depart H. M.	REMARKS
14				820	828				845			828	845	853				3055
14				45						3/5			851	—				3063
131	35 LC			90	917				935			98	935	945				601.
131	9/10 LC.			35	38				48			45	48	56				4104
14				48	48				105			56	105	19				3063
31				105	105		1013	1017	18			1019	19	24				
14				18	18				28			24	28	36				3059
14				28	28				41			36	41	49				3065
5				41	41				52			49	52	59				1469
14				52	55				1114			59	1114	1127				3067
4	50 LC			N 14	1115		N 22		28			27	27	35				79.
131	20 LC			34	37		51		51	To Dr Sdgs								587
261				57	58		1211		1214	To Loop								3315
				Friday Jan 22nd 1960														
131			X Dr Sdgs									124	124	1213				587
14				1214	1214				31			1214	31	39				3069
261			X Loop		36							39	39	47				3315
14				37	42				1258			47	58	16				3071
14				58	18				123			16	123	31				3073
5				158	23				217			23	215	225				6325.
4	17 LC			27	33		242		48			33	47	51				201
4	45 LC			51	59				310			59	310	315				2627
14				310	316				35			317	35	45				771
23				35	35				47			45	47	55				Wdfd
311				47	54				48			55	47	415				761
14				411	431				38			431	38	48				3011
14				38	40				59			48	59	57				3013
14				56	515				528			515	528	37				3017
113				28	28				36			37	37	43				3015
221				43	52		6H		610	Term to Down Shunt RR.								
				7J S Watkin Off 6 40 am														
31				641	650		70	10	76			651	75	713				
14				76	76				18			713	18	26				3021
14				18	32				46			30	45	56				3023
31				46	46		758		82	W		56	81	88				
14				82	82				12			88	12	20				3025
14				12	16				30			20	30	39				3027
		No 5 Pts trailing end disconnected B Camp Sig Engr.																

Midnight
Shift change, signalman off
Work on No 5 points

Train Register Book, Rugby Station, Up Line, Thursday 21 January 1960

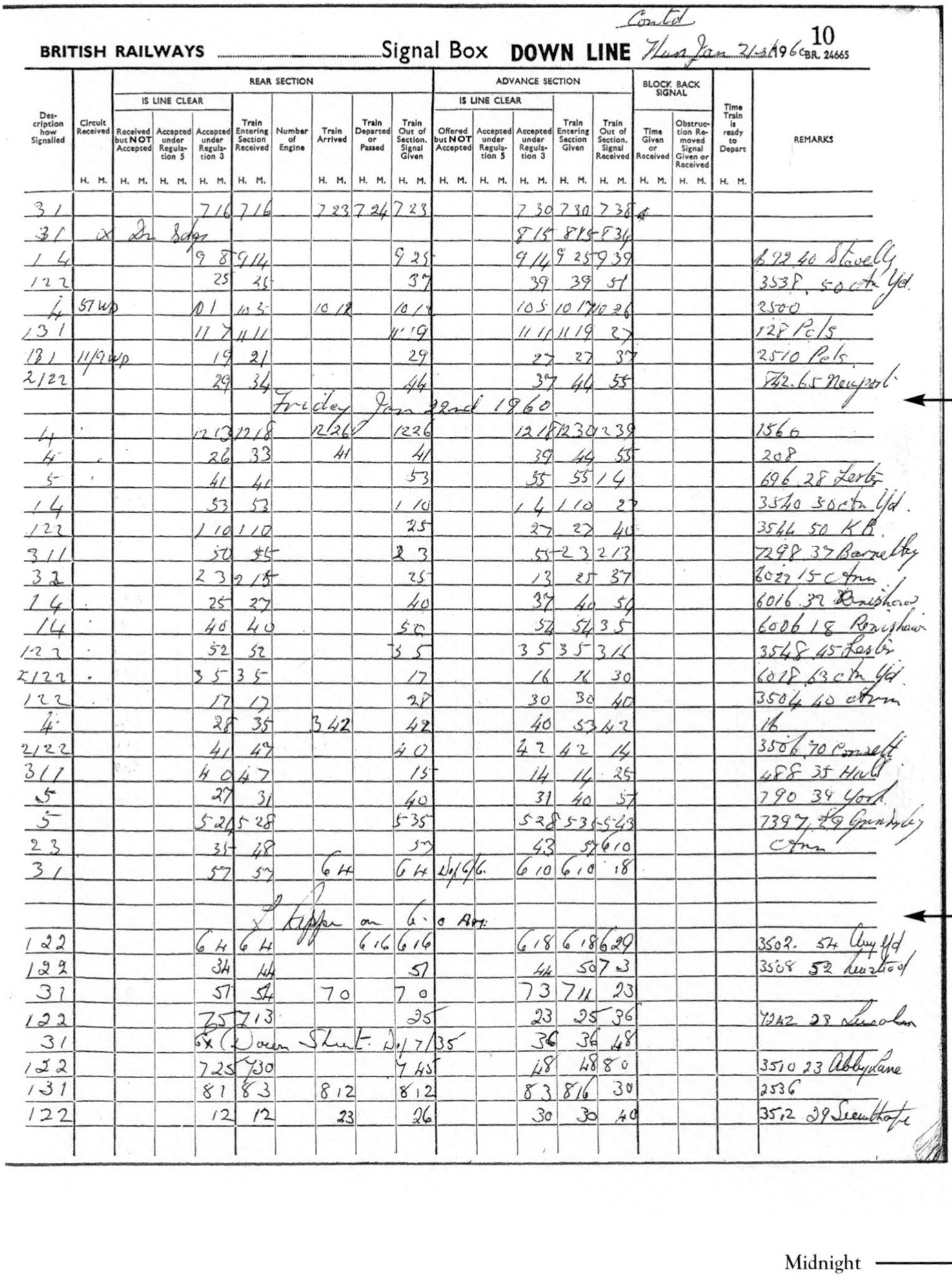

Contd 10

BRITISH RAILWAYS .... Signal Box DOWN LINE Thurs Jan 21st 1960 BR. 24665

Description how Signalled	Circuit Received H. M.	REAR SECTION — IS LINE CLEAR — Received but NOT Accepted H. M.	Accepted under Regulation 5 H. M.	Accepted under Regulation 3 H. M.	Train Entering Section Received H. M.	Number of Engine	Train Arrived H. M.	Train Departed or Passed H. M.	Train Out of Section, Signal Given H. M.	ADVANCE SECTION — IS LINE CLEAR — Offered but NOT Accepted H. M.	Accepted under Regulation 5 H. M.	Accepted under Regulation 3 H. M.	Train Entering Section Given H. M.	Train Out of Section, Signal Received H. M.	BLOCK BACK SIGNAL — Time Given or Received H. M.	Obstruction Removed Signal Given or Received H. M.	Time Train is ready to Depart H. M.	REMARKS
31				716	716		723	724	723			730	730	738				
31	x Dr Sdg											815	818	831				
14				98	914				925			914	925	939				6922 40 Stavelly
122				25	25				37			39	39	51				3538 50 Cte Yd
4	57 WP			101	103		1012		1014			103	1017	1026				2500
131				117	1111				1119			1111	1119	27				128 Pcls
131	1119 WP			19	21				29			27	27	37				2510 Pcls
2/122				29	34				44			37	44	55				7242 65 Newport
					Friday Jan 22nd 1960													
4				1213	1218		1226		1226			1218	1230	1239				1566
4				26	33		41		41			39	44	55				208
5				41	41				53			55	55	14				696 28 Lester
14				53	53				110			14	110	27				3540 50 Cte Yd
122				110	110				25			27	27	40				3546 50 KB
311				50	55				23			55	23	213				7298 37 Barnetby
32				23	215				25			13	25	37				8027 15 C Am
14				25	27				40			37	40	51				6016 37 Renishaw
14				40	40				50			54	54	35				6006 18 Renishaw
122				52	52				35			35	35	316				3548 45 Lester
2/122				35	35				17			16	16	30				6018 63 Cte Yd
122				17	17				28			30	30	40				3504 40 C Am
4				28	35		342		42			40	53	42				16
2/122				41	47				40			42	42	14				3506 70 Consett
311				40	47				15			14	14	25				488 35 Hull
5				27	31				40			31	40	57				790 34 York
5				521	528				535			528	531	543				7397 29 Grimsby C Am
23				35	48				57			43	57	610				
31				57	57		64		64	W 616		610	610	18				
					Kipper on 6.0 Arr													
122				64	64			616	616			618	618	629				3502 54 Cty Yd
122				34	44				51			44	50	73				3508 52 Heaton
31				57	54		70		70			73	711	23				
122				75	713				25			23	25	36				7242 28 Lincoln
31				6x (Down Shunt)					717/35			36	36	48				
122				725	730				745			48	48	80				3510 23 Abbey Lane
131				81	83		812		812			83	816	30				2536
122				12	12		23		26			30	30	40				3512 29 Scunthorpe

Midnight

Shift change, signalman on

Train Register Book, Rugby Station, Down Line, Thursday 21 January 1960

BRITISH RAILWAYS .... Signal Box UP LINE Contd Fri – Jan 22nd – 1960 BR. 24665

Description how Signalled	Circuit Received H. M.	REAR SECTION: IS LINE CLEAR: Received but NOT Accepted H. M.	Accepted under Regulation 5 H. M.	Accepted under Regulation 3 H. M.	Train Entering Section Received H. M.	Number of Engine	Train Arrived H. M.	Train Departed or Passed H. M.	Train Out of Section, Signal Given H. M.	ADVANCE SECTION: IS LINE CLEAR: Offered but NOT Accepted H. M.	Accepted under Regulation 5 H. M.	Accepted under Regulation 3 H. M.	Train Entering Section Given H. M.	Train Out of Section, Signal Received H. M.	BLOCK BACK SIGNAL: Time Given or Received H. M.	Obstruction Removed Signal Given or Received H. M.	Time Train is ready to Depart H. M.	REMARKS
31				8 54	9 3		9 13		9 20	Term To Down Main RR								
No 5 Points Restored 9.35 Blamp Sig Engs																		
4				9 38	9 44		9 55		9 57			9 44	9 56	10 3				2525 9/38 Leic
311				57	57				10 5			10 3	10 5	11				919
3				10 5	10 5		10 17		17	To Down Shunt								3329.
14				17	17				34			10 17	34	42				3029
14				34	34				47			42	47	56				3031
311				47	50		11 5		11 5	W		56	11 11	11 18				777 10/28 NFO
3			6x	Down Shunt Dep 11/16								11 18	18	27				3329 10 Nfld
14				11 13	11 23				11 37			11 27	11 37	11 45				789
14				47	57		12 13		12 13	To Loop								799.
311				12 13	12 13				24			12 13	12 24	12 32				3037.
14				E. Loop Arr 12/30								32	32	40				799
31				24	34		45		50	Term To Down Shunt RR								
14				50	50				1 3			12 50	1 3	1 13				3039
4				1 18	1 26		1 35		37			1 26	36	44				29 1/5 Leic
4				42	47		55		57			47	56	2 2				181 1/32 Leic
14				57	57		2 11		2 11	W		2 2	2 19	29				3041
14				2 11	2 11		23		23	W		29	31	40				3043
14				23	23		34		36	Arr 2/36		40	40	47				3045
31				52	3 0		3 11		3 14			3 0	3 13	3 20				
14				3 14	18				34			20	34	44				3047.
14				34	44				56			44	54	4 4				3051
14	Advice			4 15	4 24				4 38			4 22	4 38	46				3053
14	at 5/38		W	5 12	5 31		5 48		5 41			5 22	5 56	6 4				3061
					F.T.B.		Fothan on 5/30 pm											
31				48	49		6 2	6 4	6 5			6 4	6 4	6 12				
4	57 LC			6 5	6 11		21		24			12	23	31				2573
31				50	59		7 16		7 23	W To Dn Sdg 7/27 RR 7/33								
14				7 23	7 23				35			7 27	7 35	44				3057
14				44	52				8 7			59	8 7	8 15				3055
131	8/2 LC			8 20	8 26				41			8 26	41	49				601
131	27 LC			42	49				9 0			49	9 0	9 5				4104
14				9 0	9 0				19			9 5	19	27				3063
14				19	21				35			27	35	41				3059
31				49	10 0		10 11		10 16			10 0	15	23				
14				10 16	16				29			23	29	36				3065
5				29	29				39			36	39	46				1269

Work on No 5 points completed
Shift change, signalman on

Train Register Book, Rugby Station, Up Line, Friday 22 January 1960

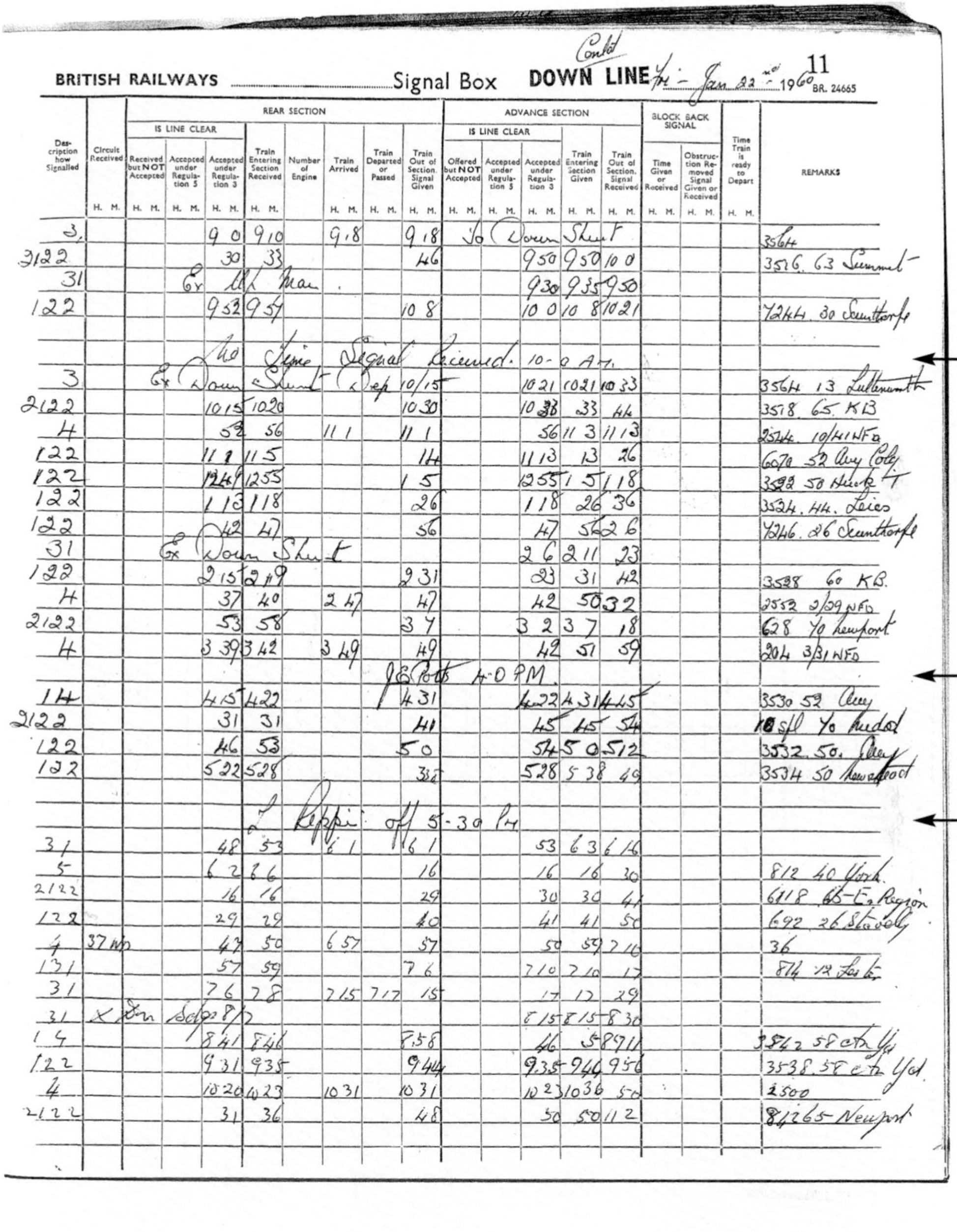

Contd

BRITISH RAILWAYS .... Signal Box DOWN LINE Fri – Jan 22nd 1960 11 BR. 24665

Description how Signalled	Circuit Received	REAR SECTION — IS LINE CLEAR: Received but NOT Accepted	Accepted under Regulation 5	Accepted under Regulation 3	Train Entering Section Received	Number of Engine	Train Arrived	Train Departed or Passed	Train Out of Section. Signal Given	ADVANCE SECTION — IS LINE CLEAR: Offered but NOT Accepted	Accepted under Regulation 5	Accepted under Regulation 3	Train Entering Section Given	Train Out of Section. Signal Received	BLOCK BACK SIGNAL: Time Given or Received	Obstruction Removed Signal Given or Received	Time Train is ready to Depart	REMARKS
	H. M.	H. M.	H. M.	H. M.	H. M.		H. M.	H. M.	H. M.	H. M.	H. M.	H. M.	H. M.	H. M.	H. M.	H. M.	H. M.	
3				9 0	9 10		9 8		9 18	To Down Shunt								3564
3122				30	33				46			9 50	9 50	10 0				3516. 63 Summit
31			Ex Up Main									9 30	9 35	9 50				
122				9 52	9 54				10 8			10 0	10 8	10 21				7244. 30 Scunthorpe
				No Time Signal Received. 10-0 AM.														
3		Ex Down Shunt Dep							10/15			10 21	10 21	10 33				3564 13 Lutterworth
2122				10 15	10 20				10 30			10 28	33	44				3518. 65. KB
4				52	56		11 1		11 1			56	11 3	11 13				2544. 10/41 NFD
122				11 1	11 5				14			11 13	13	26				6070 52 Avy Coll
122				12 49	12 55				1 5			12 55	1 5	1 18				3592 50 Hinck
122				1 13	1 18				26			1 18	26	36				3524. 44. Leics
122				42	47				56			47	56	2 6				7246. 26 Scunthorpe
31			Ex Down Shunt									2 6	2 11	23				
122				2 15	2 19				2 31			23	31	42				3528 60 KB.
4				37	40		2 47		47			42	50	3 2				2552 2/29 NFD
2122				53	58				3 7			3 2	3 7	18				628 To Newport
4				3 39	3 42		3 49		49			42	51	59				204 3/31 NFD
									JE Potts 4-0 PM.									
14				4 15	4 22				4 31			4 22	4 31	4 45				3530 52 Avy
2122				31	31				41			45	45	54				10 s/l To Hudd
122				46	53				5 0			54	5 0	5 12				3532. 50. Avy
122				5 22	5 28				35			5 28	5 38	49				3534 50 Newstead
					L Reppin off 5-30 PM													
31				48	53		6 1		6 1			53	6 3	6 16				
5				6 2	6 6				16			16	16	30				812 40 York.
2122				16	16				29			30	30	41				6118 65 E. Region
122				29	29				40			41	41	50				692 26 Stavely
4	37 WB			47	50		6 57		57			50	57	7 10				36
131				57	59				7 6			7 10	7 10	17				874 12 Leics
31				7 6	7 8		7 15	7 17	15			17	17	29				
31	X Dn Sdgs 8/2											8 15	8 15	8 30				
14				8 41	8 46				8 58			46	58	9 11				3542 58 Ctn Yd
122				9 31	9 35				9 44			9 35	9 44	9 56				3538. 58 Ctn Yd.
4				10 20	10 23		10 31		10 31			10 23	10 36	50				2500
2122				31	36				48			50	50	11 2				84265 Newport

No time signal received

Station Master's inspection

Shift change, signalman on

Train Register Book, Rugby Station, Down Line, Friday 22 January 1960

Contd

BRITISH RAILWAYS .... Signal Box **UP LINE** Fri Jan 22nd 1960 BR. 24665

Description how Signalled	Circuit Received H. M.	REAR SECTION: IS LINE CLEAR: Received but NOT Accepted H. M.	Accepted under Regulation 5 H. M.	Accepted under Regulation 3 H. M.	Train Entering Section Received H. M.	Number of Engine	Train Arrived H. M.	Train Departed or Passed H. M.	Train Out of Section, Signal Given H. M.	ADVANCE SECTION: IS LINE CLEAR: Offered but NOT Accepted H. M.	Accepted under Regulation 5 H. M.	Accepted under Regulation 3 H. M.	Train Entering Section Given H. M.	Train Out of Section, Signal Received H. M.	BLOCK BACK SIGNAL: Time Given or Received H. M.	Obstruction Removed Signal Given or Received H. M.	Time Train is ready to Depart H. M.	REMARKS
14				1039	1045				112			1046	112	1110				3067
4				112	1113		1122		29			1113	28	35				79
131	221			33	38		50		50	To Dn Sdgs								587
14				50	53				129			56	315	121				3069
				Saturday Jan 23rd 1960														
131				× Dn Sdgs								121	122	129				587
14				× Up Main								129	9	20				3069
261		Exam		129	129		1223		1227			20	26	36				3315
14				31	39				54			40	53	11				3074
14				120	128				142			128	142	57				3073
5				210	217				230			214	230	238				6315
4	361L			47	54		33		39			54	38	316				201
4				39	39				17			316	17	22				2627
14				17	17				31			22	31	40				~~779~~ 771
14				31	31				50			46	50	59				~~3011~~ 619
371				50	55				48			59	48	415				761
14				48	48				23			415	23	33				3011
14				30	40				57			40	57	56				3013
14				57	57				510			56	510	19				3015
14				527	557				54			37	54	63				3017
14				54	57				613			63	613	20				3019
				F J S Jathan off 6:30 am														
31				644	653		77		710	To Term To Down Shunt RR								
14				710	713		22		22	To Loop.								3021
31				22	22		29		32			722	731	738				
14			Ex	Loop. Dep			7/36					38	38	46				3021
31				736	747		57		80			47	59	85				
14				80	85				19			85	19	27				3025
214				28	38				50			38	50	57				3027 (70)
31				50	93		913		921	Term To Down Main RR								
23				921	21		31		31			937	937	947				E/WFO 3329
4				31	39		49		57			47	50	56				2535 9/21 Lee
221				57	55				105			56	105	1011				1820 ECS Marsh
311				105	108				20			1011	20	26				919
				Clock Correct @ 10-0 AM														
14				1020	1040				1058			1030	1058	115				3031

Midnight

Train Register Book, Rugby Station, Up Line, Saturday 23 January 1960

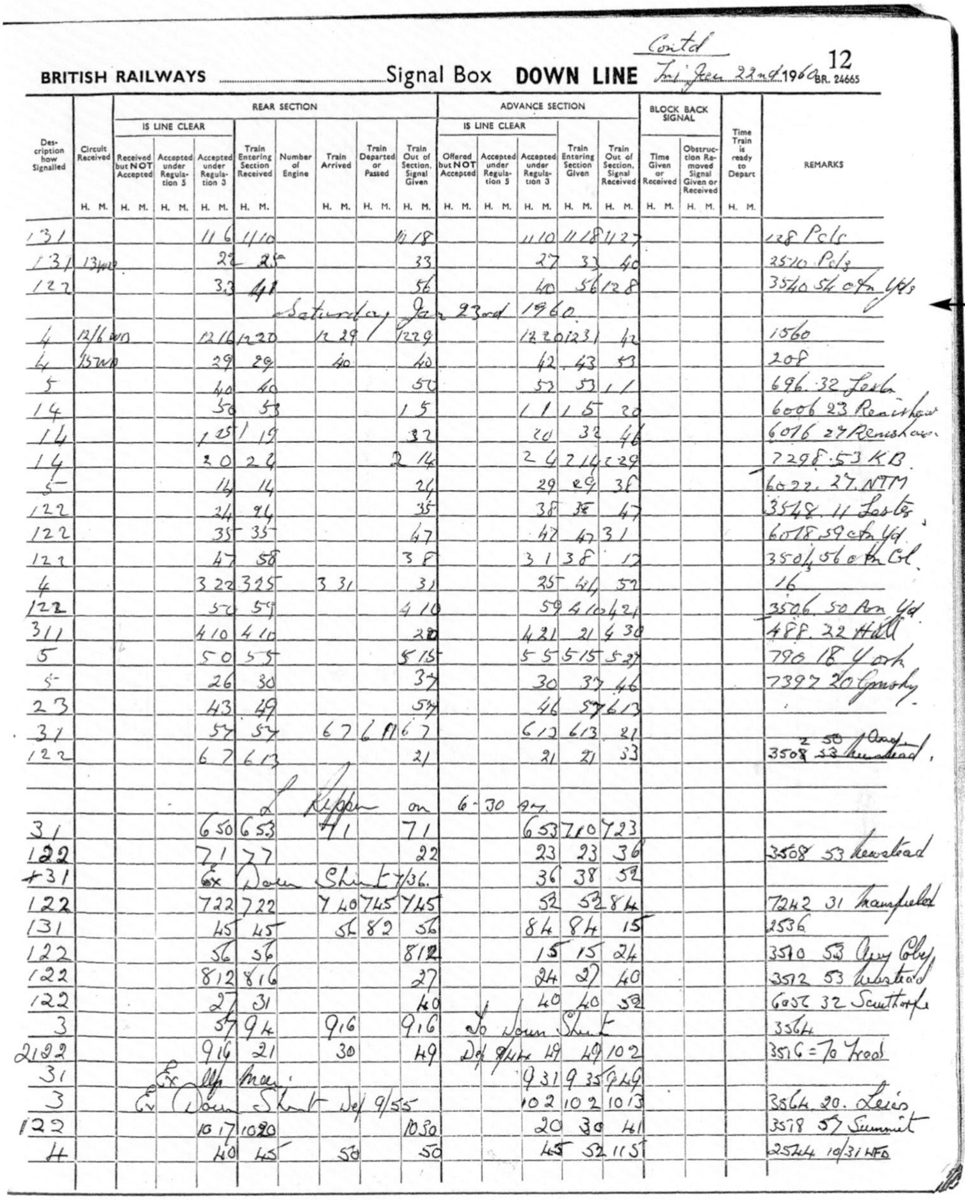

Contd

BRITISH RAILWAYS .... Signal Box DOWN LINE Fri Jan 22nd 1960 12 BR. 24665

Description how Signalled	Circuit Received H. M.	REAR SECTION — IS LINE CLEAR — Received but NOT Accepted H. M.	Accepted under Regulation 5 H. M.	Accepted under Regulation 3 H. M.	Train Entering Section Received H. M.	Number of Engine	Train Arrived H. M.	Train Departed or Passed H. M.	Train Out of Section, Signal Given H. M.	ADVANCE SECTION — IS LINE CLEAR — Offered but NOT Accepted H. M.	Accepted under Regulation 5 H. M.	Accepted under Regulation 3 H. M.	Train Entering Section Given H. M.	Train Out of Section, Signal Received H. M.	BLOCK BACK SIGNAL — Time Given or Received H. M.	Obstruction Removed Signal Given or Received H. M.	Time Train is ready to Depart H. M.	REMARKS
131				11 6	11 10				11 18			11 10	11 18	11 27				128 Pcls
131	13 WD			22	25				33			27	33	40				2510 Pcls
122				33	41				56			40	56	12 8				3540 54 ofn Yds
					Saturday Jan 23rd 1960.													
4	12/6 WD			12 16	12 20		12 29		12 29			12 20	12 31	42				1560
4	13 WD			29	29		40		40			42	43	53				208
5				40	40				50			53	53	1 1				696. 32 Leeds
14				56	53				1 5			1 1	1 5	20				6006 23 Renishaw
14				1 25	1 19				32			20	32	46				6016 27 Renishaw
14				2 0	2 4				2 14			2 4	2 14	2 29				7298 53 KB
5				14	14				26			29	29	38				6022. 27. NTM
122				24	24				35			38	38	47				3548. 11 Leeds
122				35	35				47			47	47	3 1				6018 59 ofn Yd
122				47	58				3 8			3 1	3 8	12				3504 56 ofn Col.
4				3 22	3 25		3 31		31			25	44	52				16
122				50	59				4 10			59	4 10	4 21				3506. 50 Ann Yd
311				4 10	4 10				20			4 21	21	4 30				488. 22 Hull
5				5 0	5 5				5 15			5 5	5 15	5 27				790 18 York
5				26	30				37			30	37	46				7397 20 Grimsby
23				43	49				57			46	57	6 13				
31				57	57		6 7	6 11	6 7			6 13	6 13	21				
122				6 7	6 13				21			21	21	33				3508 2 50 [illegible] ~~53 Newstead~~
					L Kipper				on	6-30 am								
31				6 50	6 53		7 1		7 1			6 53	7 10	7 23				
122				7 1	7 7				22			23	23	36				3508 53 Newstead
+31				Ex Down Shunt 7/36.								36	38	52				
122				7 22	7 22		7 40	7 45	7 45			52	53	8 4				7242 31 Mansfield
131				45	45		56	8 2	56			8 4	8 4	15				2536
122				56	56				8 12			15	15	24				3510 53 [illegible]
122				8 12	8 16				27			24	27	40				3512 53 Newstead
122				27	31				40			40	40	52				6052 32 Scunthorpe
3				57	9 4		9 16		9 16	To Down Shunt								3564
2122				9 16	21		30		49	Def 9/44		49	49	10 2				3516 = To Trent
31		Ex Up Main										9 31	9 35	9 49				
3		Ex Down Shunt Def 9/55										10 2	10 2	10 13				3564 20. Leeds
122				10 17	10 20				10 30			20	30	41				3578 57 Summit
4				40	45		50		50			45	52	11 5				2544 10/31 WFD

Midnight

Train Register Book, Rugby Station, Down Line, Saturday 23 January 1960

Had the 'Blocking Back' bell signal (2-4, ie 2 beats, pause, 4 beats) been sent to the next box to the north; had Rule 55 been properly observed with a Lever Collar (see Chapter 14) placed on the Up Home signal lever to prevent it being pulled off; had the signalmen been discharging their duties according to regulations; and had there been Track Circuits in operation (see Appendix 2), this appalling accident, the worst to have occurred on British railways, would not have happened. The two signalmen were both convicted of Criminal Negligence at Carlisle Assizes and sentenced to three years' imprisonment.

It is thus becoming apparent that being a signalman wasn't just a case of pulling levers and watching the trains go by. The procedure of opening and closing a signal box makes the point, and introduces many things covered within this narrative and in Appendix 2.

Switching In and Switching Out

Signal boxes are provided at intervals not just to safeguard the obstruction of stations and junctions, but also to improve the line capacity. The closer together they are placed, the more trains can occupy that particular stretch of railway. However, signal boxes need to be manned and the wages paid to the men working them can prove expensive should the amount of traffic not justify them. For example, fewer trains operated on Sundays and the number of signal boxes required could be reduced, thus making Block Sections much longer. In order to do this certain cabins could be dispensed with temporarily and the running signals pulled to the 'Off' position (showing line clear) and the signal box locked and left unattended until traffic intensity resumed.

Some principal signal boxes remained open continuously. On the GCR, Leicester, Ashby Magna, Rugby, Staverton Road and Woodford No 2 were never closed. The others could be Switched Out if they were not required. Some boxes were only used as and when access was required to certain facilities. Barby was opened only on weekday mornings to allow the pick-up goods to serve a Supply Depot. Rugby Cattle Sidings was also only Switched In on cattle market days in the early years of the Great Central, although it was manned as a middle turn weekday shift until the outbreak of the 1939 war. It remained closed for many years after its intended use became redundant, with livestock being transported from other centres.

The Block Switch, situated in the centre of the block shelf, provided the means whereby the cabin could be Switched Out of circuit. The electrical circuitry between the signal boxes on each side were thereby connected to each other, consequently lengthening the Block Section. However, before a signal box could be Switched Out there had, of course, to be no trains in the Block Sections.

The signalman switching out would send the 'Closing of Signal Box' bell signal (5-5-7) to the signal boxes on each side, who would acknowledge it with 1 beat and place their Block Instruments to 'Line Clear' (details of Bell Signals and Block Instruments are given in Appendix 2). This allowed the closing signalman to clear all the necessary running signals, pulling such signal levers Off to show 'Line Clear'. He then sent 1 beat on the bell to the signal box on each side, who responded with the closing 5-5-7 beats on the bell. The Block Switch could then be turned to 'Closed'. The two newly connected signalmen then exchanged 16 beats consecutively, 'Testing Block Indicators and Bells', and would announce the success (or otherwise) of the procedure on the telephone, allowing their intermediate colleague to go off duty.

The Bell Signal 5-5-7 was used when the section signals were controlled by a 'Line Clear' release from the signal box in advance. When no such controls existed, 7-5-5 was used and answered by repetition before the Block Switch was turned.

Before Switching In, the newly arrived signalman would telephone both of the signal boxes on either side of him to enquire about the traffic situation before turning the Block Switch to 'Open' and sending the bell signal 5-5-5. He would only replace his running signal levers in the frame to On (signals showing Stop) when any train in the section at the time was clear and would not be affected by them. Then he would go about his duties. Hardly the quiet life that many imagine.

And so to the bicycle rides.

3
The bicycle rides begin

Clifton Mill

With so many lines radiating from Rugby there was a considerable number of signal boxes in a comparatively small area; in fact, there were more than 50 within a 15-mile radius of the town. I found some of them easily accessible for possible visits, others with a modicum of discomfort (stinging nettles and cow-pats, etc), while some were beyond reach – the larger Rugby boxes were typical of this category, but not beyond hope! Clifton Mill on the other hand was a walkover, literally. The signal box was situated on the Up platform of the station close to the level crossing. It was on the Rugby to Market Harborough line and served the nearby village of Clifton-upon-Dunsmore. With its paraffin lamps and flower gardens it was a typical rural station, with the box an integral part of the station buildings, and it was manned by a woman!

I didn't know about such things as porter-signalmen then, but that signalwoman was responsible for everything – the booking office, goods agent, porter, and the signal box. The box was small for its 20 levers, leaving little room at each end of the frame. The Block Instruments were situated on a cupboard at the back of the box, and a door led through into the booking office. The frame fitted the cabin *so closely* that the Down Distant lever was made No 3 in order to give the signalman elbow room for a hefty pull. At the Rugby end of the station the Up and Down Lines parted company to allow the Up Line to approach Rugby Midland station via Clifton Road Junction with its flyovers. When

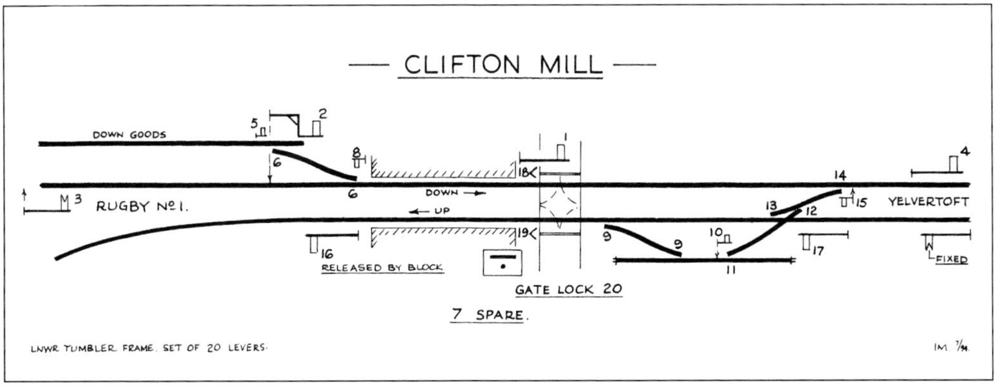

Signal box diagram, Clifton Mill

first built, the Up and Down Lines made a very complicated crossing at the south end of the junction at Rugby, and the new flyover junction solved this difficulty when it was built in the latter part of the 19th century. The Down Line became an engine line, and the original Up Line became the Down. The sharply curving Up Line necessitated the Up Distant signal being fixed at caution.

Clifton Mill worked with Yelvertoft and with Rugby No 1, the Block Instrument to the latter having two tappers to communicate with either the Up or Down signalman at that box.

The Peterborough line was not exceptionally busy and this sparseness of trains did not seem to matter at first; the ease of access and the friendly signalwoman were kindling the interest of a 12-year-old, until I happened to hear that a boy at my school had a father who was a signalman on the LMS main line. It became imperative that a friendship be nurtured!

NEWBOLD

Roger Cramphorn's father worked at Newbold, the first box out of Rugby on the Trent Valley line. It stood at the top of the embankment near the Newbold to Easenhall road bridge, from which a short footpath led up to the box, which was located just 85 miles from Euston. Normally the first impression of a place is visual; with Newbold signal box it was smell, a wonderful aroma comprising a mixture of paraffin and St Bruno tobacco smoke combined with the fuzz of the stove to create an atmosphere that could never be artificially reproduced. Perched on the window sills were a variety of strange-looking cacti in equally varied styles of flowerpots. In spite of the mild weather conditions the stove was lit in order to boil the kettle. After Clifton Mill, the most impressive thing about Newbold was the Block Shelf: there were four of the standard LNWR instruments together with two additional bells and tappers for

Newbold signal box. *D. Bullock*

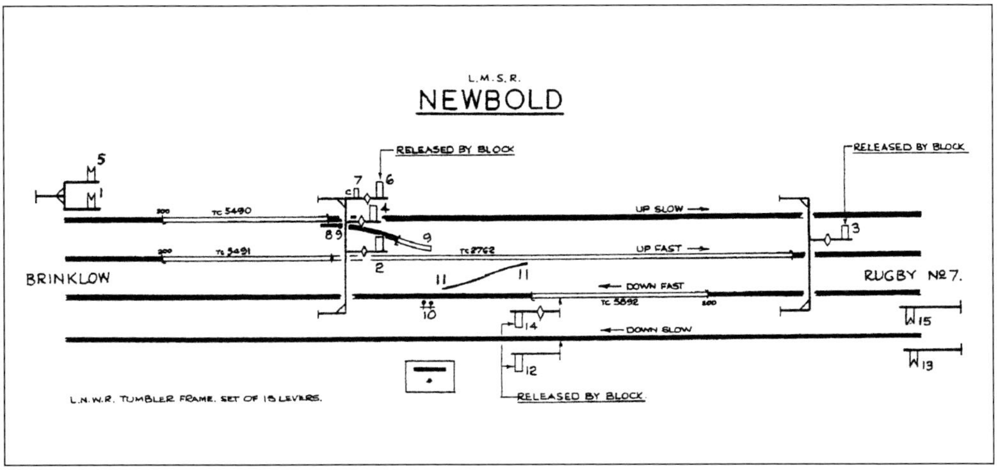

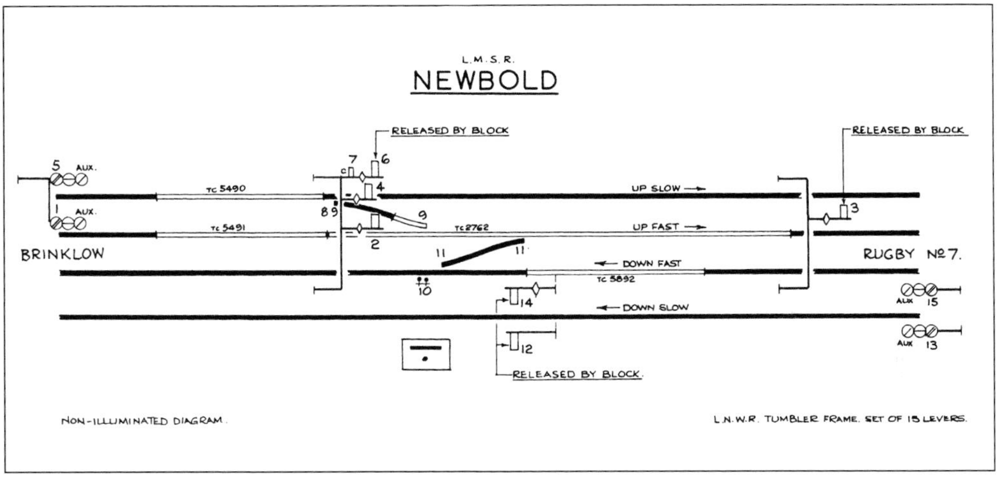

Signal box diagrams for Newbold before and after the distant signals were converted to colour lights.

communication with Rugby No 7, separated for the Up and Down sides at that box. The box overlooked the four running lines and, at that time, all the signals were vintage Crewe-pattern lower-quadrants, except for the Up Fast Starting (No 3), which was a solitary upper-quadrant Doll on the remaining section of the old gantry taken from Rugby in 1939. After the sedate tempo of life at Clifton Mill, the seemingly constant stream of trains on that Saturday afternoon was certainly an eye-opener. Present-day railways seem to close down after the commuter trains on Monday to Friday, while Saturdays and Sundays are rest days in comparison with the traffic flows in steam days. Jack Cramphorn was kept constantly busy with his 15-lever frame, his six Block Bells and his Train Register, and – of course – The Teapot.

There were two more firsts for me on that memorable Saturday all those years ago: Permissive Block Working and Routing Bell Codes. Up freight trains travelling on the Up Slow Line could be accepted one behind the other to Rugby No 7 – the 'Calling On' arm below the Up Slow Home signal made this possible. The Modified Bell Codes for the Up expresses made the biggest point of interest. An express train booked to run through Rugby and to travel via Blisworth (the 'Old

Line') was belled 4-4-4*. Similarly an express train booked to run through Rugby and travel via Northampton (the 'New Line') was belled 4-4-4-2*. These Bell Signals originated at Brinklow (the next box to the north) as a result of engine whistles given at Shilton, the next box nearer Nuneaton. During the course of the afternoon the Stafford to Rugby local passenger arrived on the Up Slow and was crossed to the Up Fast in a suitable interval between expresses. The procession of trains was ceaseless, and the Block Needles were never 'straight up' for more than a few minutes at a time on any of the four lines. This was my introduction to signal box work at its best, and it was to Newbold that I made frequent visits during the coming years.

KILSBY NORTH

Just visible from the Hillmorton to Kilsby road was the tiny Kilsby North cabin. At one time, in London & Birmingham Railway days, it was known as 'North End of Kilsby Tunnel Signal Box'. It was located on the Up side of the line in those days within a stone's throw of the tunnel mouth and close by the A5 road bridge (No 259). The details of this early structure I found on an Estate & Rating plan that had been drawn in L&BR days. It shows the box with its associated signals: the Down Distant was situated in the nearer of the two 60-foot-diameter ventilation shafts, the Down Home signal a bare 120 feet from the tunnel portal. A crossover was provided. I have no idea when this box was closed, but it was replaced by a similar cabin on the Down side of the line half a mile nearer Rugby. It is quite possible that the original Down Home provided the mast for the new Down Distant.

Access to Kilsby North was in the stinging nettle and cow-pat category, being inconsiderately positioned equidistant between two road bridges. Mike Sheppard was on duty, not more than 19 years of age and glad of a bit of company. The 10-lever frame contained five working levers and five spaces. There was a desk, a stove and three lockers, no tap, no electric light, and not a cactus in sight. But what the box lacked in size it made up for in the traffic that passed its door. There was a constant stream of express trains both Up and Down keeping Mike on his feet for much of the time, working with Hillmorton and Kilsby Tunnel South. The tunnel is 1 mile 666 yards long and is dead straight; this made it possible to see through it but for the smoke that seldom cleared because of the constant procession of trains. Both Distant signals and the Up Home were exceptionally tall. The upper arms of the

* The routing codes 4-4-4 and 4-4-4-2 were specially authorised 'Is Line Clear' codes for use on the approach to Rugby.

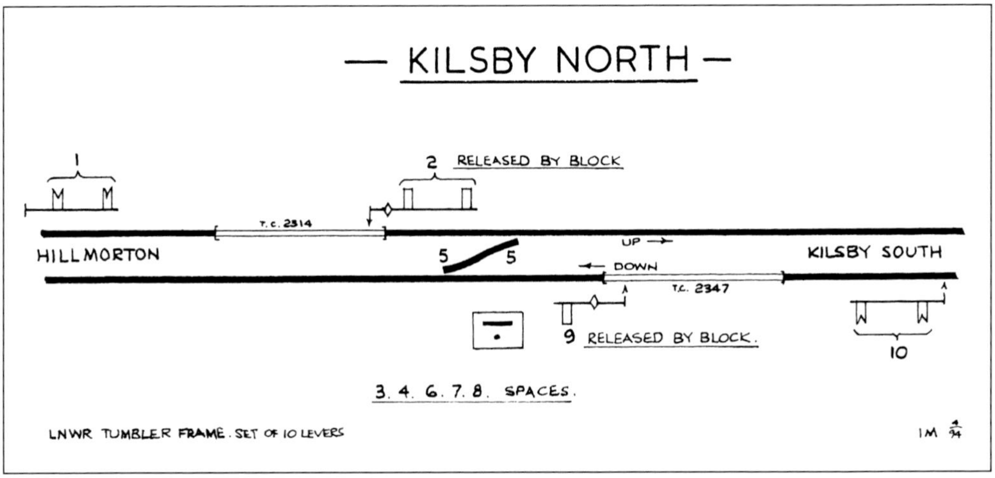

Signal box diagram, Kilsby North

Distants were visible with the naked eye from the signal box, although Signal Arm Repeaters were provided in the box.

From Rugby to Kilsby Tunnel there is a rising gradient of 1 in 370, which meant that steam locomotives were working hard on Up trains; 12- or 14-coach formations formed the normal loadings, and to hear the engines working under steam was a thrill indeed. An even greater thrill was to hear an ex-LNWR Class 'G2' coughing and wheezing its way as it ran the gauntlet between expresses with a freight train; these were usually routed via the New Line (Northampton), but one would occasionally make a run for it between the loops at Kilsby South, at Heyford, and at Blisworth. These were nail-biting times when Mike would stand, finger poised on the tapper of the Block Instrument, awaiting the 'Train out of Section' so as to 'bang in' the 4 bells and make a dash for the Distant signal lever. In those days the slightest delay caused countless heads to appear at the carriage windows to find out who had had the temerity to delay their train.

Down express trains would be 'described' in the usual way as they were offered to the North box by Kilsby South, but the 'Train Entering Section' signal would dictate the Bell Code when the 'Is Line Clear' was offered to Hillmorton. Drivers of trains not stopping at Rugby and booked to take the Trent Valley line would whistle a Routing Code at Welton, south of Kilsby South, and the 'Train Entering Section' would be sent 2-2-2. Kilsby North would then offer the train forward as 4-4-4. Similarly, trains for Birmingham would become 2-2-2-2, offered forward as 4-4-4-2.

In the 1950s the semaphore signals were replaced by colour lights, and both North and South boxes had an additional Distant signal provided at the further end of the tunnel in both cases. This meant very rapid work by each signalman as drivers were looking at those Outer Distants well in advance.

Nowadays there are no traces of the two boxes that guarded the murky depths of the West Coast Main Line's longest tunnel. Electric traction whisks trains through in less than a minute, faster and more efficient maybe, but lacking that something extra.

4
The Great Central

So far I have made no mention of the 'other railway' at Rugby. It was much closer to my home than the LMS and I could lay abed at nights listening to the various trains and trying to identify the engines by their sounds. It was at Rugby Station that I became an unpaid assistant at a very early age. Foremen Croxford and Harding turned a blind eye to my closing carriage doors prior to the departure of trains. In fact, I think they welcomed the help as my young legs enabled me to run the length of a train in next to no time. It all went badly wrong one day when a train of all LMS stock arrived with a special to some South Coast seaside resort. Guard's doors on Gresley stock opened inwards, whereas doors on 'the other line' opened outwards. Having done my duty, the station staff looked along the length of the train and gave the guard the 'Right away'. With a shrill on his whistle and a flourish of his flag the train began to move away – but the guard found that his door had been closed, and he was last seen clinging to the grab rail while trying to open the door with his other hand with the train heading countrywards.

I couldn't claim unfair dismissal, but my presence was not welcomed for some considerable time as a result. Looking back, the incident may sound amusing, but it was

Rugby Station as seen from the top of the Down embankment, behind the signal box, in 1966. The curved roof to the left is Travis & Arnold's saw-mill shed, then comes the GCR Goods Shed. The Booking Hall, missing its left-hand chimney, is on the Hillmorton Road bridge with the staircase to the buildings down on the island platform. The white-painted house on the top of the Up embankment beside the bridge is the Station Master's residence. The S&T (Signal & Telegraph) cabin is in the right foreground beside a platelayers' hut. The signal box is out of shot, to the right. *A. Franklin*

The station booking hall and offices on Hillmorton Road. It is interesting that the name on the awning is Rugby Central. The red/orange brickwork of the booking hall, the station buildings on the platform, the signal box and water tower was in contrast to the dark brown brickwork of the offices to the left and the dark blue and red to the right of the bridges. *I. Mackenzie collection*

very unfortunate and could have had a very different ending.

Finding my way into signal boxes on the LMS had proved to be fairly easy, but this could not be said of the boxes on the Central. Appeals 'to have a look around' were always steadfastly refused by the signalman at Rugby Station – until one day when a Class 'A5' tank engine 'spread the rails' in the siding at the back of the box. The usual gang of kids who were resident at the top of the bank couldn't believe their luck when they were invited to 'cab' the unfortunate locomotive while it waited for the 'clanger wagon' to arrive from Woodford. Not only did we board the engine, but the signalman, not to be outdone, had a tribe of us up into the box. It was my first meeting with Relief Signalman Charlie Baumber. More of that later.

Everything about the Great Central signal box was different. It was more spacious; the levers had catch handles rather than the

The spotters' spot. *A. Franklin*

A trackside view of 'Rugby Station' box, looking south. The passing 'Duchess' gives an indication of the specials that ran over the line in the later years before closure. *I Mackenzie collection*

stirrups so favoured by Crewe; the Block Instruments seemed to occupy the entire length of the Block Shelf, despite there being only two main lines; and the Illuminated Track Diagram was a first for me.

There were glass cupboards along two walls, which housed very complicated-looking instruments (relays), and there was a fireplace instead of the ubiquitous stove. (A stove replaced the fireplace in the early 1950s.)

SHAWELL

One day a bicycle ride took me through the village of Newton and on to Shawell, where the GC line crossed the A5 road by a brick arched bridge. Shawell signal box stood about 200 yards north of the bridge on the Up side of the railway line. I found my way to the box by way of the field opposite and made my acquaintance with the man in charge, one George Dillow. I must explain now that George Dillow was always known as 'Johnnie' in view of the fact that he was on the same shift as George Wilson at Rugby. A splendid view of the railway could be had as the line was straight for a good 2 miles to the south, this straight section ending northwards when it curved away in a cutting towards Lutterworth. The box stood on an embankment and, as was usual in such cases, was constructed of wood. It contained a Railway Signal Co frame of 12 working levers with 8 spaces. There was a 'refuge' siding on the Down side, which could accommodate 65 wagons. In keeping with all remote cabins of this sort there were no 'mod cons'. Illumination was by Tilley lamp and the toilet was the nearby bushes. It had, however, a constant supply of fresh water, which emerged from the ground in the form of a spring in the nearby field. This provided the coldest, sweetest drinking water it is possible to imagine.

Fred Marvin was Johnnie's mate on another shift, and he lived in Lutterworth and rode to work each day by the 4-mile direct route via the main roads. This route presented problems after sunset, however, as it took him via the Gibbet Crossroads on the A5. Fred was known

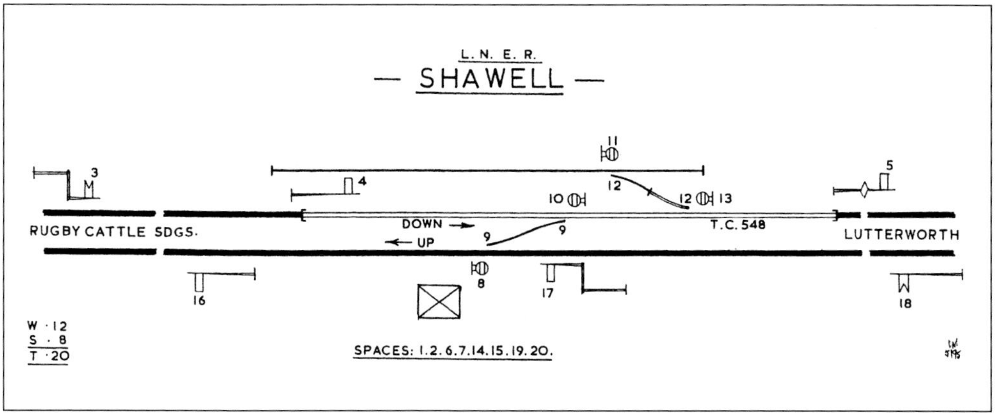

Signal box diagram, Shawell

to go in the opposite direction and travel many more miles than needed in order to avoid the chance of meeting the ghost of some poor unfortunate who had perished at that spot. It was Johnnie who experienced what he thought was a ghostly train one foggy night. He could hear an engine letting off steam when there were no trains within miles. He walked the line as far as the Up Home signal – but no train. He looked in the opposite direction on the Down Line – no train. But he could still hear steam escaping from this unseen source. It was then that he remembered putting the kettle *into the oven* of the stove, and the spectral presence was exorcised. Just one of the odd things George Dillow was prone to do. George Wilson gave me this story when I got to know him later, and this was thanks to Johnnie, who kindly arranged for me to visit Rugby Station box and Lutterworth. This was a bonus indeed.

RUGBY STATION

It is impossible to describe the elation I felt that Saturday afternoon so many years ago. This was the moment I had dreamed about; this was the signal box that I had wanted to visit more than any of them, and, after announcing my presence from the foot of the embankment, I received the longed-for invitation.

George Wilson was the signalman and it is to him that I owe a debt of gratitude for the help he gave me, not only with my hobby but with the invaluable knowledge he shared to help me in my future career. George was a Londoner and had started work as a porter at Finsbury Park. He was also a fully trained first-aider and was a keen member of the Railway Division of the St John Ambulance Brigade.

Until his promotion to Rugby Station, George had worked on the LNWR/GNR Joint Line at Harby & Stathern. He had a wonderful sense of humour and was completely unflappable. There were times when the box seemed to be surrounded by trains, telephones were demanding to be answered, and block bells were ringing, but George took it all in his stride, with never a sign of impatience or temper. He seemed to know the names of all the train crews passing his door and it instilled in me the knowledge that railway work is teamwork – no one man is more important than another. George also taught me to observe, to watch every train as it passed – a wave to the crew, then door handles, axle boxes, tarpaulins, any goods insecure and a host of other things that might be the cause of an incident. A nod to the guard, check the tail lamp, then to the blocks and bells, replacement of signals and completion of the Train Register. 'Always keep your booking up to date' – a dictum that I followed throughout my career in the box.

Rugby Station box was Class 3, open continuously. It worked on the south side with Barby, and on the north with Rugby Cattle

George Wilson (his arm on the Block Shelf) with Denis Fiander in Rugby No 7, some years later. *I. Mackenzie collection*

Sidings. The latter was rarely opened and the section was normally to Shawell, the next box towards Leicester. Barby was also only switched in for the pick-up trains on weekdays, so Braunston & Willoughby was the next box that was normally open. Rugby had a 40-lever Railway Signal Co frame, with 27 working levers and 13 spare spaces. There was an Illuminated Track Diagram and standard three-position Block Instruments as used on the GCR: a 'pegger', 'non-pegger' and Block Bell for each running line. The Accepting Instruments were modified to the Welwyn Block principle (see Chapter 9). The track layout provided an Up Passenger Loop, which could accommodate 85 wagons, and a Down Refuge Siding with a capacity of 95 wagons. There was an additional water column between the Up Main and Up Loop, which allowed many freight trains (which we called 'runners') to take water before their next high-speed run to Woodford. There were platform-mounted water columns for passenger trains.

The Reporting system

Rugby was a 'Reporting' box. The GC line was divided into sections, the local sections being Grendon Junction –Woodford No 4 – Rugby – Leicester Goods South – Loughborough. The principal box at the start of the section was responsible for keeping all of the boxes in the forward direction informed of freight train loadings and passenger train passing times in order to minimise delay to all traffic.

To make this a little clearer, let us imagine Woodford No 4 ringing a 'circuit' to Rugby. This was an Omnibus Telephone System that linked all boxes on an 'open circuit' and the code '2 short, 2 longs, 1 short' (. . - - .) would summon all signalmen in that section to the telephone and they would announce their presence. Woodford No 4 would then say, 'The ord right time Woodford; the Yorkie right time Grendon.' Woodford No 1 would then report the freight trains leaving the yard, for example: '3544 65 Frodingham, 3548 60 Wath, light engine Leicester.' All signalmen were then aware of what traffic to expect and would work out their margins accordingly to waylay freight trains out of the paths of faster traffic.

Not all the boxes were equipped with Refuge Sidings or loops but, when they were, the signalman concerned, knowing the capacity of his siding, would know from the 'circuit' whether or not he could accommodate a particular train. This information was supplemented in the 'Is Line Clear' codes of goods trains. A 3-2 conveying more than 60 wagons would be described as 2-3-2, while a 1-4 would become a 2-1-4. A train conveying bogie bolsters (as did many of the steel trains destined for South Wales) would

Right **These two pictures show that 'foreign' cross-country workings were quite normal on the Great Central. The first provides a good view of the station, a typical Great Central arrangement. The second was taken at Rugby Cattle Sidings. The bridge brickwork at Rugby was different from other GCR builds. The dark blue faces of the bricks were laid in one course and the next course was usually showing dark red, and this was repeated. Corners or edges were dark blue.** *Both I. Mackenzie collection*

7905

be described, for example, as '=60' in length, the unit being the standard coal wagon at the time. The passing times of all trains at these principal boxes would also be reported to the Control Office at Nottingham Victoria.

The Telegraph System

At this point signalmen from 'other' railways, particularly ex-GNR men, may be wondering why we didn't use the telegraph system. Many people will be wondering what this system was used for, as knowledge of it seems to have disappeared into the mists of time.

The Great Northern Railway used a single-needle telegraph between stations and also between signal boxes, which was superseded by Omnibus Telephones in later years. The Great Central Railway used the single-needle telegraph between station offices, and they were still in use in the middle of the last century. The codes used in the telegraph system were based on those of the Morse code, but used high and low notes made by a needle striking a 'pin' when moved to the left or right – the headphones of the usual Morse code operator were not needed. Movement to the left produced a 'tink' sound, that to the right a 'tonk'. The tone and loudness could be altered, unofficially, by cutting a slot in tobacco-tin lids and placing one over each pin. The Morse for 'V' is 'dot dot dot dash', the equivalent in telegraph being 'tink tink tink tonk'. The instrument was a similar size to a Block Instrument with a long needle and the sounding pins on either side of it. Below it was a shelf for the operator to place the hand-written message to be sent while using the machine. Below the shelf were two protruding striker plates, one to move the needle to the left and the other to move the needle to the right. Some instruments had a handle, as on a 'pegger' Block Instrument. Messages could be sent and received at considerable speed: 18 words per minute was the requirement.

Peter Watson was the Junior Clerk at Rugby Station. He and I were great friends and he would practice his telegraph skill using two cups and a pencil. Placing the two cups, each filled to a different level, or two empty cups of different sizes, so that the left was the high note and the right the low, he would proceed to send messages to an imaginary recipient by striking the cups with the pencil, thus making the correct sound. Pete was Junior to the Chief Clerk, Roy Chambers, and the Station Master was Ernie Potts. Now there's a coincidence.

The Telegraph System involved abbreviations for railway titles and addresses (station names), and code words that allowed sometimes long and complicated messages to be reduced to a few words. The ciphers were contained in a book to which I was not privy. I do not remember many of the codes used now, as they were mainly to do with running the station as a whole, not just signalling, but here are some examples:

CAPE	Undermentioned train will not run. Advise all concerned.
FUNGUS	No trace of forwarding the following.
REMCOL	Arrange packing and collection from house of undermentioned removal on date and time named.
GUITAR	Wire particulars and confirm by letter.
KIPPER	I have advised all concerned.

THE TELEGRAPH CODE

A	B	C	D	E	F	G	H	I	J	K	L	M
\/	/\\\	/\/\	/\\	\	\\/\	//\	\\\\	\\	\///	\/\	\/\\	//

N	O	P	Q	R	S	T	U	V	W	X	Y	Z
/\	///	\//\	\\/\	\/\	\\\	/	\\/	\\\/	\//	/\\/	/\//	//\\

\ = needle to the left ('tink') / = needle to the right ('tonk')

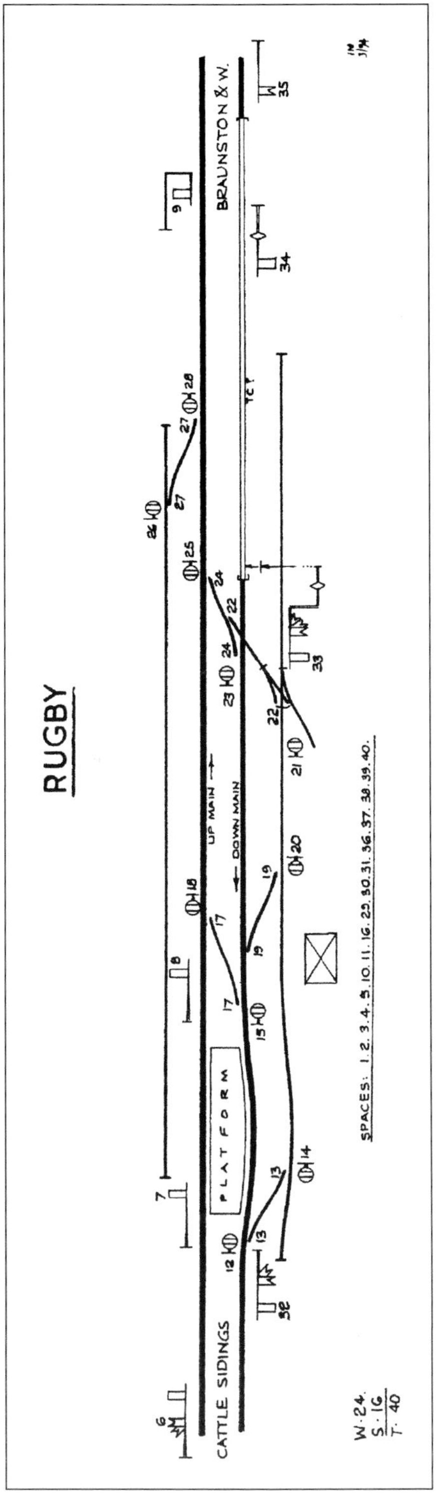

Signal box diagram, Rugby Station, pre-1941

For some reason I also recall DEEPDENE and GROVE; they were for Royal Trains, one carrying Royal personages and the other dignitaries from another country, but I cannot now remember which was which.

By the time the details of date, train, station and times had been added, some messages could be 200 words long. A 1958 copy of the Standard Codes for Telegrams lists some 1,200 code words for 76 subjects. It does not mention the operating abbreviations, such as SN, 'End of message'.

Rugby was an interesting box to work. Free acceptance of trains was nearly always possible with the Down Outer Home Signal and the Up Loop providing the requirements of Regulation 4, that a train could not be accepted unless there was sufficient clearance beyond a signal at danger. Signal 34 was essential when crossing a train from the Up Main Line into the Down Sidings, as was often the case with 'hot boxes' (over-heating axle bearings) being detached into the cripple siding. No 5 points at the end of the Up Loop were motor-operated, and to supply power for the point machines in the event of a mains failure a hand generator was provided at the No 40 end of the frame. George referred to this machine as 'The Mangle'. An Annetts Key was also provided if all else failed. The Up Intermediate Home signal, No 10, was Barby's Home signal No 20 when the latter box was open. It cut the section between Rugby and Braunston & Willoughby almost exactly in half and certainly helped to keep wheels turning.

Progressive improvements over the years at Rugby Station, later Rugby Central, were devoted mostly to the Up line.

The pre-1941 layout

I remember the layout and signalling as it was prior to these major alterations, before the conversion of the Up Siding into a running loop. The three Up signals as shown in the pre-1941 diagram were all lower-quadrants. The First Home signal (7) at the Leicester end of the Up platform was extremely tall to sight the arm above the Hillmorton Road bridge and to allow early sighting on the curve beyond Lower

The Down Inner Home/Down Cattle Sidings Outer Distant (33/3) can be seen in this old photograph. In front of the signal post is the Fogman's hut, tipped over waiting for the next spell of duty. The brick pump house and water tank is on the extreme left – the water bag can just be seen. *A. Franklin*

Hillmorton Road bridge. The Second Home signal (8) stood opposite the end of the Up platform and provided protection for points 17, 24 and 27. First and Second Home signals were used from the very early days – the terms Inner and Outer Home signals came later. The Starting signal (9) was a lower-quadrant 'gallows'-style bracket signal approximately opposite the Down Outer Home signal (34), between Catesby Road bridge (south of the station) and the next road bridge at Ashlawn Road. The entrance points into the Up Siding (27) were just beyond the south crossover (24) in those days. At that time all Down signals were equipped with lower-quadrant arms except the Down Inner Home/Down Cattle Sidings Outer Distant (33/3), which had been converted before my spottings began.

The bracket post carrying Up signals 1 and 7, with the sighting boards behind them. *A. Franklin*

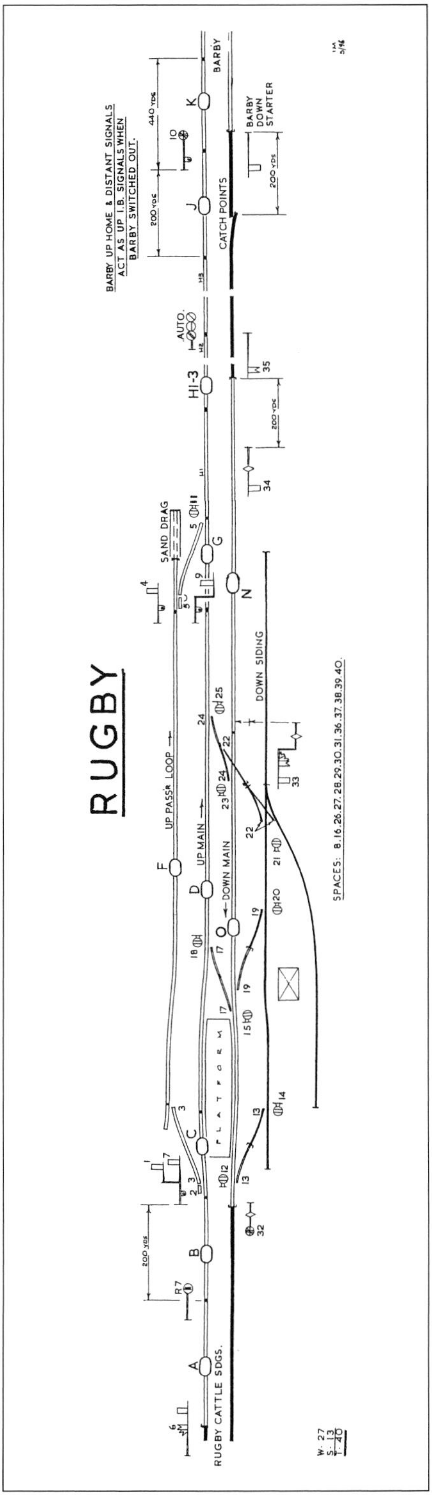

Signal box diagram, Rugby Station, post-1941

The post-1941 changes

The early war years saw dramatic changes to the layout on the Up side when earth-moving equipment removed large quantities of the embankment towards Catesby Road bridge to allow for the extension of the Up Siding into a Loop. A relatively small amount of the embankment was removed from the north side of Hillmorton Road bridge for the entrance to the Up Loop, and a small retaining wall built.

With the resignalling in 1941, the layout of the Up Main was changed extensively when it was track circuited throughout from the Up Starting signal at Rugby Cattle Sidings to the new Home signal at Barby Sidings. This signal acted as the IB (Intermediate Block) Home signal (10) when Barby was switched out. The Down Line remained unaltered for a few more years. All of the GCR signals were abolished and replaced by appropriate upper-quadrant signals except Nos 32 and 35, which were renewed later. Levers 1, 2, 3, 4, 5, 10 and 11 were added to the frame, whilst Nos 8, 26, 27 and 28 were removed. To allow for complete utilisation, the new loop was designated as a Passenger Loop so that trains of that category could use it. Signal No 1 controlled the entry to the loop and was bracketed from the post of No 7. As these signals were close to the Hillmorton Road bridge they had white sighting boards, as seen in the accompanying photograph.

A Banner Repeater (R7) was situated roughly halfway between Clifton Road bridge and Lower Hillmorton Road bridge and forewarned drivers of the indication of No 7 signal – because of the curvature of the line and the overbridge, sighting was impossible. It did not repeat the position of signal No 1 as trains were required to enter the loop at reduced speed. A Banner Repeater is a centrally pivoted black semaphore arm in a circular glass-fronted case. This one was mounted on a pitch-pine post and had a ladder fore and aft; the rearmost ladder was provided to service the paraffin lamp, the foremost to give access to the apparatus.

A small but easily overlooked device could be found on the Trap Points (3) at the entrance end of the Up Loop. Known as a

Track Circuit Interrupter, it was a matchbox-sized device fitted to the crown of the (unused) rail. In the event of a runaway going over it to become derailed, the device would be broken which would operate Track Circuit 'C', thus locking both the Home and Loop signals 1 and 7. The other end of the loop was protected by a 'sand drag'.

Mention must now be made of some of the electrical controls that the introduction of track circuits imposed on the signalman. Facing Points have always presented a hazard to safe working, and in the early years of railways were avoided as much as possible; they face trains in the direction of travel, allowing them to be diverted from one running line to another without the need to stop, as is necessary with Trailing Points, which have to be reversed over. The problem of the blades of a Facing Point moving while a train was passing over them was solved by the provision of a Facing Point Lock (FPL). Although allaying one fear to a degree, there was still a danger that a signalman could change his mind and alter the route while a train was *within* the safe stopping distance from the points. However, with the Approach Track Circuits occupied, should the Stop signal be 'put back' prematurely, the controlling lever could only be replaced part-way into the frame, electrical 'back-locking' preventing a full restoration, thus maintaining the integrity of the mechanical interlocking but allowing sufficient movement for the signal arm to be returned to Stop. This provided a margin that allowed the approaching train to either stop, or to over-run on to the route originally signalled. A timing relay was operated to clear the back-lock on the Stop signal lever after a pre-set period, usually 30 seconds to 1 minute. The back-lock position operated on levers 1 and 7 with Track Circuit 'B' occupied, preventing the FPL (2) from being operated. This, in turn, locked the Facing Points (3).

The points at the 'country' end of the loop (5) were motor-operated. When a train entered the loop and occupied Track Circuit 'F' a timing relay was energised controlling an electric lock on lever No 5 to prevent the exit points being reversed until the train had been brought to a stand at the Starting signal (4). Thus the Up Loop, with its speed restriction, could not be used as an alternative to the Up Main for through trains without their being brought quite or almost to a stand at No 4 signal.

With the replacement of my favourite signal, the Down Starter became a colour light and the Down Line was track circuited between signals 33 and 32, the letter 'O' being added to the diagram.

Another addition was made with the provision of a 'backing' signal for freight trains being shunted into the Down Refuge . These 'runners' were invariably 60 or more wagons in length and it was impossible for the drivers to see the ground signal, or 'dolly' (12), by Hillmorton Road bridge when the engine was on the curve between the Lower Hillmorton Road bridge and Clifton Road bridge. A hand signal by the guard had been the accepted method of 'calling back', but this was superseded by the provision of a post-mounted Ground signal almost opposite the Up Main Banner Repeater. It was worked by lever No 16.

IB signals were installed and the Down line track circuited when Shawell signal box was closed. No 31 was the final addition to the frame. Similar arrangements were added at Lutterworth.

The lengths of trains detained in the Up Loop were usually such as to prevent the signalman from observing the all-important tail lamp for 'clearing back' purposes. A lineside telephone was therefore provided for the guard's benefit so that he could declare his train complete to the signalman. This equipment was rarely used as the men concerned preferred to use hand signals, being quicker and less involved than leaving the brake-van to phone. Telephones were provided at signals 1/7, 4 and 9, and at IB 10. The LNER favoured white 'D' signs on the signal post to indicate signal telephones. Nowadays this would be a 'T' superimposed on a white diamond sign.

Due to the close proximity of the bracket signal No 9 to the water column, the effects of the smoke from engines taking water caused serious decay to the metal of the original signal and it was eventually replaced by a similar but less elegant structure. No 9 was sufficiently tall to take advantage of a sky background above Catesby Road bridge. However, No 4, being shorter, was provided with a white panel painted on the brickwork of Catesby Road bridge behind it to assist sighting. The white panel can still be seen on the bridge today.

Although I was no longer involved by that time, the final layout at Rugby completes the signalling story, so it has been included.

My account of Rugby Central would not be complete without mention of the Station Master, Ernie Potts. He had been brought up Great Central and knew the system thoroughly well. He was a kindly man and his railway stories kept me enthralled. One in particular might be worth recounting here.

Above A view looking south from the pump house. The Down Inner Home signal (33) is in the foreground, and the white painted panel can be seen on the Catesby Road bridge. *A. Franklin*

Right The southern end of the Up Passenger Loop showing the sand drag. Bracket signal No 9 and Starting signal No 4 with the 'D' sign on the post are in front of the water tank. Note the point rodding and the telegraph poles, once an integral part of the railway infrastructure. *A. Franklin*

Ernie was SM at a station in Nottinghamshire at the time and the station house was close to the line at the foot of the embankment. His coal shed was nearly empty, and he had told Mrs Potts to 'order the coalman in the morning'. During the night he was awakened by a terrible noise on the line outside. When going to investigate he found that a coal train had been derailed and had deposited five wagon-loads of coal into his garden!

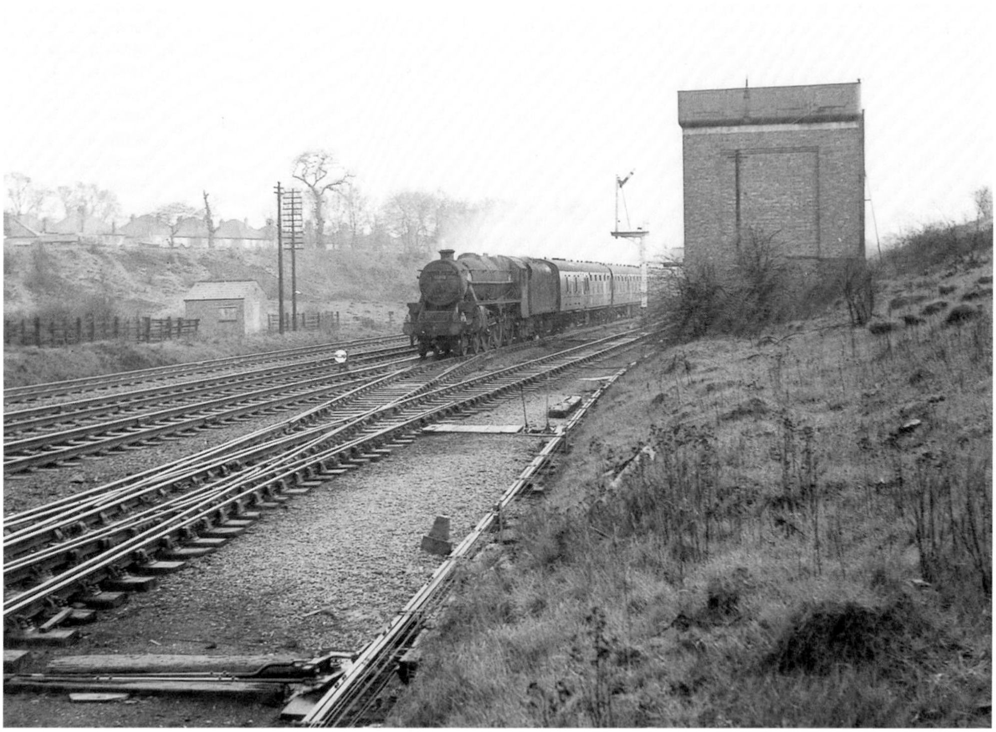

Above This view looking south shows the double-slip point No 22, Down Inner Home signal No 33 and the substantial pump house and water tank on the Down embankment. The point rodding, cranks and rods for points Nos 22 and 24 are in the foreground. *A. Franklin*

Left This is signal No 33 from a different view, but it is included because of the arrangement of guy wires stabilising the signal post. They can be seen stretching across to each embankment from the Doll, and from the signal landing or gangway down on to an anchor point between the Down Line and the siding. There are further guy wires from the top of the signal post to anchor points on the embankment. *A. Franklin*

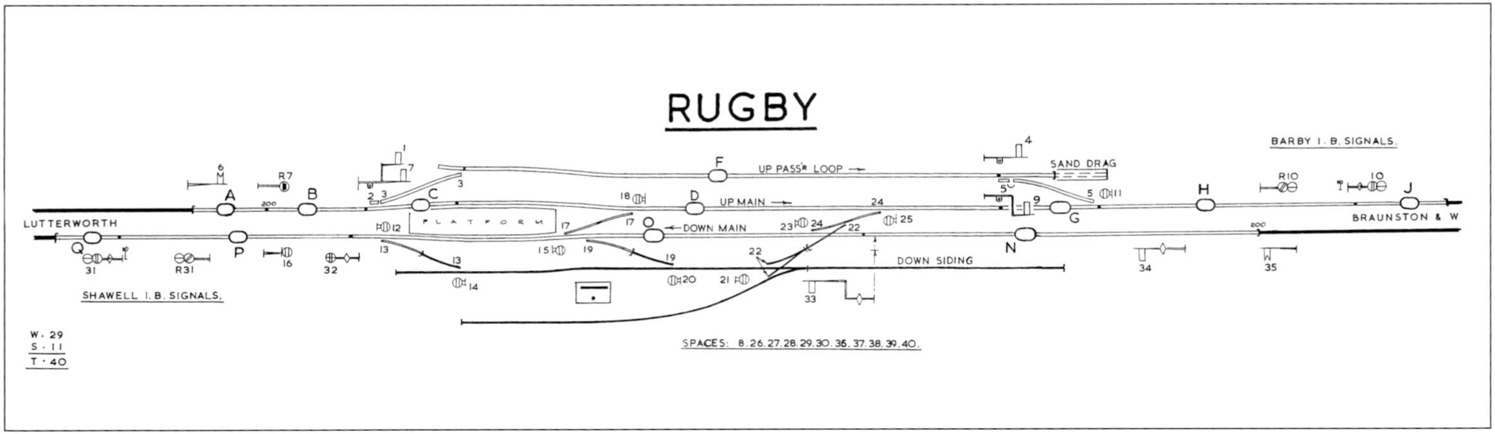

Signal box diagram, Rugby Station, the final layout

City of Truro stands at the north end of the platform, and Station Master Potts, smartly dressed in his uniform, can be seen consulting his watch. *I Mackenzie*

RUGBY CATTLE SIDINGS

On the north side of Rugby Station, just before the line was carried over 'the other railway' on the girder bridge, was Rugby Cattle Sidings box. The cattle docks were provided by the GCR when the line was first built as being conveniently close to the cattle market. The traffic went into decline before the war of 1939 and the box was left almost permanently closed. I can just remember the signals being operated – I must have been 6 or 7 at the time – but the box was only a middle-turn working even when it had a regular signalman. Cattle Sidings was situated about 200 yards south of the girder bridge on the Up side of the line. It had a brick base with wooden superstructure and contained a 30-lever frame, 17 working levers with 13 spare spaces. There were no track circuits and only three Signal Repeaters: Distants 3, 4 and 28. I was able to visit the box on one occasion only, when Signal & Telegraph fitters from Leicester were preparing for the replacement of the Inner Distant No 4 with a colour light. This, incidentally, was the demise of my favourite signal in the late 1940s when Rugby's Down Starter No 32 became a 'searchlight'-type colour light signal. Rugby Cattle Sidings was dismantled in the mid-1950s.

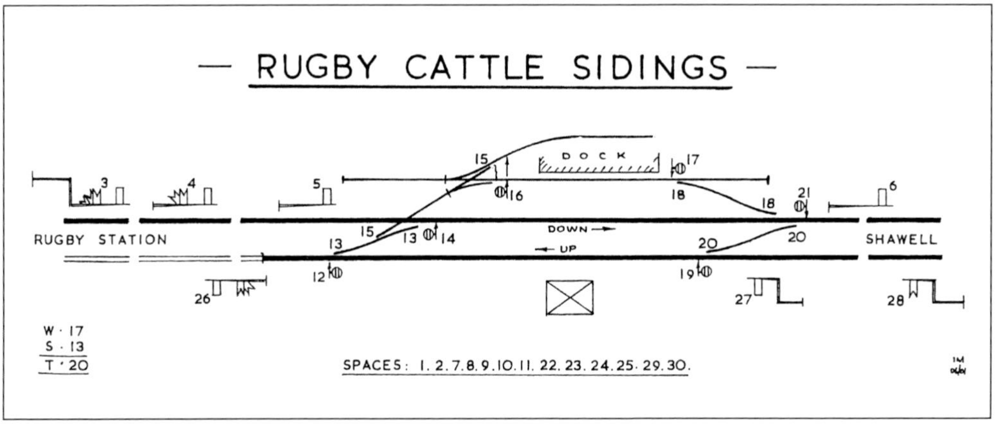

Above Signal box diagram, Rugby Cattle Sidings

Below Rugby Cattle Sidings box. *A. Franklin*

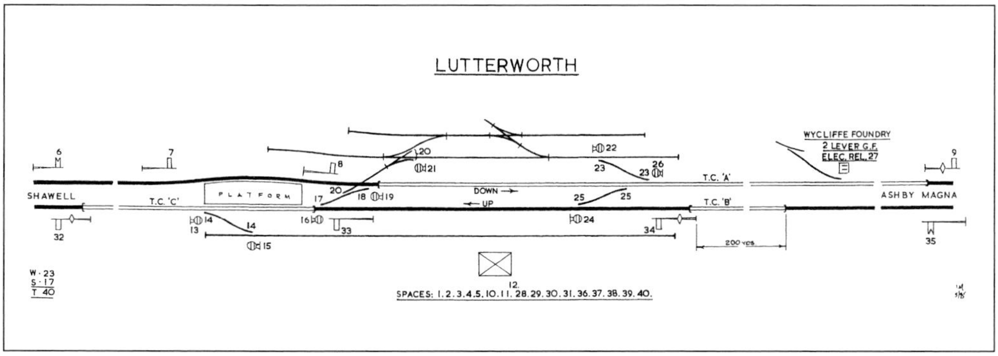

Signal box diagram, Lutterworth, circa 1946

LUTTERWORTH

The signal boxes that I was most keen to visit were now becoming further away from Rugby, and the distances involved made it impossible except on Saturday afternoons. Lawrence Sheriff School insisted that I attend during Saturday mornings, followed by a dash for home, a quick dinner, then – well, it could be somewhere like Lutterworth. There were many signal boxes that I was able to visit only once, and Lutterworth was one of them. Johnnie Dillow had paved the way for me and Wilf Day met me at the door with two small sections of carpet on which I had to shuffle on the highly polished linoleum. This was the cleanest box on the Great Central and to prove it everything shone. Lever handles were burnished, the frame black-leaded, brasses gleamed, and the kicking board (the long board that rested along the front of the lever frame) was scrubbed into submission, the whiteness of surrender! There was the customary 40-lever frame with levers 6, 7, 8 and 9 working the Down signals, and 32, 33, 34 and 35 the Up signals. Even the crossovers had predictable numbers in the almost standard arrangement of GCR boxes. This accounts for relief signalmen on the district being called 'keyhole signalmen' because a peep through the keyhole was sufficient knowledge to work the box. Talking of relief signalmen, I have often wondered how they coped in the pristine conditions at Lutterworth as they weren't always overfond of cleaning.

ASHBY MAGNA

The next of my jaunts took me to visit Percy Reynolds at Ashby Magna. The box was a carbon copy of Rugby Station, but here there were Down and Up Passenger Loops and the Up Line between Whetstone and Ashby Magna, worked by automatic signals, was Track Circuited throughout. Whetstone described the trains as they entered the automatic section using the prescribed bell codes, but there were no 'Train Entering Section' or 'Train Out of Section' bell codes. It was a very interesting box and I was able to see a totally different method of train operation for the first time. It was in fact an insight into what was to become standard signalling practise in the later modernised railways – Track Circuit Block.

I was able to visit many signal boxes on a one-off basis, all within cycling distance of Rugby. But one more visit must be included to close this chapter of my experiences before I left school in July 1947.

STAVERTON ROAD

Having been laid low with the flu, I was forced to stay at home to recuperate. After a time, as my health returned to normal, I became bored. To relieve this boredom I foolishly decided to bicycle out to Staverton Road. Now, Rugby Station to Staverton Road is roughly 8½ miles by rail, but by road via Dunchurch and Daventry the distance is 17 miles, the route taking the form of a Z.

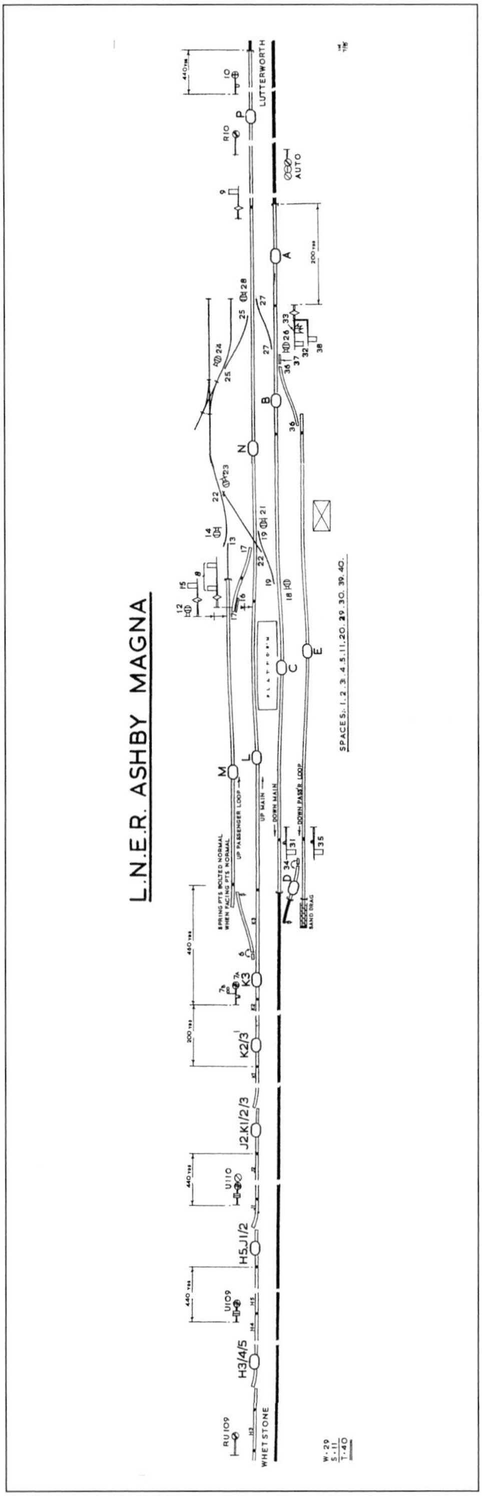

Above Signal box diagram, Ashby Magna, circa 1946

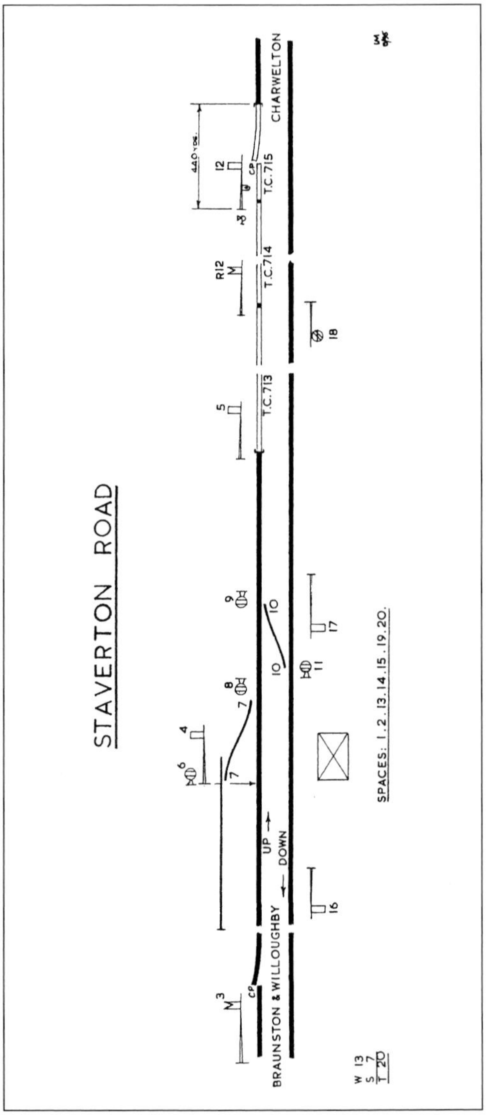

Left Signal box diagram, Staverton Road, circa 1946

Staverton Road cabin stands on the embankment with the parapets of the A425 bridge in view. Signal No 4 frames the view, showing the smoke deflector plate on the underside of the gantry and Doll to protect them from the corrosive effects of smoke. The restraining wires can be seen, and that the signal ladder is positioned so that anyone using it has a clear view of any oncoming trains. The 'dolly', No 6, at the base is for the catch points of the siding. On the Down Line is signal No 17. A typical telegraph pole carrying the many wires is as usual on the Up side of the formation. It must have been a bleak spot in winter. *D. Bullock*

The box stood on an embankment above the A425 Daventry to Southam road. It was on the Down side of the line where the railway was on a sweeping curve on a rising gradient of 1 in 176 up towards Catesby Tunnel. There was a frame of 20 levers, 13 working and 7 spaces. An Up Refuge Siding was provided, which could accommodate trains of up to 72 wagons. There was also a crossover road. It had unusual Intermediate Block Signals on the Up Line, which were semaphore signals worked by motors. There was also a Down Distant that was a mechanically operated colour light. Both IB signals and the Down Distant were replaced by orthodox signals in 1959. The 3,000-yard Catesby Tunnel was in the section between Charwelton and Staverton Road and a telephone was provided in the tunnel for train crews to use in the event of an emergency.

Having noted the relevant details, I thanked signalman Vernon Morley for his hospitality only to realise that I was in no fit state to tackle the 17-mile return journey. I had been extremely stupid venturing this far, but help was at hand. Vernon stopped a 'down runner' and bundled me into the brake-van with instructions to the train crew to 'Drop him off at Rugby'. I shall never forget the kindness shown to me by those railwaymen – quite unofficial and highly irregular, but they were Good Samaritans that day.

OTHER GC BOXES VISITED

To describe all the signal boxes visited would be tiresome, so the diagrams are included for interest, with a schematic layout diagram to show their relative positions and orientation. They are given in sequence travelling northwards from Brackley to Leicester Central, away from London Marylebone, the principal station.

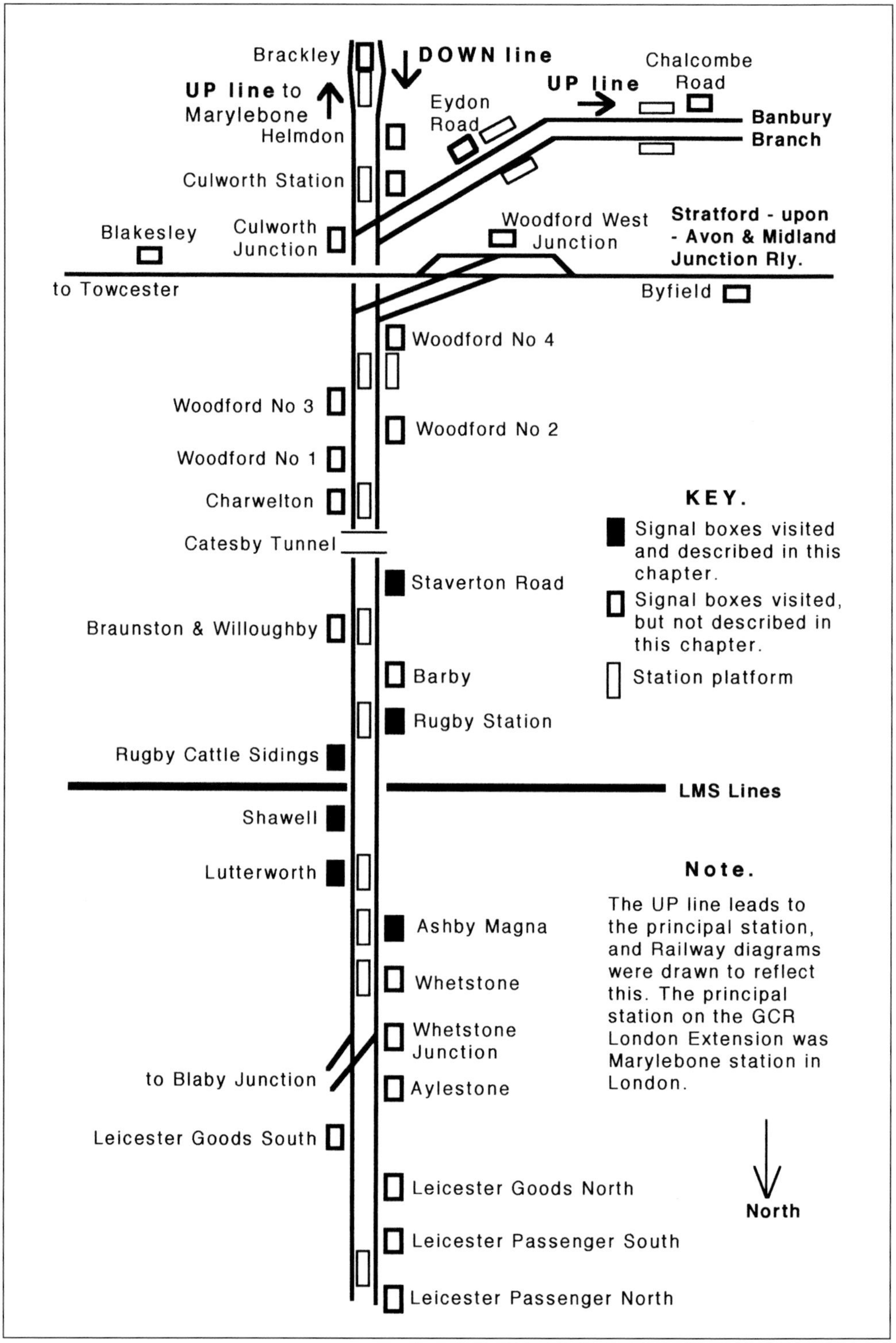
Brackley
DOWN line
UP line to Marylebone
Helmdon
Eydon Road
UP line
Chalcombe Road
Banbury Branch
Culworth Station
Blakesley
Culworth Junction
Woodford West Junction
Stratford - upon - Avon & Midland Junction Rly.
to Towcester
Byfield
Woodford No 4
Woodford No 3
Woodford No 2
Woodford No 1
Charwelton
Catesby Tunnel
KEY.
Signal boxes visited and described in this chapter.
Signal boxes visited, but not described in this chapter.
Station platform
Staverton Road
Braunston & Willoughby
Barby
Rugby Station
Rugby Cattle Sidings
LMS Lines
Shawell
Lutterworth
Note.
The UP line leads to the principal station, and Railway diagrams were drawn to reflect this. The principal station on the GCR London Extension was Marylebone station in London.
Ashby Magna
Whetstone
Whetstone Junction
to Blaby Junction
Aylestone
Leicester Goods South
Leicester Goods North
North
Leicester Passenger South
Leicester Passenger North

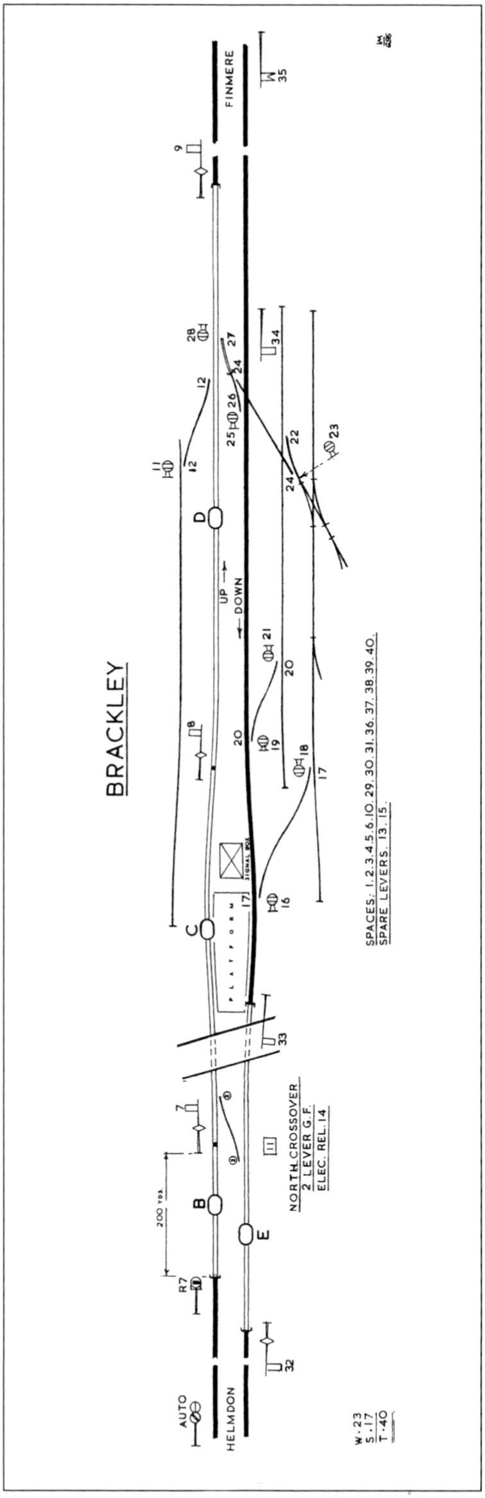

Signal box diagrams, Brackley and Helmdon, circa 1947

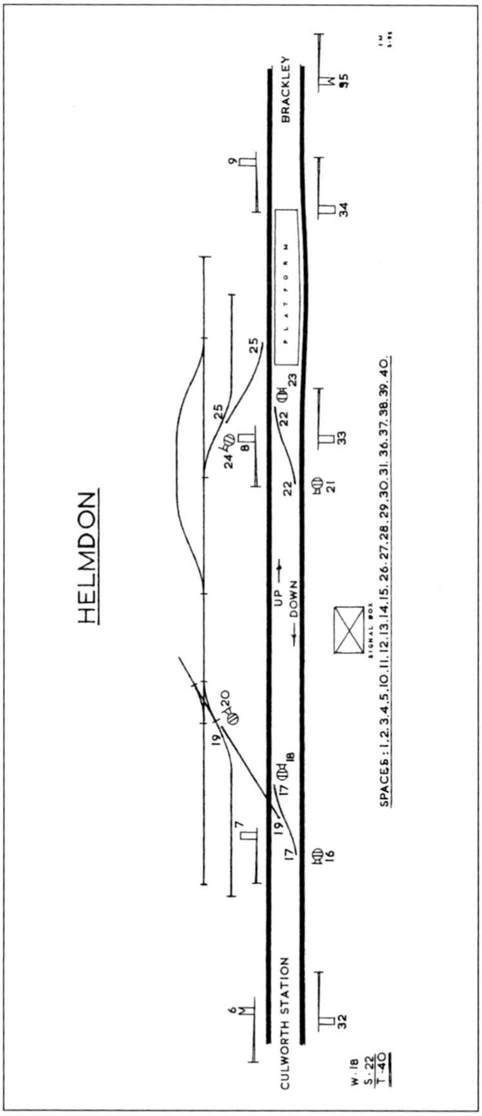

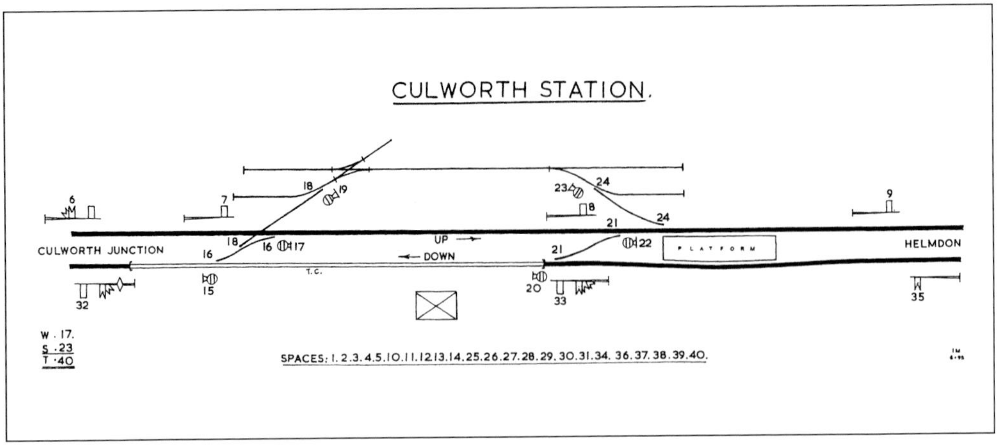

Above Signal box diagram, Culworth Station

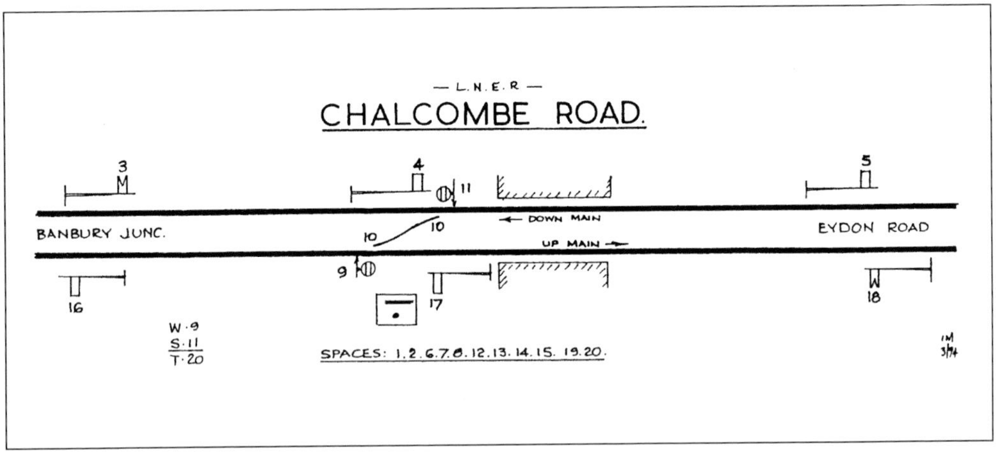

Above and below Signal box diagrams for two boxes on the Banbury branch, Chalcombe Road and Eydon Road

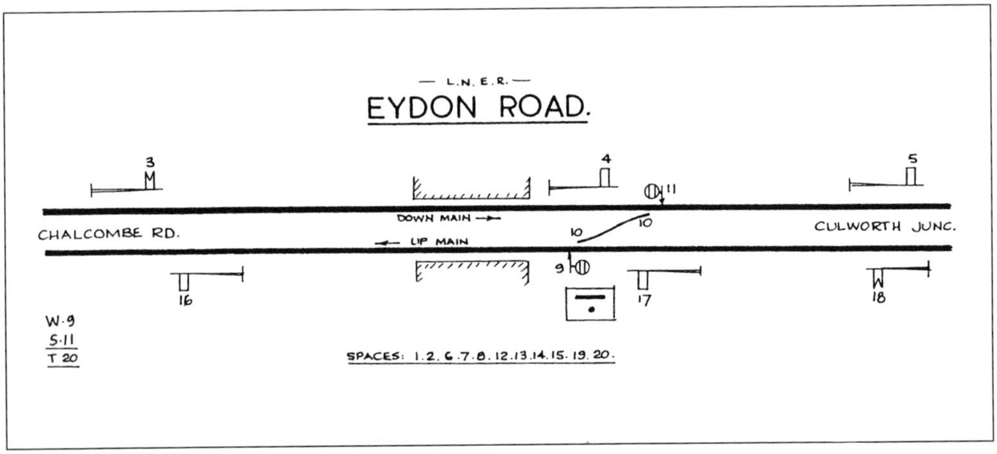

Left Signal box diagram for Culworth Junction, where the Banbury branch joined the main line south of Woodford

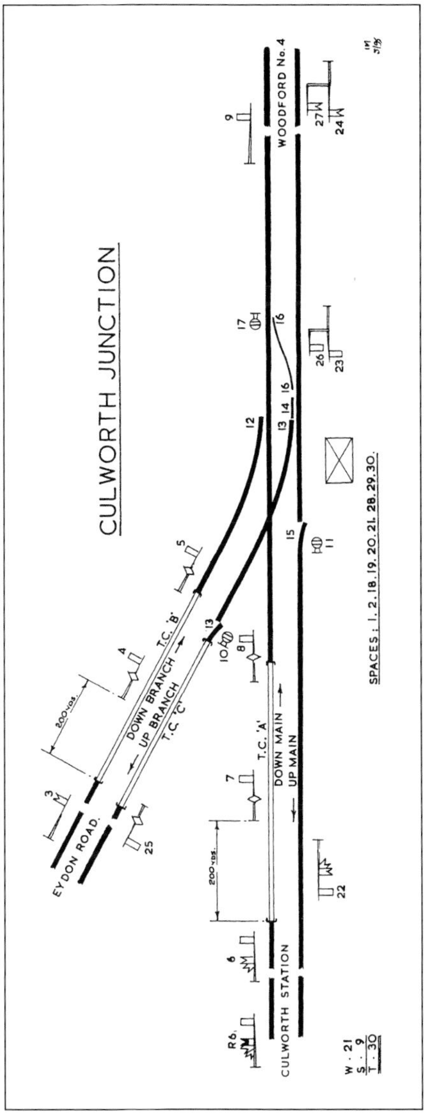

Below Signal box diagram for Woodford No 4 circa 1947, showing the junction for the Stratford-upon-Avon & Midland Junction Railway at Woodford West Junction (see Chapter 6)

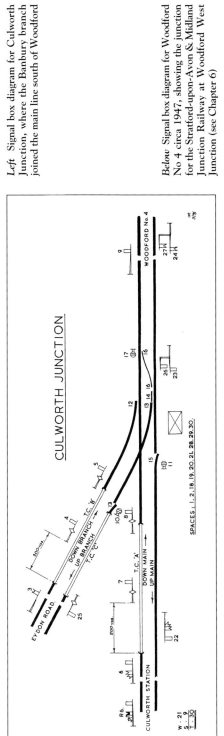

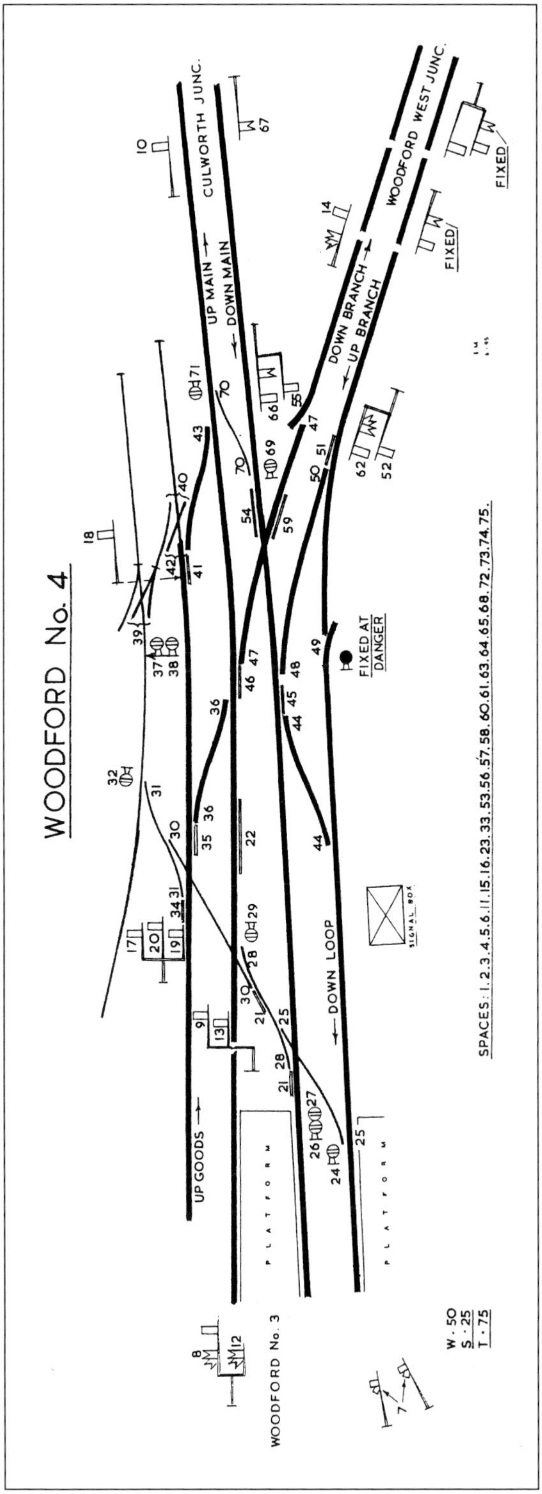

Signal box diagrams, Woodford Nos 3 and 2, circa 1947 and 1948 respectively

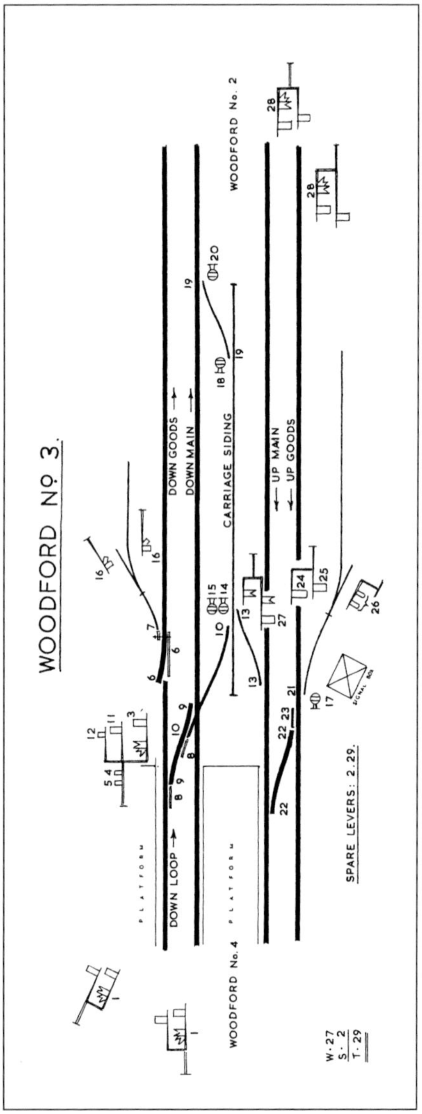

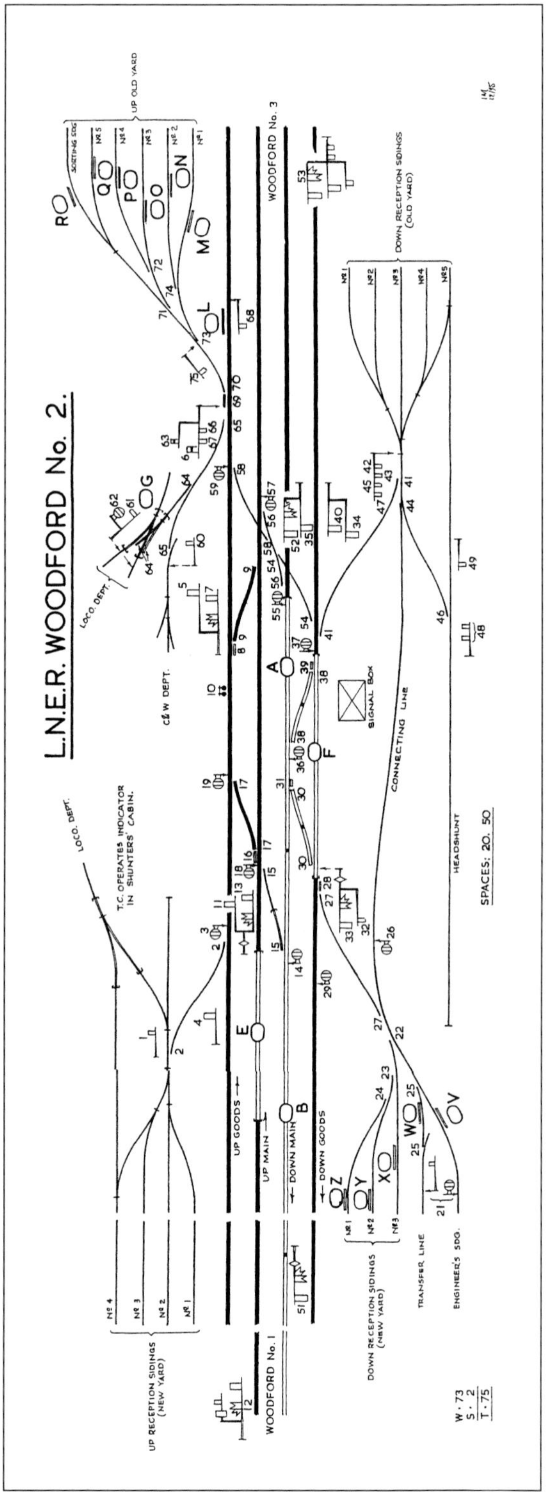

Left Signal box diagram, Woodford No 1, circa 1948

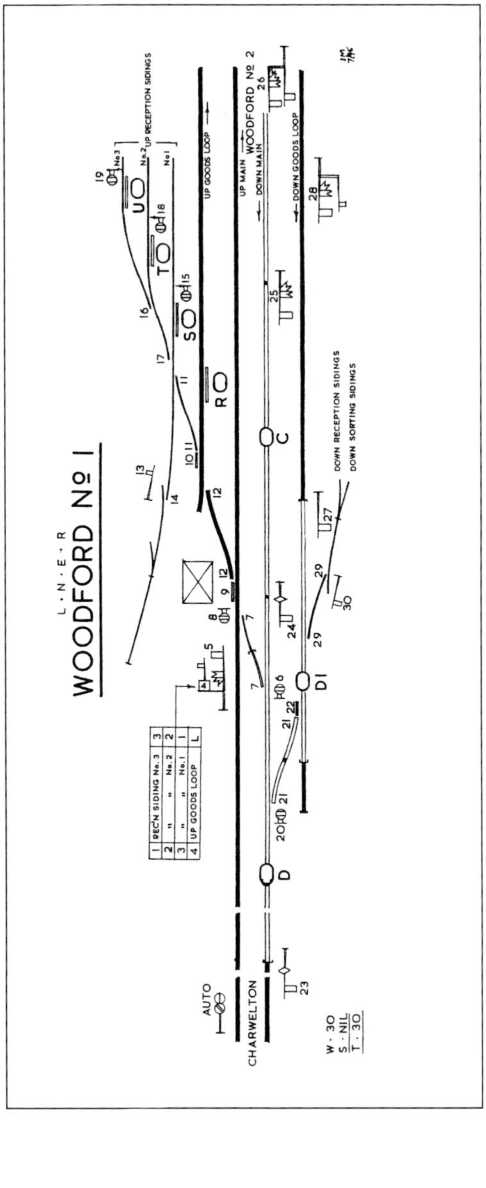

Below Signal box diagram, Charwelton

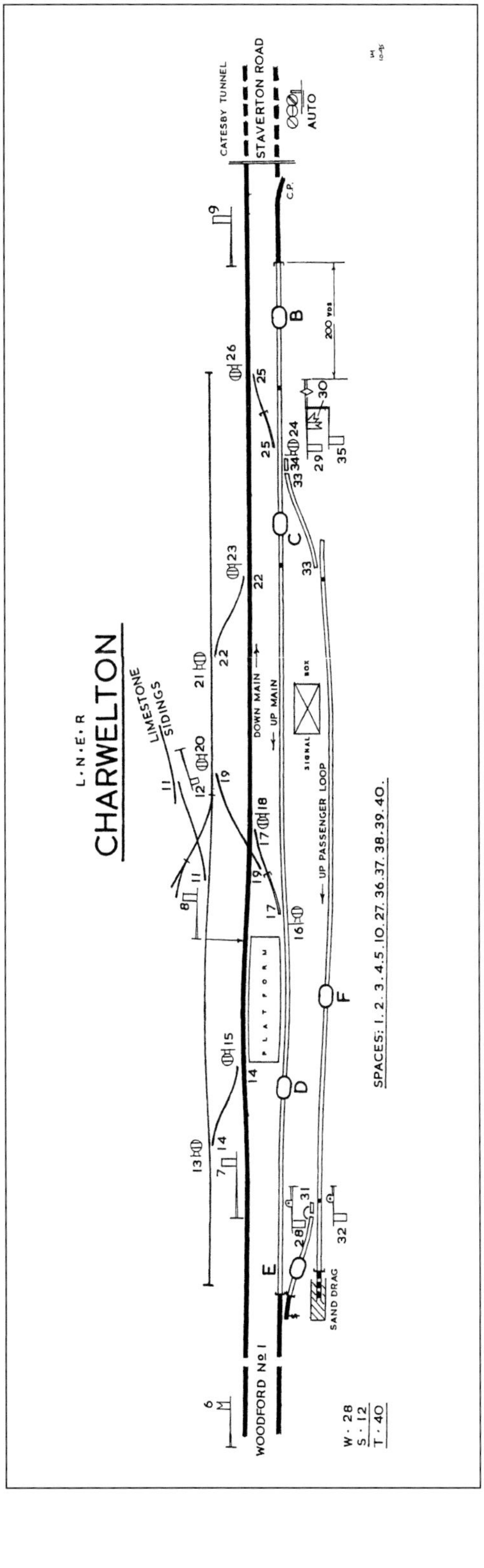

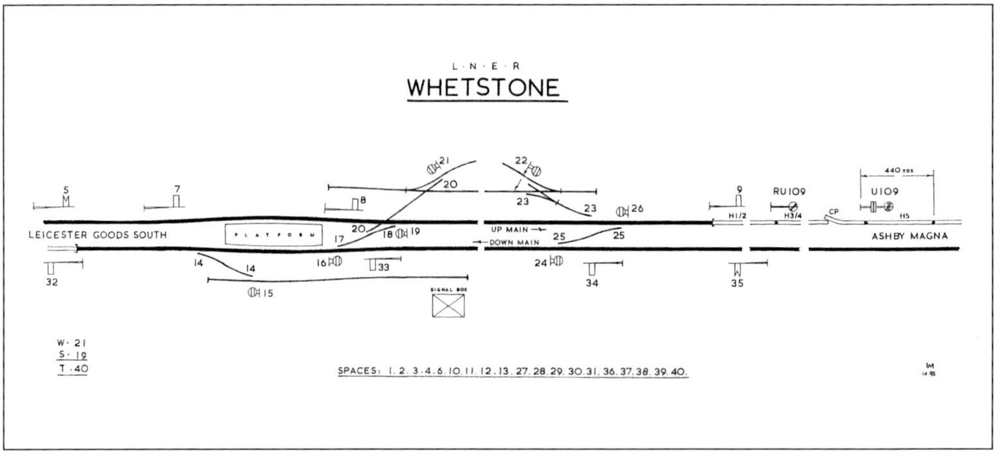

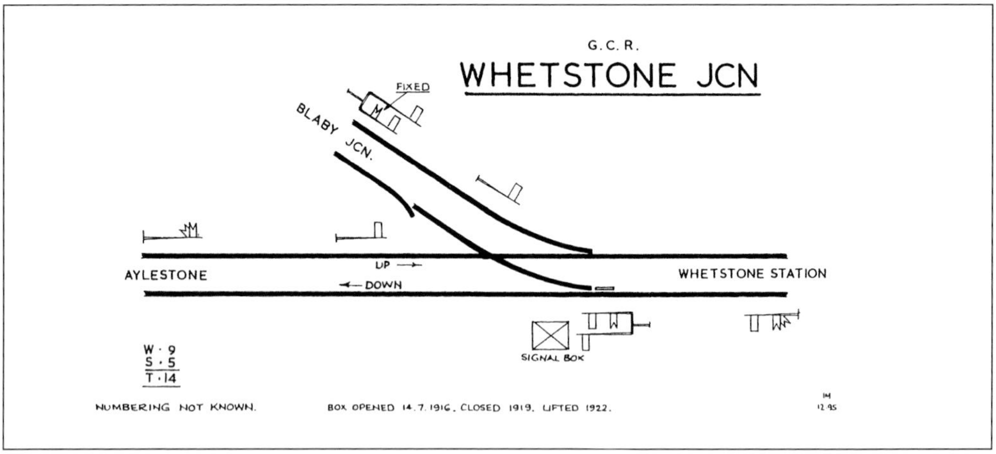

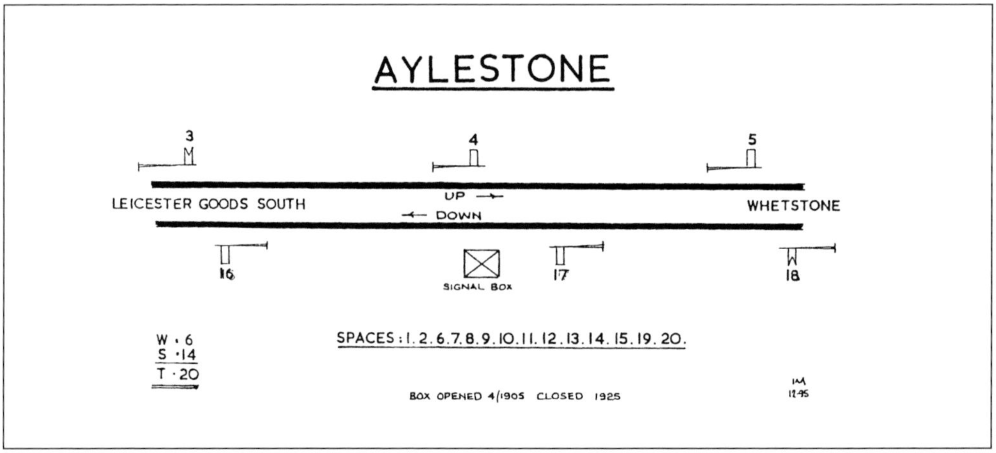

Moving now to the north of the Rugby area, signal box diagrams for Whetstone (circa 1946), Whetstone Junction and Aylestone, details for the last two supplied by M. Back.

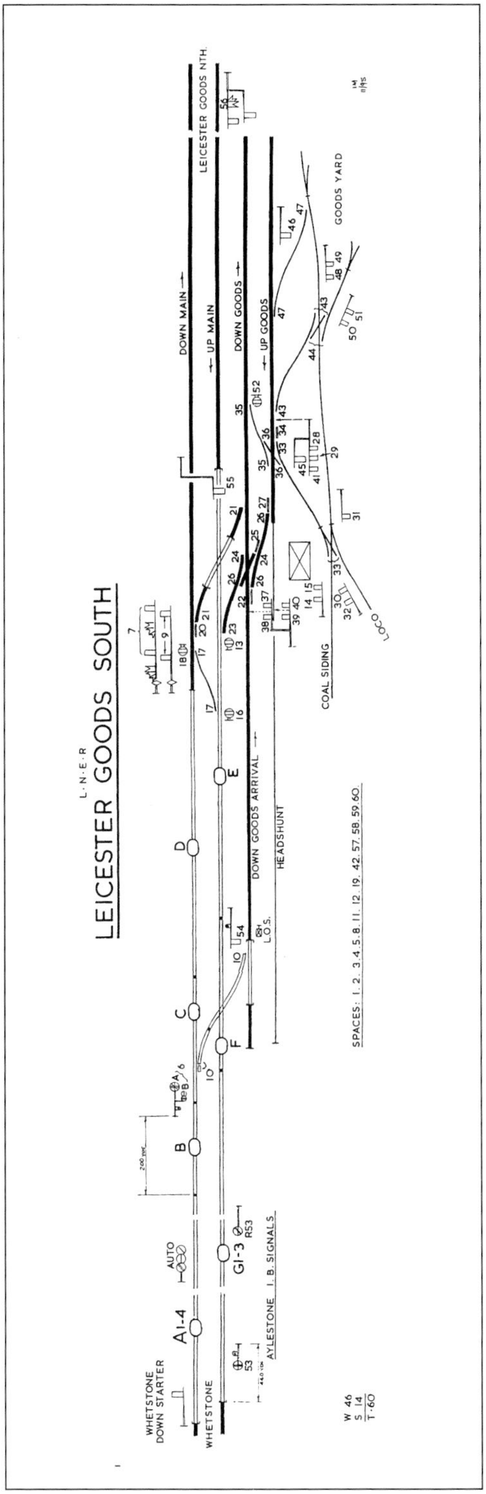

Signal box diagrams, Leicester Goods South and Leicester Goods North

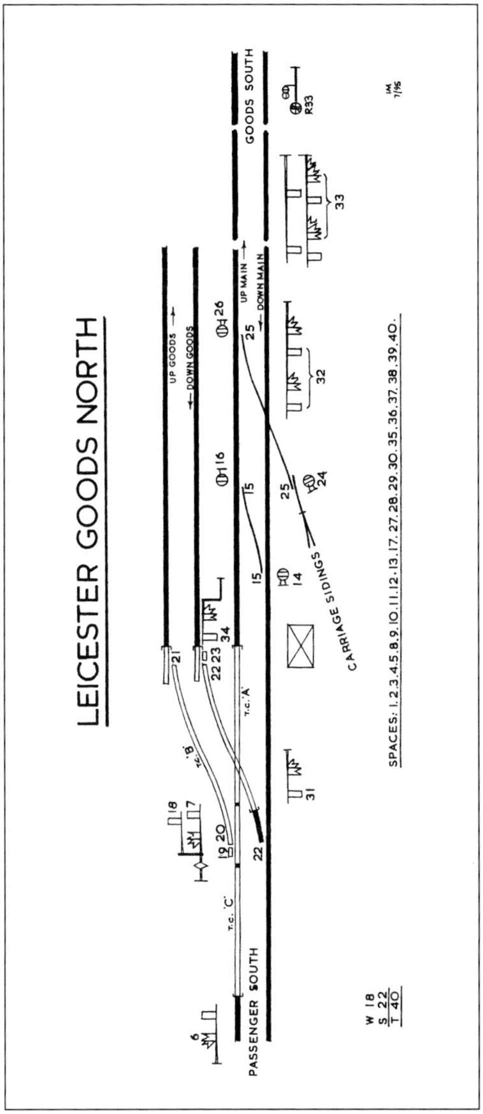

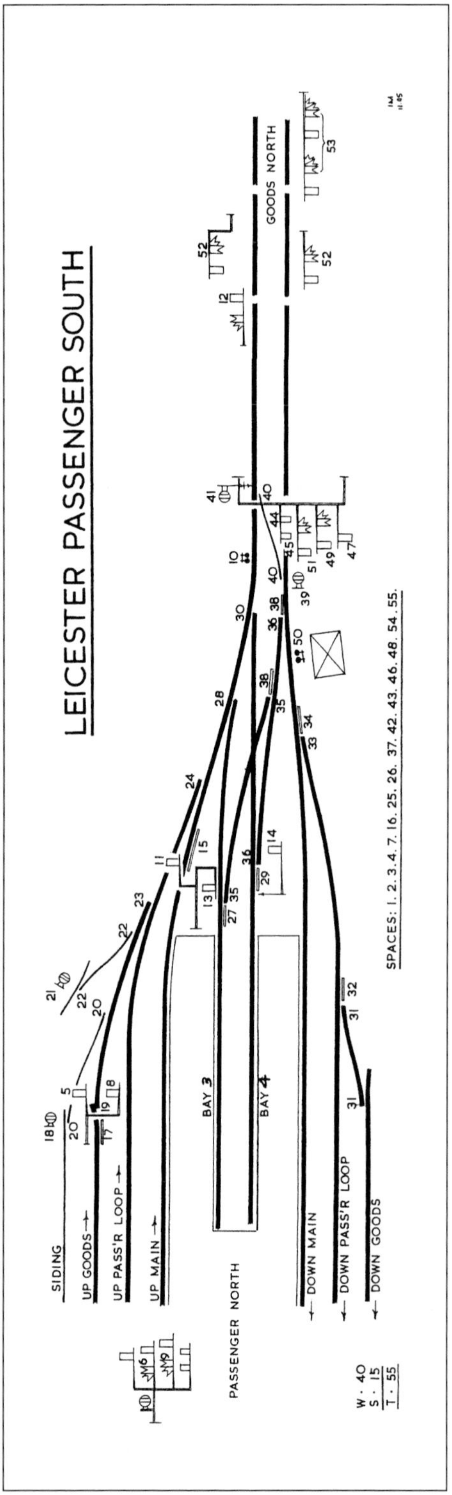

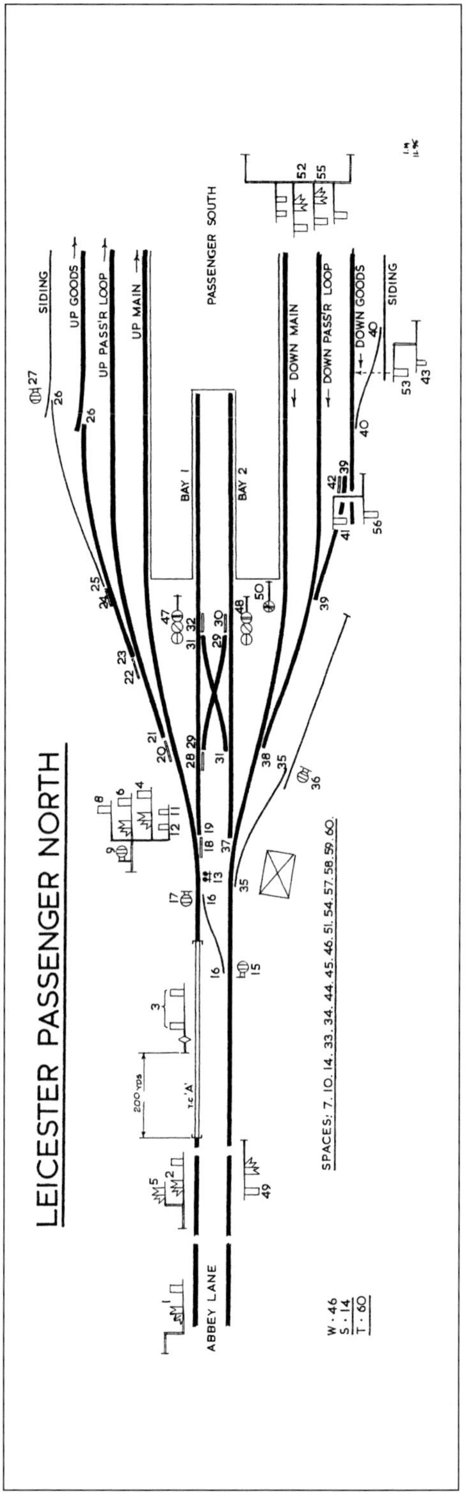

Signal box diagrams, Leicester Passenger South and Leicester Passenger North

5
Back to the 'Midland'

In these days of strict controls, of safety awareness, when each and every person who walks or works anywhere near to a railway line must have a Personal Track Safety qualification, and PICOWs and PICOPs (Person In Charge Of Work and Person In Charge Of Possession) are the order of the day – how did we manage in the old days? Safety and the preservation of human life is absolutely essential, and it is satisfying to know that these stringent measures have been established and rigorously imposed. But there were days, not so long ago, when signalmen at remote boxes were obliged to walk or cycle along the 'cess' to reach their places of work, there being no road access as there is to modern signalling centres, and the push-bike has given way to the BMW. Two examples of a) the hazardous approach and b) the remote situation are Rugby No 5 and Kilsby Tunnel South End. Rugby No 5 was accessible only by crossing all of the running lines at the approach to Rugby Midland station, which was curving at that location. Kilsby Tunnel South End, on the other hand, was situated midway between the A5 road at Welton station and the Ashby St Ledgers road, which crossed the south portal of the tunnel. From either direction it involved a cess-side trek of some half a mile. No doubt there were thousands of similar situations in the days of mechanical signalling, and it was accepted as a way of life by the men who worked those isolated watch-towers.

Kilsby Tunnel South End

In my young signal box visiting days the remote cabins presented a challenge that would set the adrenaline flowing. Kilsby Tunnel South End (hereinafter referred to as KTSE) could be seen from the road that crossed the tunnel mouth, but it was a long way off. Its Up Distant signal, an elderly LNWR lower-quadrant, was sited a few yards beyond the tunnel mouth, on the Down side of the line, thus providing a better sighting for engine crews as they emerged from the smoky depths. The elliptical shape of Kilsby Tunnel provides a headroom of some 24 feet above the running rails at the centre-line of the structure, thus the signal situated on the off side of the railway could be seen easily from the foot plate as the train neared the end of the tunnel. A platelayers' hut placed adjacent to the signal provided ample shelter for the unfortunate Fogsignalman whose lot it was to keep a lookout at that spot during fog or falling snow. I was less fortunate, as I was presented with the choice of either risking my neck on the trackside, or risking my clothing on barbed wire and brambles. I chose the latter! Anyway, the signalman would hardly be welcoming if I approached along the cess – he would more likely summon up the constabulary!

I found Signalman Bill Smith in a receptive mood and I was invited to share a pot of tea with him. KTSE box was a typical LNWR building and was sited on the Down side of the line just short of 76¼ miles from Euston. There

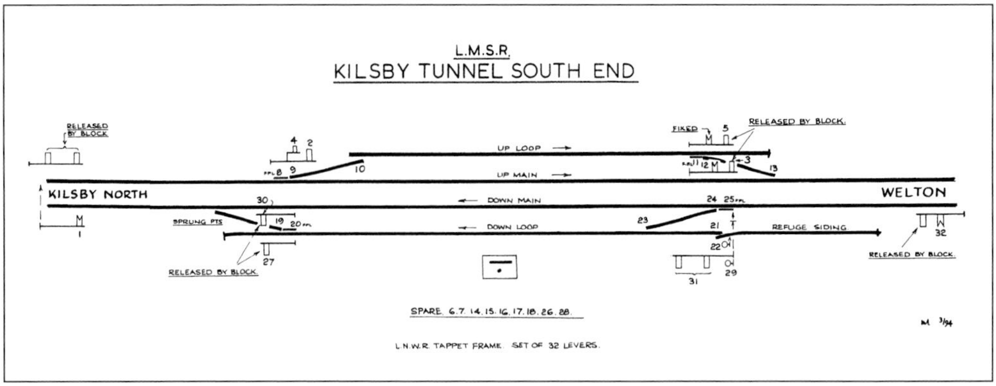

Signal box diagram, Kilsby Tunnel South End

were Up and Down Goods Loops but no crossover between the Main Lines. Prior to 1913 there was merely a Refuge Siding on the Down side, but this became a rearward extension of the Down Loop when that was installed in that year. The Down Home was a typical tall LNWR signal with co-acting arms, the Down Main to Loop signal was a 'dummy' (ground signal) situated at the foot of the main post. The only upper-quadrant signals at that time were the Up Main and the Up Loop Starters, both of which carried Distant arms for Welton, which was barely a mile away further south. There were special bell codes in operation for Down train routing purposes, which were initiated at Welton. Special 'Train Entering Section' signals were received and forwarded to Kilsby North for trains not stopping at Rugby as described earlier.

In view of the difficult approach to the box, I made very few visits there, but to complete the picture of the area I was able to obtain an invitation from the signalman at Welton to visit him. This visit presented a more serious hazard – road traffic.

WELTON

To reach Welton station it was necessary to cycle along the A5 road with all the dangers that that entailed. You can keep out of the way of trains, but lorries and cars present more serious problems. So Welton station was a one-off visit, just enough for me to take a few notes and enjoy the customary cup of tea.

The box itself was accessible from the end of the platform on the Up side at Welton; there was a timber yard served by sidings on the Down and a goods shed with sidings on the Up. At one time there were sidings that connected with the wharf of the Grand Union Canal, which was adjacent at that point; in fact, the canal passed under the railway just south of the station where the London & Birmingham Railway had provided a very ornate iron bridge. The station platforms were staggered and separated by an overbridge that carried the road to the village of Watford, which was but a stone's throw from the station, whereas Welton was some distance away nearer to Daventry.

It was at Welton that I encountered my first set of IB signals on the LMS, which were at Brockhall in the section to Weedon No 2. There was also the locomotive crews whistling (or hooting would be a more apt description of a Stanier engine) their routing requirements at Rugby.

DUNCHURCH

I had an aunt who lived at Cawston quite close to the station at Dunchurch. This was on the Rugby to Leamington line and, typically, was a mile or so from the village of Dunchurch. Adjacent to the station yard was a building carrying a sign proclaiming 'Laughing Dog Brand Dog Rusks'. I've never seen these delicacies offered for sale anywhere and have now accepted it as a mystery that

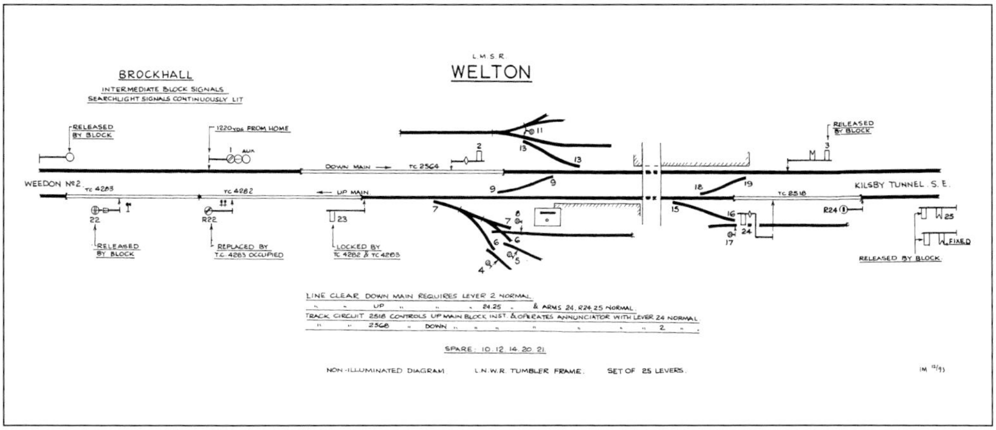

Signal box diagram, Welton

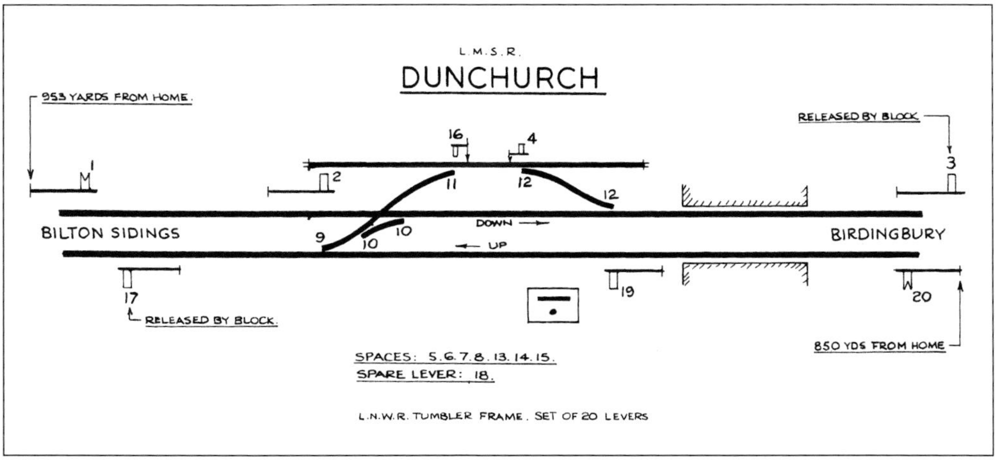

Signal box diagram, Dunchurch

must remain unsolved. Trains at Dunchurch were thinly spaced, and interest in the line was thus not of the greatest. I remember Dougie Burge at the station, who later became a relief signalman. In later years I also remember seeing the very elderly locomotive *Lion* in steam along the line at Dunchurch. It was built in 1838 for the Liverpool & Manchester Railway and was being tested prior to taking part in the filming of *The Titfield Thunderbolt*. The engine crew were dressed in period costume and were filmed as they drove backwards and forwards along the Up Main Line, which shows the infrequency of the service on that line.

Rugby No 1

From the somewhat quiet backwater of Dunchurch to the mammoth that was Rugby No 1 is a study in contrasts. Naturally, Rugby No 1 was by invitation only and strictly supervised. I was met at the end of Platform 2 at Rugby Midland and escorted along the trackside by Frank Renshaw, the Senior Signal Fitter at Rugby. This enormous box stood in splendid isolation between the running lines and numerous sidings at the south end of the station. Entrance was by way of two flights of interior stairs through the locking floors of the box to emerge at the end

Lion at Dunchurch station. *I. Mackenzie*

of a lever frame the length of a cricket pitch – 185 levers, all but three working! Two men were responsible for the operation of this busy box, and on the day of my visit they were Joe Bond and Bert Rennocks. Joe was 'Upside' and Bert was 'Downside', and both were constantly toing and froing, pushing and pulling levers along their respective ends of that enormous frame. I know there have been bigger boxes in the UK, but this was the biggest that I had seen. I understand that during the course of a day's duty these men would walk the equivalent of 13 miles and make 3,000 lever movements in the process – a day's duty being, of course, a normal 8 hours. In those days the box was graded a Special Plus in the marking system, a system that graded the work done and decided the pay scale for all boxes.

Joe was a tall man, very upright in stature, who walked with a strange sort of shuffling gait. Maybe it was the slippers he wore that made him keep his feet almost on the floor. It seems that from lever number 68 to 181 constituted the Up man's responsibility, and from 1 to 67 the Down. During the re-signalling of 1939, when Clifton Road Junction was abolished, a further four levers were added, designated A, B, C and D, and Bert was at that end. He was of medium height and ambled about almost like a friendly gorilla with a cap! I can never understand why some signalmen wore caps while at work, but there were many who did and Bert was one such.

The signal box diagram for Rugby No 1 can be found on pages 12-13. I was 15 when I visited the box. I had a basic idea about the principles of railway signalling and had understood what it was all about upon first crossing the threshold of ordinary signal boxes, but what I was witnessing now was no ordinary signal box; the levers stretched in a seemingly never-ending line, and these were the first things to claim attention. Then there were the Block Shelves, one at each end with its dominant Illuminated Track Diagram, and the Block Instruments – six on the Down side shelf and nine on the Up shelf. Six different bell tones was bad enough, but nine demanded a critical hearing to differentiate one from another. A booking boy was responsible for the telephones, and even his task was sufficiently demanding that the normal Train Register Book was not kept (except for out-of-the-ordinary occurrences) and he was occupied by only recording the engines as they entered or left the sheds, and with wiring the various freight train movements to Control and other interested parties.

From the elevated position three floors above the rails it was possible to obtain a bird's-eye view of the track layout and the seemingly endless shunting that took place at that end of Rugby Midland. There was also a wonderful view of the Great Central 'Birdcage' bridge, which spanned the LMS at that point. That great gantry, the 'Bedstead', which I described earlier, had long since been dismantled, but there was still a goodly number of mechanical signals to be seen at that time, which provided the observer with some idea of what the area would have looked like in truly semaphore days. Sadly these are but memories of a rapidly vanishing past, but on the plus side there is the seldom considered fact that the signalmen of today are not subject to hernias as were many of their forerunners in boxes such as Rugby No 1. Obesity is probably today's problem.

THE OTHER RUGBY BOXES

The diagrams for the other Rugby signal boxes are included to give an historical overview of signalling at this complex station. They were drawn from visits made in the late 1940s and as such are an important record of Rugby's railway history.

SUBSIDENCE AND POINT OPERATION BY DOUBLE WIRES

Before leaving the former LMS line, one unusual item of signalling apparatus is worthy of mention, the Turnover frame at Brandon Ballast Pit signal box. This box provided access to Binley Colliery (near Coventry), the workings of which produced serious subsidence with its associated problems. The box was a standard LMS design but had been built on a foundation that could be jacked up when sinking occurred; heavy lifting equipment provided by the Motive Power Department would be employed to restore the signal box to its correct level as and when necessary.

Subsidence also played havoc with the operation of the Down Loop exit points and the associated Facing Point Lock. These could not be operated by point rodding but instead were worked by a system favoured by railways on the Continent, double wires. The Transportation Corps of the Royal Engineers trained their signalmen in the use of this type of frame at Longmoor Downs in Hampshire. The double wires were operated by what is called a Turnover frame, which was about 2 feet 6 inches long with its fulcrum about 3 feet above the floor. The operating travel of the lever was 180 degrees.

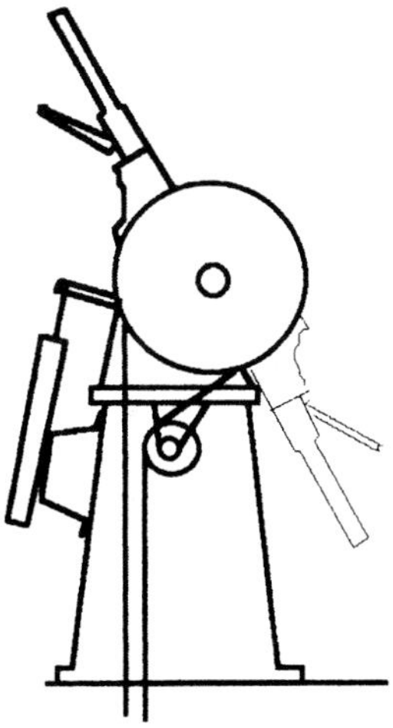

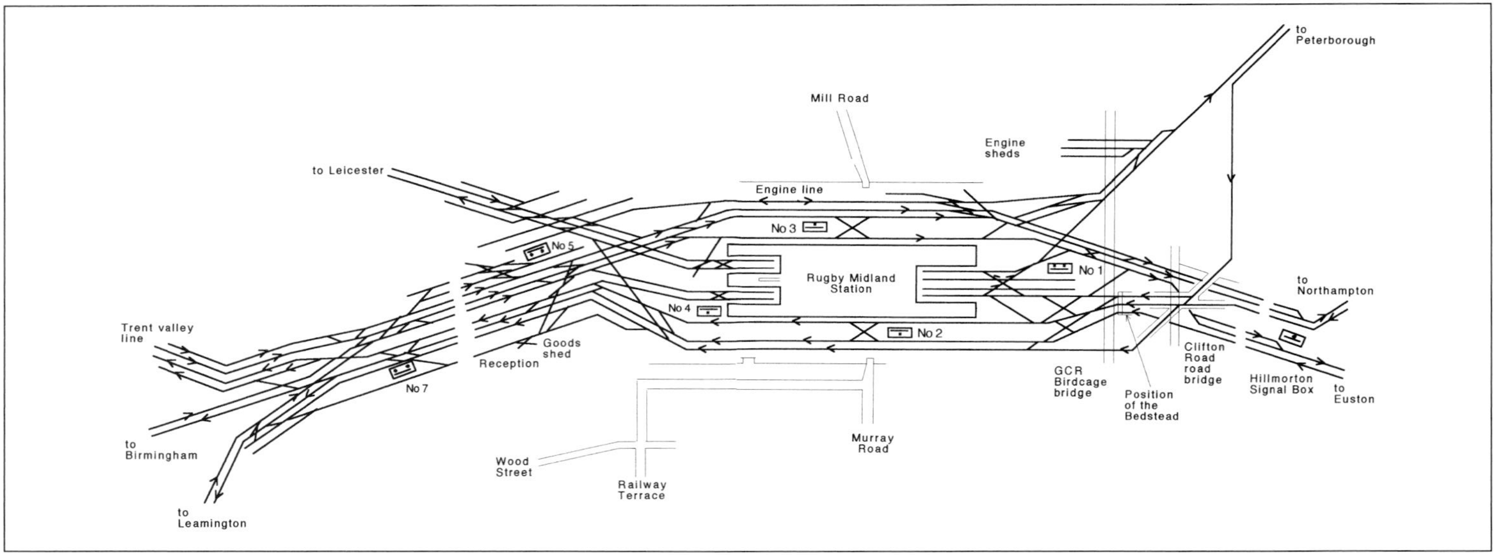

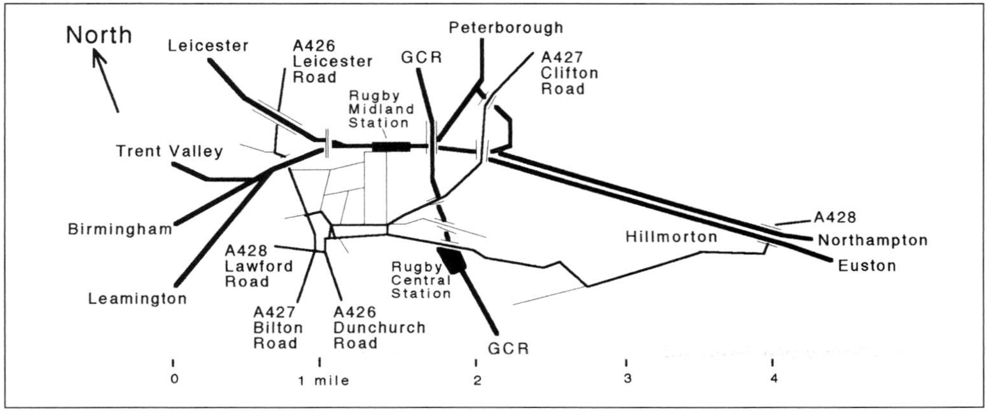

Above Schematic diagram showing the running lines and signal boxes at Rugby (not to scale). (No 6 box was never replaced.) *PJW*

No 1	185 levers, 2 signalmen
No 2	32 levers, 1 signalman
No 3	28 levers, 1 signalman
No 4	90 levers, 1 signalman
No 5	175 levers, 2 signalmen
No 7	135 levers, 2 signalmen

Left Scaled map of Rugby in the 1950s, showing railways and major roads. *PJW*

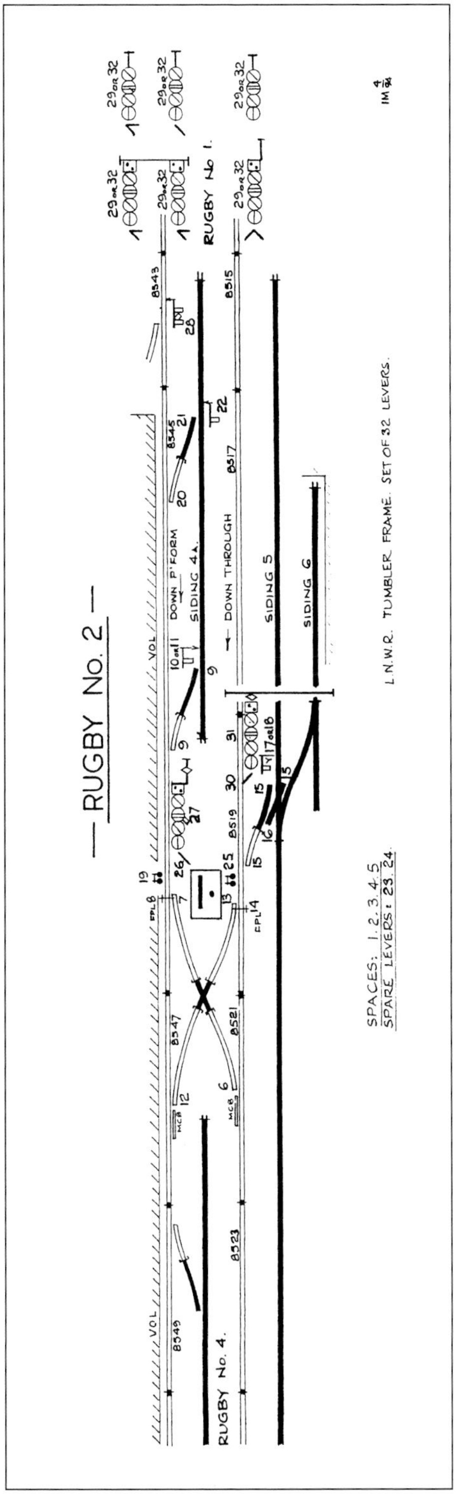

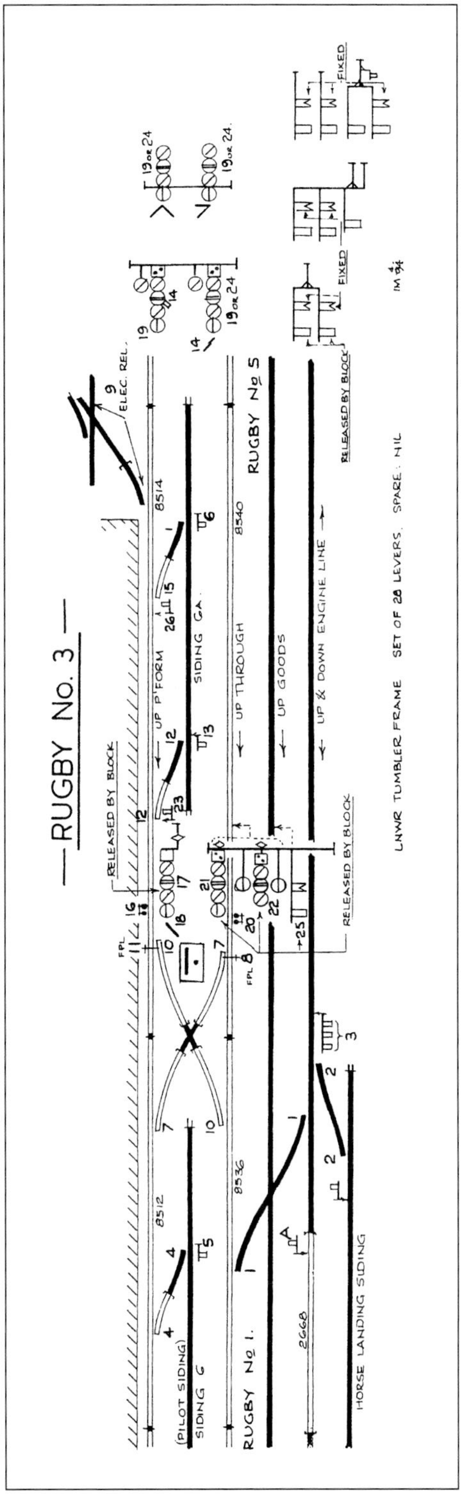

Signal box diagrams, Rugby No 2 and No 3

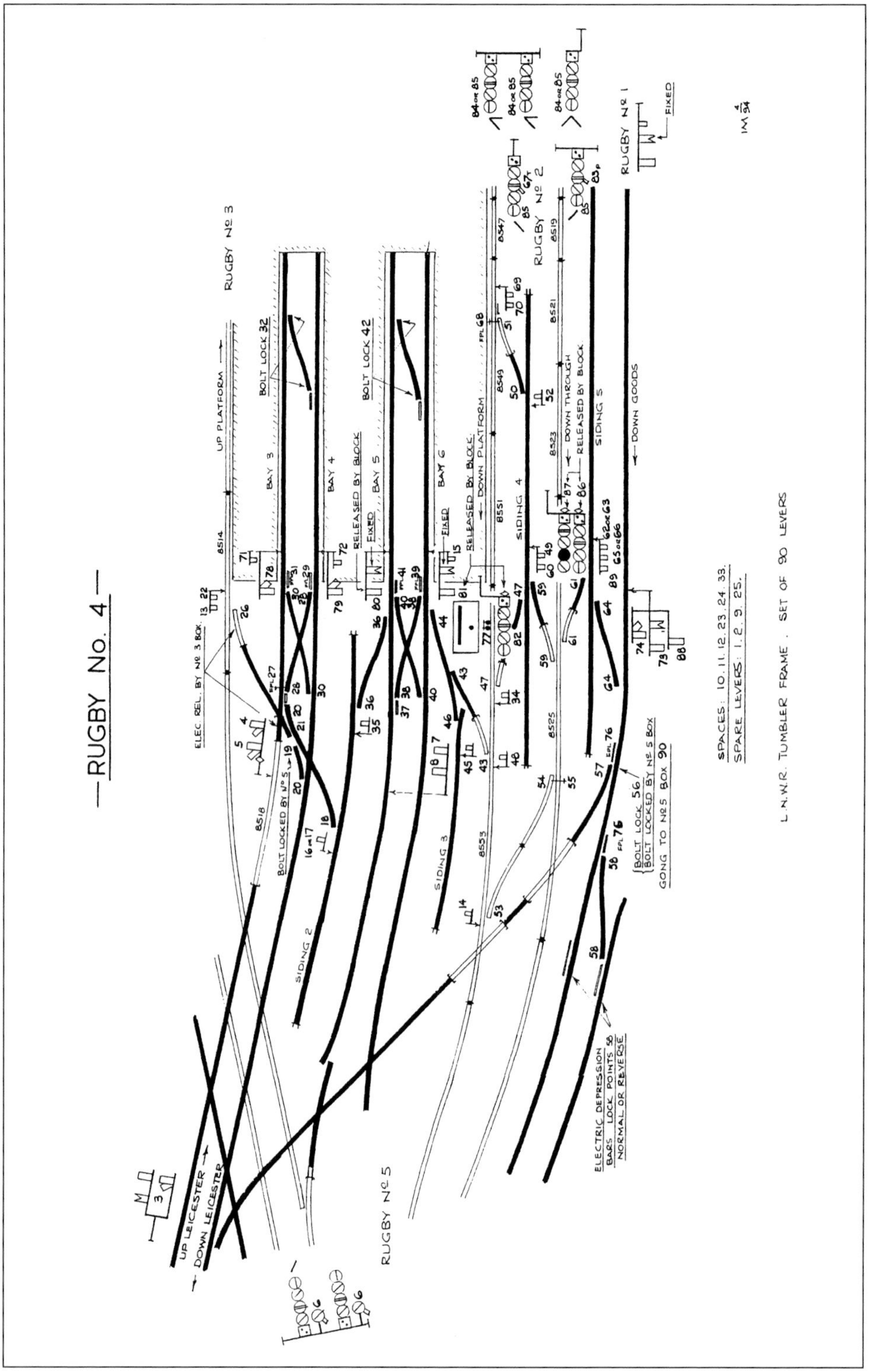

Signal box diagram, Rugby No 4

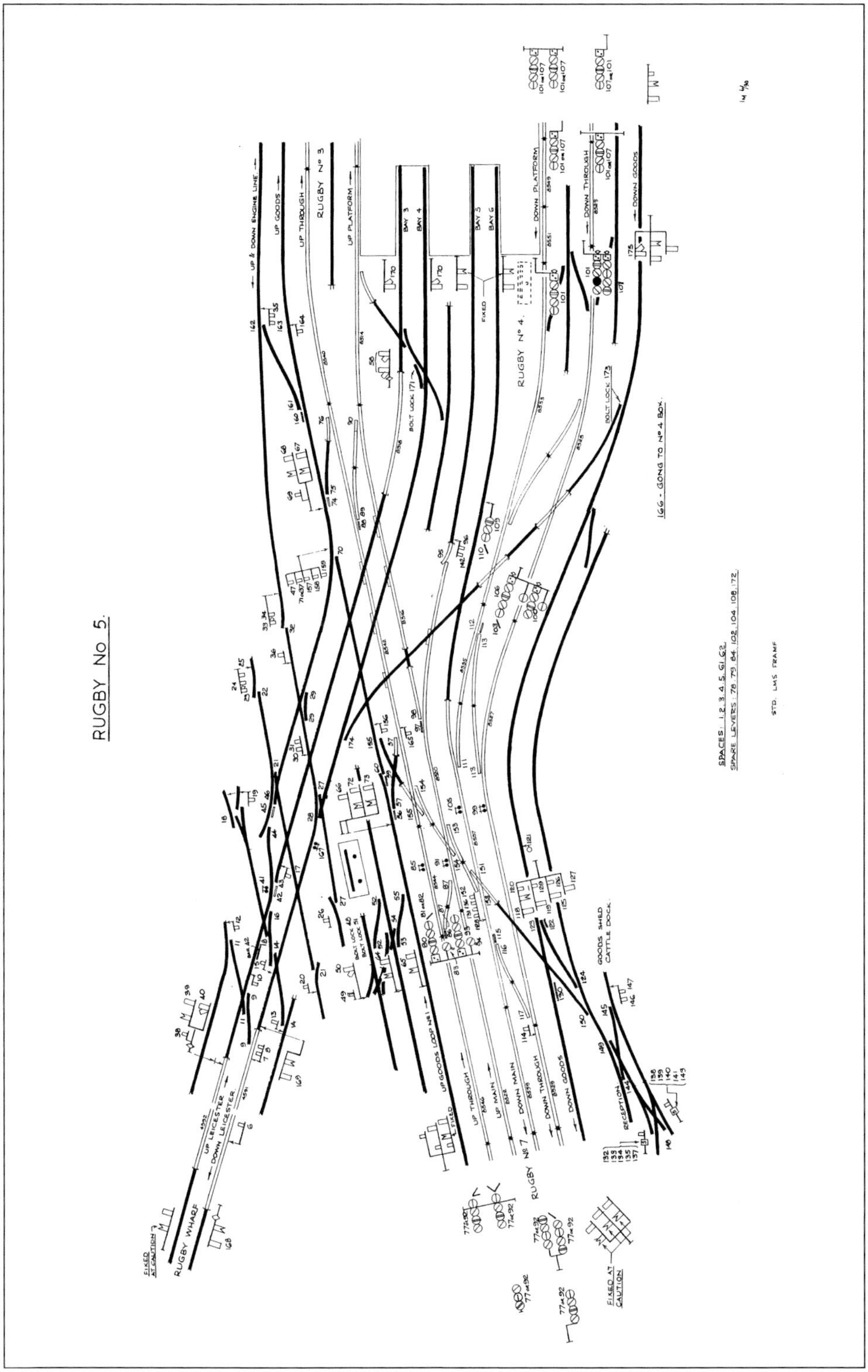

Signal box diagram, Rugby No 5

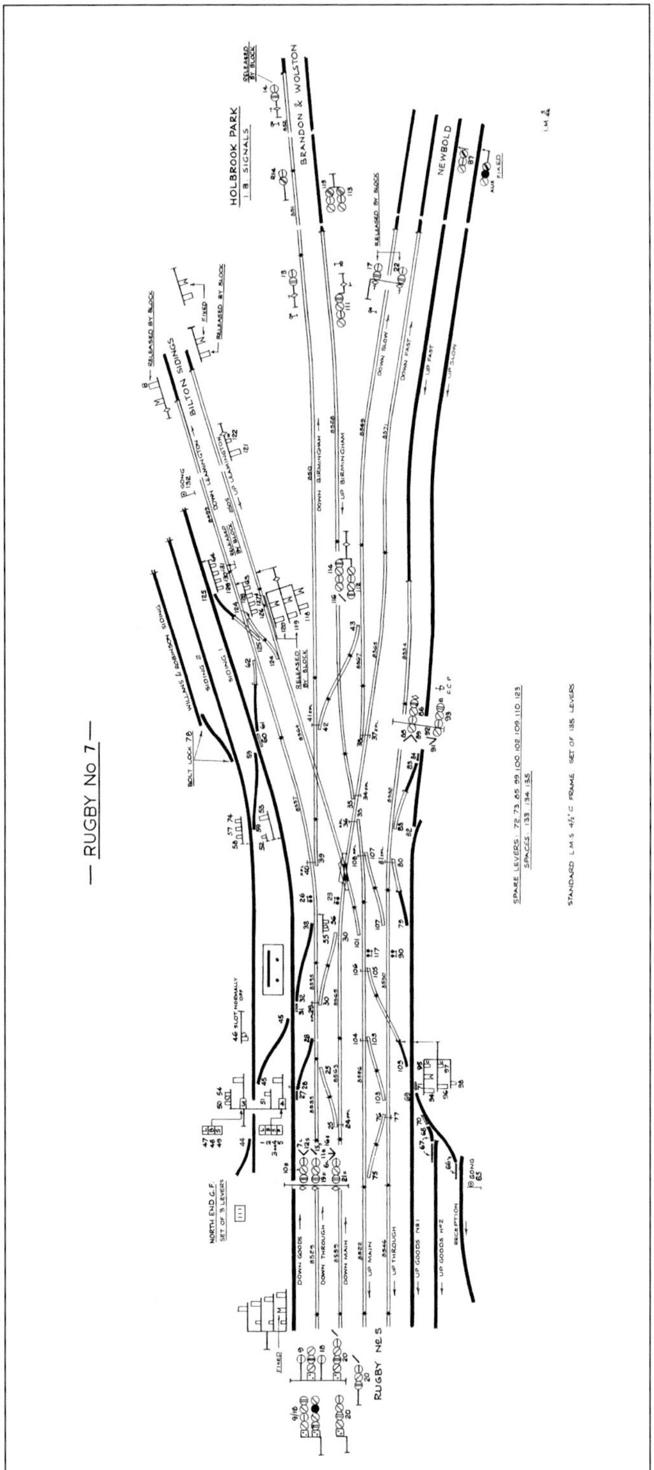

Signal box diagram, Rugby No 7

6
STARTING WORK

It was 1947, and my school days were drawing to a close; gone were the days when pedagogues would make their endless demands on me to recall the facts of the hypotenuse and, worse still, the seemingly endless variations of rules that the French built into their use of verbs. In some subjects there was much truth in the jargon, the rubber-stamp comments made in end-of-term reports by some school masters. I HAD NOT reached my full potential, I HAD NOT worked as hard as I could, but I had always been top in Woodwork, and in Art, and very nearly top in English occasionally. Anyway, the only use I could find for 'la plume de ma tante' was for keeping my Train Register up to date. Chances lost, but I had been sorely bitten by the railway bug, which had made increasing demands upon my waking hours during recent years.

My interest in railways was insatiable, focusing mostly on signalling, although my maternal grandfather had fostered an interest in railways from his point of view from an early age. He had served faithfully the London & North Western Railway as an engine driver, retiring from the LMS in 1936. His influence at Rugby Sheds was still sufficient that he was allowed to take me to look at the engines even after he had retired. I hadn't the heart to tell him that I favoured the other railway that crossed his by means of the girder bridge at Rugby. The day was to come when he would have to be told, and that day arrived shortly after I had been declared medically fit by the railway doctors at Liverpool Street. I had become an employee of the London & North Eastern Railway. As there were no opportunities for Train Register boys in the signal boxes of the Great Central, and as I had no enthusiasm for platform work, I opted to take employment as a cleaner at Woodford Halse until such time as I could become a signalman. My grandfather knew I had left school, and he also knew that I had applied for a job on the railway. What he didn't know was *which* railway! The conversation on that eventful day went something like this:

'You got a job on the railway?'

'Yes.'

'You starting down the shed?'

'No.'

'Where then?'

'Woodford Halse.'

'*Woodford Halse*! Why, that's on the bloody *Great Central*!'

There was to be no further communication between my aged grandparent and myself for a considerable period of time – there was even talk of deletions from his will, which showed the enormity of his displeasure.

ENGINE CLEANER AT WOODFORD

Accordingly, I started work in September 1947 at the Motive Power Depot at Woodford Halse for the remaining months of the much-lamented LNER. I was an engine

Gresley 'B17' *Grimsby Town*. *P. J. Wortley collection*

cleaner and was employed with a gang of other engine cleaners of similar age to myself. We worked under the watchful eye of the Chargehand Cleaner who, although spending much of his time anywhere other than with us, had the unhappy knack of turning up at any moment from any direction, making skiving a risky business. A variety of engines were shedded at Woodford, but only a few qualified for the attentions of the cleaners. Naturally, passenger engines took pride of place, with the comparatively new pair of 'B1s' at the top of the list, No 1066 in its splendid apple green livery and No 1078 in lined black. I remember spending some time polishing the footballs displayed under the name *Grimsby Town* on one of the 'B17s' that strayed down from Leicester on the 'ords'; we always liked to pay some attention to the namers as none were allocated to Woodford after about 1938. The 'B17s' that did come on shed were based at Colwick. *Derby County*, *Darlington* and *Huddersfield Town* were all names that I recall seeing on the trains of the time. They were not particularly popular engines among the crews as they could be rough riders when ready for overhaul, but that's another story.

The 'V2s' on the other hand were splendid machines and, although none were actually allocated to Woodford at the time, we did have visiting members of the class to grace our doors. When given the opportunity I would sit in the driver's bucket seat of a 'V2', simmering on the back road of the shed, and imagine myself as the driver. Boys never seem to grow up! The back road was very close to the Running Foreman's office and was considered to be a danger area. There were three Running Shift Foremen, and one of them, 'Pom' French, was of boxer-like stature and not to be tangled with. Why he had earned the sobriquet 'Pom' I was not to discover, but I watched in amazement at his reaction to taunts of 'Pom-tiddley-om-pom' by three reckless members of our team. Fortunately youth is faster off the mark than a middle-aged man even in prime condition and they escaped what would have been a good hiding.

Besides 'Pom' French, one of the other foremen was Cyril Jordan, who, I believe, saw the opening of the Great Central and died soon after its closure. The shed master was R. H. N. Hardy, who was to become a Senior Manager on British Railways later on.

Engine cleaners are the most lowly of all grades in the pecking order of the Motive Power Department. Nevertheless, by their efforts the standards of the depot could be judged by the travelling public – if they were interested, that is. Also, while working on the locomotives we were learning much about the working parts of the machines with which we had chosen to work. The first step up the ladder would be to Passed Cleaner, then to Fireman, and finally, if we stayed the course, to Driver. With the shortage of staff just after the war the first step was fairly rapid and the day soon came when I stood on the carpet in Mr Hardy's office to pass out on The Rules.

PASSED CLEANER

Passed Cleaner was a grandiose title for a person who could now be called upon to perform many more menial tasks, albeit more varied. Firing duties could now be expected and even some really responsible ones in the event of a more senior fireman failing to come to work. Perhaps the least pleasant task at Woodford was relieving the Annesley crews on their engines as they arrived in the Up New Yard, taking the engine on the shed, cleaning the fire, the ashpan, the smokebox, coaling, watering and turning ready for its next turn of duty. Attending to the fire was hot and tricky work using the long clinker shovels and prickers. Raking the ashpan was a terrible job done from underneath in the pit, and on a windy day the task could be horrendous. Equally difficult in a high wind was the removing of ash from the smokebox; after that, watering, coaling and turning were simple jobs. Considering that each Annesley 'runner' had to be met by a team of Woodford men throughout the 24 hours, it was a remarkable example of team work that made the GC Section freight trains the fastest in the country – bar none. The Annesley crews left their charges with the relief crews, then walked from the Up New Yard across to the mess rooms of the Down New Yard to await the delivery by Woodford men of a fresh engine to work their next Down 'runner' (I have never got used to the expression 'windjammer', having always thought of these trains as 'runners', hence my preference).

There were no washrooms or shower facilities in those days, so a bucket of hot water drawn from the boiler of an engine to provide the means to rinse off some of the muck accumulated during the course of the 8 hours was all we could expect. Travelling home with such grime made it unacceptable to use the 'cushions' (carriage seats), so I joined the train at the front and walked slowly along its length (providing it wasn't over full) and alighted at the rear by the time we reached Rugby. One Saturday I was walking the train when I was met in the corridor by my recent headmaster, Colonel Wheeler; he recognised me, shook me by the oily hand and wanted to know all about the work I was doing.

It was not unusual for Woodford Loco to pay host to visitors from other railways. The Great Western was frequently represented in view of the closeness of Banbury and the trips along the branch. The LMS would also stick their nose in with an occasional '4F' or something similar popping in from the SMJ. This single line, which linked the Midland Railway to Stratford-upon-Avon, was known locally as 'The Nibble' – why, I shall never know. A real stranger came on shed one day in

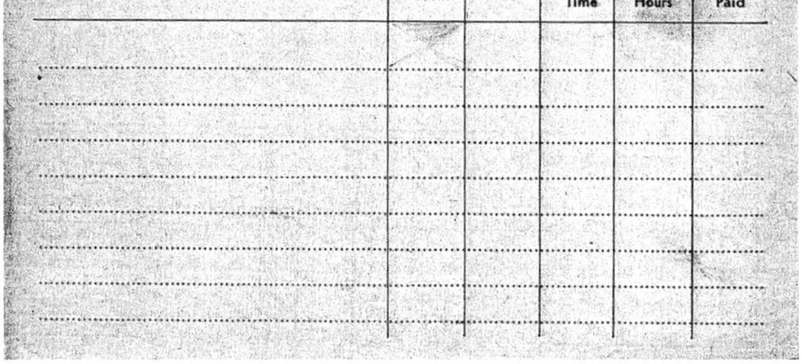
L.R.S. 7821

L.N.E.R.

DAILY WORK SLIP Locomotive Running Department

....Depot ....194....

No.................. Name.. Grade..........................

Work Performed	Time Worked		For Locomotive Accountant's Use		
	From	To	Total Time	Allowance Hours	Hours Paid

the shape of Southern Railway 'Schools' Class *Kings Wimbledon*. I have always regretted not having a camera to record these events, but film wasn't plentiful and, to be honest, I was too lazy to carry my camera – something I regret to this day. Most of these foreigners came on shed merely to turn prior to returning to their own lines. Engine-turning at Woodford was accomplished by means of the triangle that occupied land to the north-east of the shed yard and was normally a simple operation involving no physical effort by the engine crews. The ex-WD 2-8-0s presented a problem when they first appeared as their tenders occasionally derailed on the sharp curves, but eventually this was solved when it was discovered that a full load of coal and water was sufficient to keep the tender on the rails when the engine was running tender-first.

As time progressed and experience was gained I was being rostered to somewhat more interesting duties, which were certainly less dirty, comparatively speaking. Manning the various yard pilots was an easy enough job, but even that demanded the skill of judging the amount of fire needed to perform a particularly busy shunt followed by a period of idleness when there might be a problem with excess steam, causing blowing off, a nuisance and a waste. The two Robinson 2-6-4Ts, Nos 9050 and 9069, were ugly brutes compared with the usually handsome lines of other Robinson designs (only my opinion), but they possessed a cab like a dining room with space enough for me at 6 feet tall to stretch full length on the cabside seat during rest periods in the early hours. An allocation of a couple of Class 'N5' 0-6-2Ts were also used as pilots in the various yards. They were useful engines and, together with the ubiquitous 'J11' ('Pom-Poms'), made a valuable contribution as they were all popular machines with their crews.

Mention must be made of the gourmet breakfasts enjoyed on the footplates of these various engines. A well-scrubbed shovel with a little lard added would provide the tastiest of eggs and bacon in very little time when cooked just inside the firebox door. Mushrooms could also be added according to season. But the footplate meals I could not get accustomed to were the hunks of bread and cheese (OK so far) but accompanied by slices of raw onion that had been grown on the local allotment. At first these onions *appeared* to be very tempting, but their tear-provoking, mouth-burning effect was not so enjoyable. Good for colds, I was told. There was little chance of catching any infection from anyone who ate onions such as those – you couldn't get close enough to them to catch anything.

After midnight on Sunday mornings there was a gradual reduction in the number of trains having to be re-marshalled, the consequence being the gradual disappearance of the personnel involved with the shunting. Behind Woodford No 2 signal box was a short spur on which brake-vans were parked. This siding ended at the top of an embankment with nothing more than a couple of sleepers interlaced to prevent over-runs. Fate was unkind one Sunday morning when the points into the brake-van siding were inadvertently set and a heavy shunt sent the brake-vans off the end and on to the soil embankment. No one was hurt beyond a few bruises, but there were a number of very embarrassed shunters who had had their dormitory so suddenly discovered.

Incidents on the line, particularly accidents involving loss of life, were the subject of much long-winded discussion in the enginemen's mess room at Woodford Halse, typical of anywhere where locomotive crews assembled to have a brew-up and get their grub. A serious derailment occurred between Barnstone and Loughborough when an Up 'runner' plunged down the embankment, killing both driver and fireman in the process. The Permanent Way Gang had undertaken to turn rails and had not provided adequate protection for the work. Having removed a length of rail they were in the act of turning it when the goods train bore down on them, having had little warning of the extreme danger facing them. The engine rolled down the embankment followed by much of its coal train.

On another occasion a Leicester driver was bringing his train into the Down platform at the city's Central station and was surprised to see some waiting passengers swooning while others were turning their faces away in horror!

The cause, as he discovered, was the head of a Platelayer grotesquely positioned in the centre of the buffer beam of his engine. The man had been run down at Ashby Magna and the fact had gone completely unnoticed by either of the footplate crew.

Returning to more cheerful topics, I must mention the problems that beset me when travelling to and from work. Going on duty was usually a simple matter of thumbing a lift with the guard of any 'runner' that had stopped for water at Rugby. Coming home was a different kettle of fish, as 'runners' did not stop on the Down, and passenger trains did not always fit in with my home-time. Consequently I was obliged to spend much time 'kicking my heels in either Woodford No 3 or No 4 signal box. If I had an inordinately long time to wait, I would wander around to Woodford West Junction to witness life on 'The Nibble'.

WOODFORD WEST JUNCTION

Woodford West Junction was a standard Great Central wooden cabin that had been provided to signal the short-lived south-to-west spur that had allowed direct running for trains from Marylebone to Stratford-upon-Avon, as well as the north-to-west spur from Woodford Halse station. The single line of the Stratford-upon-Avon & Midland Junction Railway linked the Midland Railway's Bedford-Northampton line in the east with the same company's line at Broom Junction in the west. The surviving spur at Woodford was used in later years as a useful link for inter-regional freight between the Eastern and Western Regions; iron-ore trains from Charwelton and trains of steel ingots made much use of the route until the early 1960s. The intended direct link was a very short-lived venture: the double-track junction at Woodford South closed in 1904 and the tracks were truncated to form a siding from West Junction. The passenger service on the line had been introduced in March 1899 and ceased in August of that year, while goods trains continued to use it until the end of 1899.

The single-line equipment in Woodford West box comprised a two-column Electric Train Staff between Blakesley and West Junction, a two-column Electric Train Staff

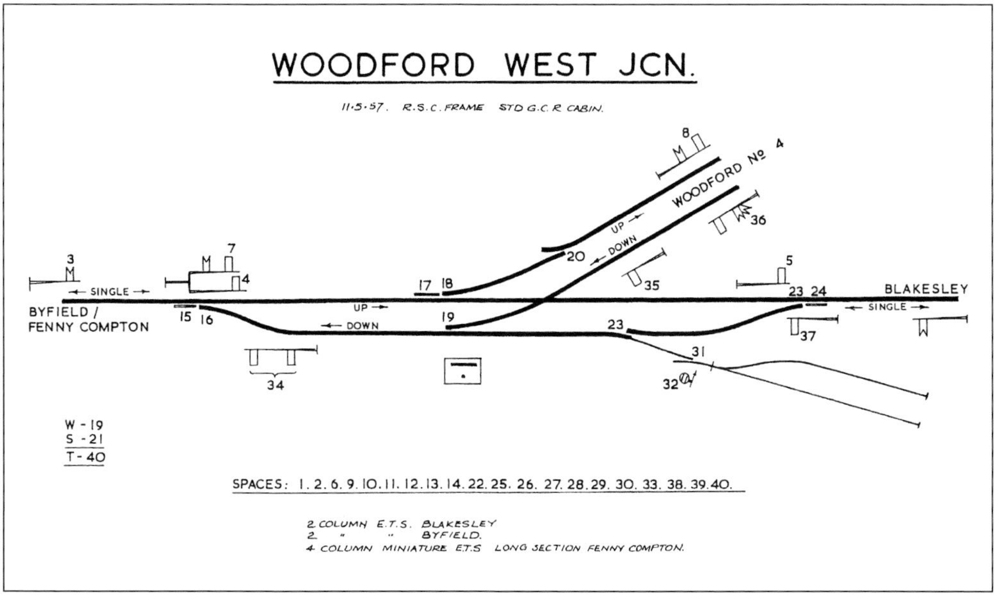

Signal box diagram, Woodford West Junction

between Byfield and West Junction, and a miniature four-column Electric Key Token between Fenny Compton and West Junction when Byfield was closed and long-section working was operated. These notes refer to 1958; I did not take detailed notes in 1948, when there was a Staff section at Morton Pinkney, although that station was closed in 1951; it had been the station that served Sulgrave Manor and was roughly midway between West Junction and Blakesley.

There was always a very strong rivalry between the LMS and the LNER and this manifested itself in the derision that showed itself at places where the two systems crossed – as at Rugby. To the uninitiated the whistles that the engine crews exchanged were merely forms of greeting, but to those in the know it was not so innocent. The cadence is not easy to describe, but imagine if you will a highly pitched note followed immediately by a slightly lower note and you have something that suggests an indelicate expression – 'a soul', or something that sounds rather like it. It was always amusing to listen to the exchanges, as the LMS men had difficulty returning the compliment on their ship-style hooters.

Gestures were also useful ways of conveying messages to crews of passing trains. George Wilson had several that he used to good affect. If he wanted a driver to put a move on he would use a pedalling action with both hands. Also, in the days of grease-lubricated axle boxes on goods wagons, the grease would melt if subject to fast running, and would then ignite and produce a foul smell. George would put his index finger and thumb to his nose and the engine crew would immediately understand that there was a 'hot box' on their train. This helped quite a lot as it was very difficult to shout and make oneself heard above the noise of an engine blowing off steam.

My interest in signalling did not dwindle in the time I spent on the footplate, and on several occasions I was able to leave the engine simmering while I sat having a cup of tea and a chat with the signalman at Woodford No 1. This was a new box, constructed when the yards were extended a few years earlier, and was of brick with a flat roof. The frame was at the rear of the cabin as was usual with all boxes built at about that time. Other boxes I was able to visit before I was finally transferred to the Operating Department were Culworth Junction, Culworth Station, and Helmdon. The latter two were closed at the time and I had to be satisfied with a look through the windows in the doors. These were all visited on a day when, discovering that I was rostered 'spare' and unlikely to be allocated duty, I walked along the track southwards to the remoteness of Culworth Junction; the only access to this box was along the track. The others I viewed because I had nothing better to do and fancied a walk. I shudder to think of the reactions such an idea would produce nowadays, particularly with Personal Track Safety and PICOWS, introduced to discourage such irresponsible behaviour. But with sunshine, the birds singing and youth, what could have been nicer?

The end of 1948 saw the end of my short career with the Traffic Department, and my transfer to the Operating Department. I had learned a lot and had been made fully aware of the rigours of footplate work, which would not be overlooked when I was snug and warm in the confines of the signal box.

7
SIGNALLING SCHOOL

I had made a lot of friends during my stay at Woodford Motive Power Depot. In some ways I was sorry to be leaving, even though it was to start on the job that was really my first choice, but a few weeks prior to my 18th birthday I took my place at the Signalling School in the building on Platform 1 at Nottingham Victoria station. I had read about and seen pictures of signalling schools, with the trainees playing trains with elaborately equipped model railways. How far these imaginings were from reality were proved upon arrival on my first day. I reported to Instructor Ernie Brown in the attic room under the roof over Platform 1 to find no model railway, just a long room with fanlight windows, a table down the centre with chairs, and a shelf at the far end of the room on which were displayed a set of the typical Block Instruments as used on the GC. The instruments were full-size working examples but the trains used in conjunction with them were blocks of wood which were pushed unceremoniously along a narrow shelf at waist height to the operators. Simple, cheap, and (in the event) very effective.

Ernie Brown was an avuncular character who guided us through the intricacies of the Rules and Regulations with infinite patience. There was, as there always will be in such cases, a 'thickie' who seemed incapable of grasping even the most elementary of principles, and after a couple of painful days there was an empty chair at the table – had he fallen or was he pushed? For the rest of us it was business as usual, the phrases 'When it is necessary to…' or 'In the event of…' cropping up so often that it seemed that no regulation would be complete without them. 'Except where instructions are issued to the contrary … or during fog or falling snow … or where there is a tunnel in the section…' are indelibly printed on my brain even after all these years. But it was all enjoyable. During my lunch breaks I was able to launch myself out into the unknown with sneakily taken visits to the East

LONDON & NORTH EASTERN RAILWAY.

RULES

FOR

OBSERVANCE BY EMPLOYEES.

1st January, 1933.

(Reprint 1945 including Supplements Nos. 1 to 14.)

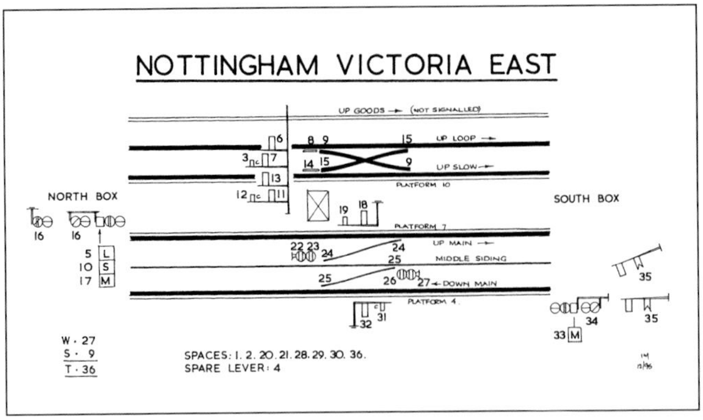

Signal box diagram, Nottingham Victoria East

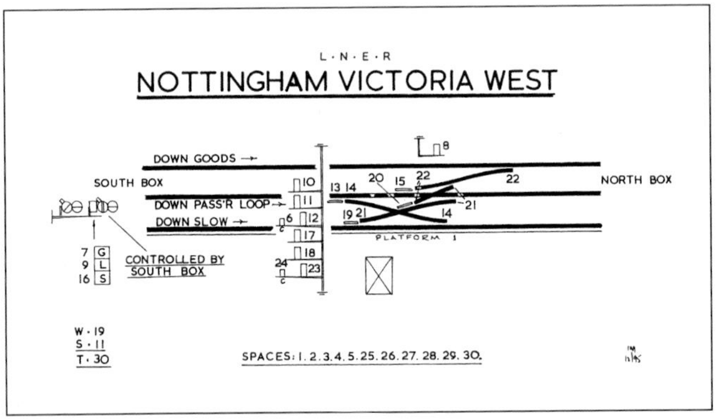

Signal box diagram, Nottingham Victoria West

and West signal boxes on the platforms at Victoria; I even ventured out as far as Arkwright Street and Carrington, but the visits had to be brief in view of the limited time available. North and South boxes were out of bounds because of their positions and the problems that visits to busy boxes entailed if unofficial.

During the course we were taken out on an official visit to Bulwell Forest. I cannot remember exactly how we arrived at that Great Northern outpost – I seem to think we travelled to Bulwell Common and walked to the Forest. I am not certain after all these years, but I found the signal box to be rather dull, there being very few trains along the Leen Valley Line when we went there, which was probably why Ernie chose that spot in the first place, it being inadvisable to have a host of visitors in a busy signal box. He did stress the importance of the word 'Private' that greeted the eye of all visitors at the door – they can provide a most dangerous distraction! Ouch – I'm glad now I hadn't disclosed to him the number of boxes in which I had been a distraction over the years!

The period of chalking and talking came to an end, and after an end-of-term examination we were all sent out into the world to put into practice all that we had learned … or most of it. Ernie dispatched us to various points of the compass: to Aslockton, to Chesterfield and Mansfield, Staverton Road and Braunston & Willoughby. I had been offered Swithland at first, but the problems of lodging caused me to opt for Braunston & Willoughby, where there was a vacancy following the retirement of Sammy Russell, whom I had visited some years earlier.

To back-track a little, Sammy was a rather portly little man who wore a cap perched over his forehead leaving a bald pate exposed at the back. He was also a keen taker of snuff as witness the copious quantities deposited down his waistcoat. He was a typical countryman and tended an allotment in the field at the

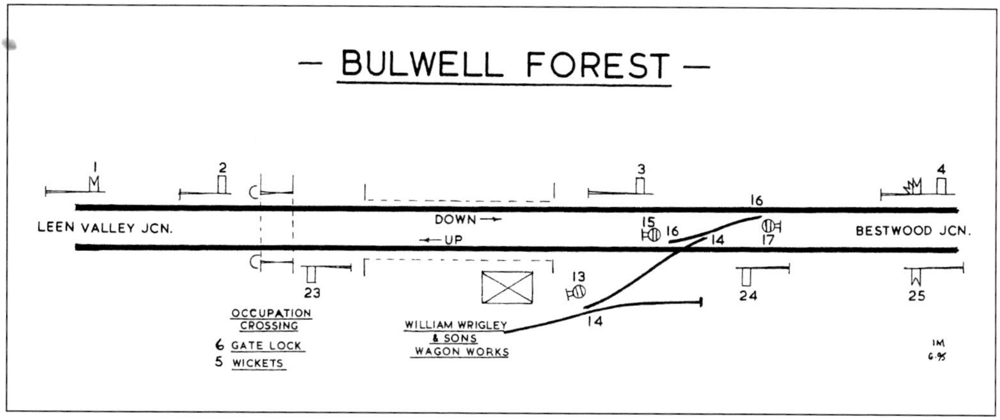

Signal box diagram, Bulwell Forest

back of the box. Some signalmen will assume that visitors will be awe-struck by the effort needed to pull a particularly difficult lever. It was so with Sammy, who suggested I should 'have a go at No 28'. To a novice it would have presented problems, but I had learned a thing or two from George Wilson. No 28 wasn't easy but I hung on as I'd been taught and I'm afraid I rather spoiled Sammy's thunder. Sorry Sammy, wherever you are – I couldn't help showing off a bit.

Digressing still further, some years ago I was on duty in a signal box situated on the platform on a preserved railway when a visitor stuck his head around the door and asked to be allowed to pull a lever. In view of the Line Manager's office being in close proximity, I refused the request. The visitor remained undaunted and persisted. In the end I agreed and gave him the lever cloth. Making sure the office door was closed I selected a suitable lever and let him pull it and put it back. He told me it was as good as a week at the seaside to work a lever again. He went on to say that he was a signalman at Euston Power Box, and used to work at Willesden No 1. 'You must visit me one day.'

But back to the Great Central. With my lunch-bag packed (the ubiquitous Army service gasmask bag that had been demobbed), I boarded the 8.01am Nottingham-Marylebone stopping train for my first day at B&W. I was to be 'sandwiched' between the two Freds – Fred Humphries and Fred Trathan – who both lived in the nearby village of Braunston. Percy Warr, who had been at Signalling School with me, was learning at Staverton Road and we would eventually be on the same shift. I believe he went to Coventry Power Box many years later. Learning the nitty-gritty of the frame, the special instructions and the traffic was a very happy experience, but a distant voice on the telephone told me that I was to 'let him know when I thought I was ready'. This was the District Inspector, and the visit that would launch me officially into my new career – that is, unless my built-in fear of examinations didn't put a spanner in the works. The very thought of the impending grilling was enough to put me off, but it had to be done and it wasn't the end of the world. I considered a week spent on each shift to be sufficient – after all, I had been acquainted with the traffic and the timetable for some time already and it was the rules and the frame that were my main concern ... and the calculation of margins, which are the times needed for trains to pass through a section. The latter did not enter into it, which I discovered on the day. So I sent for him, sat back and awaited his arrival a day or so later.

Inspector Williamson stepped off the train from Leicester and made his way up to the box. This was it. I pretended to be totally indifferent as he came into the box, but my stomach was telling a completely different story. The diurnal order of Lepidoptera (otherwise known as butterflies) were playing havoc with my guts. He indicated that I should sit beside him on the locker for the first part of the interrogation, which started with:

'What is the first thing you do on Monday mornings?'

This wasn't fair. My mind went blank and I stammered a few things that might be considered relevant. Things became serious as the word 'No' followed each of my ideas. What then? An appealing look at the resident signalman who had supervised my training period revealed nothing as he seemed to be concentrating on something beyond the windows. Ah well, tell me the worst…

'Light the fire and put the kettle on!'

From then on it was plain sailing. It was obviously a ploy to put the unfortunate examinee at ease, and it worked in my case because all the ensuing questions were almost the same as those asked by Ernie Brown a few weeks previously.

8

ABSOLUTE BLOCK REGULATIONS.

(ii) Except where special instructions to the contrary are issued, the **Train entering section** signal must not be forwarded until the train approaches the intermediate block home signal.

(iii) During fog or falling snow, except where special instructions to the contrary are issued, no train must, unless Fogsignalmen are on duty at the intermediate block distant and home signals, be permitted to pass the starting (or advanced starting) signal and proceed towards the intermediate block home signal until the **Train out of section** signal or **Obstruction removed** signal has been received from ~~and the line is clear to~~ the signal box in advance and the block indicator worked from that box is in the normal position; nor must the **Blocking back** signal (3—3) or (2—4) from the box in advance be acknowledged if permission has been given for a train to proceed towards the intermediate block home signal until such train has come to a stand at that signal.

4. LINE CLEAR OR GIVING PERMISSION FOR A TRAIN TO APPROACH.—(*a*) Except where special instructions to the contrary are issued, the line must not be considered clear, nor must a train be allowed to approach from the signal box in rear, in accordance with Regulation 3, until the preceding train has passed at least ¼ mile beyond the home signal, nor until all the necessary points within this distance have been placed in their proper position, subject to the provisions of clause (*f*), for the safety of the approaching train, and the line is clear for at least ¼ mile ahead of the home signal.

Where an additional home signal is provided at least ¼ mile in rear of the inner home signal the **Is line clear** signal may be acknowledged when the line is clear to the inner home signal. This permission will not apply during fog or falling snow unless Fogsignalmen are on duty at the distant signal and at the outermost home signal.

(*b*) Where the signal box in advance is less than ¼ mile ahead, permission for a train to approach must not be given to the signal box in rear until the **Train out of section** signal or, when the signal **Blocking back outside home signal** (3—3) has been acknowledged, the **Obstruction removed** signal, has been received from the signal box in advance.

Should the block apparatus between two signal boxes less than ¼ mile apart have failed, no train must be accepted by the Signalman at the rear box until it has been ascertained that the line is clear to the home signal of the signal box in advance. If this cannot be done the train must, provided the line is clear as far as can be seen and all points necessary for the safety of the approaching train have been placed in their proper position, be accepted in accordance with Regulation 5, the Signalman to whom this signal is sent being advised previously of the circumstances.

(*c*) After permission has been given for a train to approach in accordance with this Regulation (4), no obstruction of the line on which such train requires to run or, at a junction, of the line for which the facing

9

ABSOLUTE BLOCK REGULATIONS.

points are set, must be allowed within a distance of ¼ mile ahead of the home signal or within any other prescribed clearance point, until the train has been brought to a stand at the home signal, or has passed into the section in advance, or the **Cancelling** signal (3—5) has been received.

(*d*) If the line be not clear, or if from any other cause the Signalman be not in a position to give permission for the train to approach when the Signalman in rear forwards the **Is line clear** signal, that signal must not be acknowledged until the Signalman to whom the signal has been sent is prepared to receive the train, when he must give permission for it to approach in accordance with the prescribed Regulations.

(*e*) (i) During fog or falling snow, except where special instructions to the contrary are issued, if a Fogsignalman is not on duty at the distant signal, the **Is line clear** signal must not be acknowledged in accordance with this Regulation until the **Train out of section** signal or the **Obstruction removed** signal has been received from and the line is clear to the signal box in advance, the Signalman acknowledging the **Is line clear** signal has placed all the necessary points in their proper position for the safety of the approaching train, and, where a block indicator worked from the box in advance is provided, such indicator is in the normal position, nor must the **Blocking back** signal (3—3) or (2—4) from the box in advance be acknowledged if permission has been given for a train to approach from the box in rear in accordance with this Regulation.

Where an additional home signal is provided at least ¼ mile in rear of the inner home signal, the **Is line clear** signal must not be acknowledged in accordance with this Regulation during fog or falling snow when the line is clear only to the inner home signal unless Fogsignalmen are on duty at the distant signal and outermost home signal; if, however, a Fogsignalman is on duty at the distant signal only, the **Is line clear** signal may be acknowledged in accordance with this Regulation provided the line is clear for at least ¼ mile beyond the *inner* home signal. Except where special instructions to the contrary are issued, if a Fogsignalman is not on duty at the distant signal, the **Is line clear** signal may be acknowledged in accordance with Regulation 5 provided the line is clear to the inner home signal and the line in advance of the *inner* home signal is also clear for at least ¼ mile, or, if the box in advance is within that distance, provided the line is clear to the inner home signal and the line in advance of the *inner* home signal is also clear in accordance with clause (*b*) of this Regulation (4).

(ii) During fog or falling snow, where intermediate block signals controlled from the signal box in rear are provided, until the Fogsignalman is on duty at the distant signal for the box controlling the intermediate block signals, trains may be accepted by the Signalman at that box from the signal box next in rear provided the line is clear to the intermediate block home signal and the overlap track circuit in advance of that signal is also clear.

C_2

Rules and regulations are vital to any organisation and, for obvious reasons, they need to be written using legal terminology; this means that they are invariably incomprehensible to the layman. The most basic Signalling Regulation 4, illustrated here, becomes a nightmare to understand unless it can be explained in simple terms to a person accustomed only to speaking plain English. There were, in all, 36 similar sets of laws in the 1933 edition of the LMS's Instructions to Signalmen to cover all possible eventualities and mishaps. Signalling Schools were vital in training new recruits to the system, and Instructors made the most involved jargon more easy to understand. Improvement Classes were also held in the evenings at important railway centres where men could study the rules and improve their knowledge of them, which helped with their prospects for promotion.

8
Signalman at Braunston & Willoughby

I took over on early turn the next day and the remainder of that first week was uneventful. The same cannot be said of the week of nights that followed. It is common knowledge that troubles never come singly, and this was certainly the case when I received 6 bells from George Wilson at Rugby for an Up 'runner' with 'hot boxes'. The train was stopped at Barby's IBs before being allowed to proceed with a 7 bells 'Stop and examine' sent to me as part of the process. The train arrived with no fewer than six hot axle boxes on various wagons in the train, and Murphy's Law decreed that no two wagons were together. The entire train was shunted into the Up Refuge Siding, from where each wagon had to be detached and propelled across the road into the Down sidings as traffic permitted. It was a long and pitifully slow job – I was as sick of the train as the crew must have been of me by the time it was finished. In the years that followed I sometimes had two hot boxes, but *never* again did I experience six. It was a testing time for me. Six, and on nights – and my first week of nights into the bargain. Never again!

The 'out and home' working employed at Annesley for the freight trains to Woodford imposed a great strain on the wagons involved; the constant running at high speeds soon exposed any flaws in wagon maintenance. This was particularly so in days of 'fat boxes' when wagon axle boxes were filled with grease. The high speeds would melt the grease, it would run out of the axle box and what was left would ignite, rendering the wagon a cripple. There were occasions when, if the top flap of the box was left open, crows would take a fancy to a little grease in their diet with disastrous results when the wagon was in transit. It was all very primitive compared with modern standards in rolling-stock design, but some of these facts are not now remembered. Crippled wagons would be detached and sidelined until a visit by a Carriage & Wagon Engineer corrected any defect and the vehicle was sent on its way on the next pick-up goods.

The 'out and home' working mentioned above produced some high-class engine crews, but because their work was with freight trains, they never gained the fame that the more highly recognised passenger drivers achieved, and Annesley didn't command the same interest as places like Leicester. There were lots of drivers whose exploits I could recall here, but Reubin Taylor is the one I most distinctly remember. His appearance also imprinted itself on one's memory, as he had the biggest ears I have ever seen on a man – ever. It was a standing joke that Reubin had to keep his head inside the cab while the train was in motion – to put his head *out* would have reduced the speed by at least 50%! Joking apart, when he drove a train, even a goods train took on express speeds. An incident that illustrates this happened one Saturday when I was on early turn. I had a 'runner' approaching on the Down, which I intended to shunt to allow the 10.15am

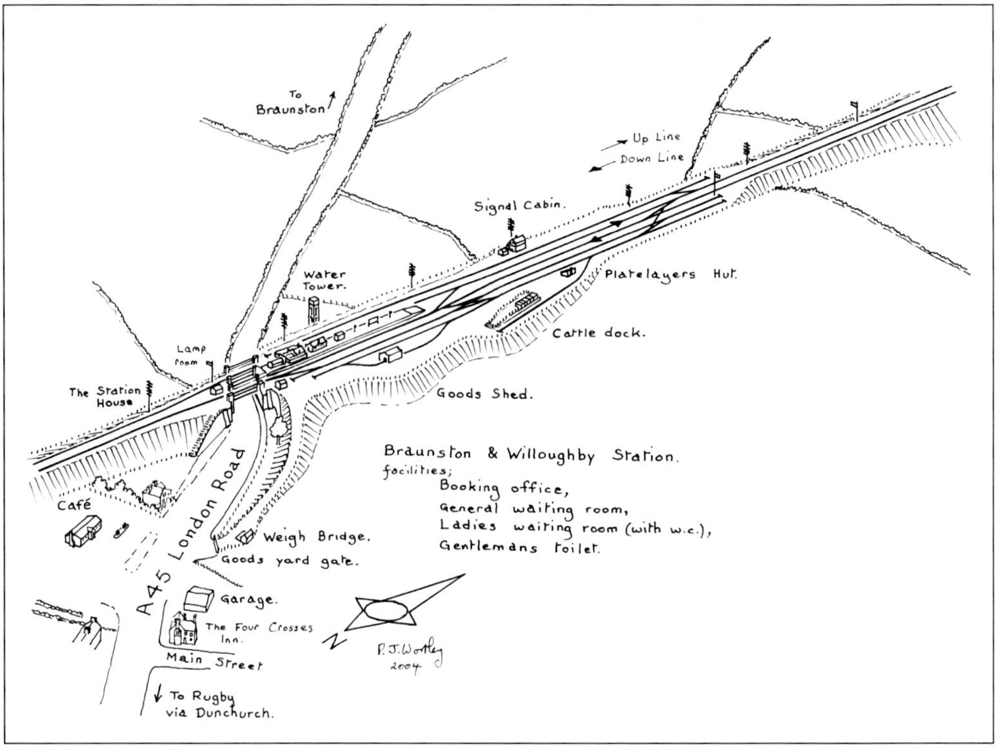

A sketch showing the arrangement of Braunston & Willoughby station. Entry to the station was by a staircase from road level between the piers for the two girder bridges. Note the steps from the Station House garden up the embankment, allowing easy access for the Station Master. *PJW*

Marylebone-Manchester to pass. The latter was 'right time' at Grendon and was well past Brackley by this time. I indicated 'inside' to the driver (a duster waved from side to side was the usual signal) when I realised it was Reubin Taylor. He slowed almost to a stop and shouted:

'Give us the road, Bobby – I've got a wedding at 3 o'clock.'

I got the road and 'pulled off', giving the message to George at Rugby, who passed it along the line. Reubin took off like a rocket. My last impression was of the guard hanging on for dear life as his little caboose rocked perilously from side to side in the wake of the train going hell for leather northwards. My faith was not betrayed. Reubin Taylor reached Leicester Goods South in his headlong flight before he had to stop for water. It was here that the express eventually managed to catch up and overtake him.

Somewhere in this narrative – the exact time is uncertain – I was called away to serve His Majesty in a little pastime called National Service. That I went to the Royal Engineers and was stationed at Longmoor on the Military Railway is neither here nor there – in typical military fashion, where a dustman can become a Brigadier or a dentist a cook, I was installed in the medical inspection room as medical orderly. This paragraph is sufficient to cover that two-year interlude – but it was enjoyable none the less.

Railway work has always depended to a very large extent upon teamwork. It was teamwork that made the high-speed home run possible so that a driver could attend his daughter's wedding, and this was only the tip of the iceberg – there being thousands of cases where a special effort had to be made in order to produce a satisfactory result. It was all part of the job. I am tending to use the past tense far too much – railways will always depend upon teamwork among their employees. It is only politicians who seem to pull in different directions. Sadly, there are always exceptions to the ideal I have just outlined, and a certain Station Master who sat in authority at Willoughby for a short time was one of the exceptions. He did not intend to be difficult, he was just made that way, and being recently demobilised from one of His Majesty's Services after the war with the elevated rank of Sergeant in the RAF made him all the more difficult to please. The saying 'If it moves, salute it – if it doesn't, paint it' fits this gentleman's attitude to life. Some of the following little incidents illustrate the 'Everyday Story of Railway Folk' with a difference, but they are not fictional as is the long-running Radio 4 programme.

The start as far as I am concerned is to provide the man with an identity, albeit fictitious and a nickname that will help in all of the following narratives. It was his particular desire to appear in public in his gold braid that set it all off. Fridays were 'go-into-Rugby-to-collect-the-money-for-the-wages-from-the-bank' day – a very ordinary task, but it involved a 7-mile journey on Midland Red bus service 572 to get there, and a similar journey to return. Farmers, local ladies going shopping, all ordinary folks dressed in their ordinary clothes, were suddenly joined by a Pickwickian figure dressed in his Station Master's uniform, not unlike an Admiral of the Fleet! To get to the point of the story, he apparently left the Midland Bank a little too late to catch the return bus service home and was relieved to find it held up at traffic lights at the top of the High Street. Heaving himself on to the vehicle he was confronted by an employee of the 'friendly' Midland Red in the shape of the conductor. This is an account of the proceedings that ensued:

'And where do you think you're going?'

'I'm late and I don't want to miss the bus.'

'It is illegal to board the bus at traffic lights.'

'But I am the Station Master at Braunston & Willoughby.'

'I don't care if you're Napoleon – you don't get on here!'

The conductor concerned told me about the altercation a few days later, and from that day forward it was decreed that his name shall be – Napoleon!

I have mentioned earlier the names of my two mates, the two Freds. Now, there is one thing that Fred Humphries could do that has *never* been equalled anywhere at any time in my life so far – he could make the most mouth-watering rice puddings in our stove, which would have made the Head Chef at the Dorchester green with envy. He told me the recipe, he demonstrated the method, but the results were never the same. Hot or cold, it was delicious. While on the subject of the culinary arts, there was a local farmer who had a wagon-load of potatoes arrive from Lincolnshire with which to feed his cattle.

'I don't care if you're Napoleon – you don't get on here!' *PJW*

They were jolly good baked in the oven with butter and cheese as filling – the very size of them made one into an entire meal, and much better than sandwiches. Then there was Tubby's Cafe. This was (maybe still is) a typical chips-with-everything lorry drivers' caff, but one that provided me with ample nourishment when things didn't go according to plan and I was landed with an unexpected 12-hour shift with no grub. There was always someone who would nip down and fetch something to eat. In a real emergency Control would authorise a short switch out of circuit so that I could replenish the larder. One good turn deserved another.

Control was on a telephone that was connected only with the brains at Nottingham. The Controller on my shift was Leonard Pennington, known affectionately as 'Len Pen, The Man With All The Gen'. He was only a voice to me – I was never able to meet him. Unlike some railways the Controller acted as a kind of unseen hand that almost dictated every move. Fortunately, Len Pen was there to receive information and collate it when things were running smoothly – it was only when things went wrong that he took over, and you did as you were told in those conditions.

While on the subject of train control, and things running smoothly, the means of achieving this end needs explaining. The Working Timetable wasn't the only instruction to railway staff. Towards the end of each week Napoleon would make his routine daily visit, but this time he would be carrying the orders for the next seven days commencing Sunday. These orders comprised of a timetable of Special Trains, the Special Notices and the latest Vacancy List.

In the years immediately after the war the railways catered for many different organisations who required trains to convey their members to various destinations in the United Kingdom. The timings, loadings and crewing arrangements would be detailed in the Special Trains Timetable and it was important that signalmen involved on the routes of these trains be made aware so that delays were avoided, and destinations reached at the appointed time. Each train was provided with a Reporting Number, which was displayed on the front of the locomotive for identification purposes. Such a special train might be a schoolgirls' hockey team, the entire school with supporters travelling from, say, Mansfield to Wembley for the Big Match. Supporters' trains were quite common for football clubs playing away. There were also pigeon specials, which usually ran on Saturdays, the 'passengers' being released from their baskets to find their own way back home. Rugby Station Goods Yard often catered for these trains, made up of a rake of full-brake coaching stock. The baskets were off-loaded and the pigeons released at a set time.

The book that concerned loco crews more than anything was the Special Notices, which gave details of signal alterations, track relaying, speed restrictions, etc, for the following week and, if necessary, for weeks ahead. This information was relevant to signalmen only if it affected their particular patch. It did give an indication that if there were any restrictions nearby then drivers would be wanting to make up time. Single-line working would be detailed, giving the signal boxes between which it would be in operation, which line would be blocked, and which was to be the single line. Relief signalmen were usually called upon to act as pilotmen in these cases, a nice little earner for the chosen few.

The Vacancy List came with other items, including any of the dreaded 'Please explains' from the office of the District Superintendent, Mr Probert.

There were two other books, apart from the Train Register, which were part of the everyday working of the signal box. These were the Occurrence Book and the First Aid Book. The former was a record of minor happenings that failed to justify a place in the Train Register, while the First Aid Book was to record and account for all the medical supplies that were used, every bandage, sticking plaster and safety pin.

Even when the wheels were turning smoothly, trains running to time, and there was no sign of Napoleon, life wasn't boring, far from it. There was always something going on. Bill Homan was the Ganger and his length began at the station and ran southwards towards Staverton Road. George Green was the Ganger on the length northwards from the station towards Rugby; I saw little of him because he worked further away from the signal box. Bill Homan's gang were always working on some kind of track maintenance, scything the banks, mending fences, tasks that don't get a mention nowadays. Their cabin stood on the Down side of the line right opposite the box and I could always watch their comings and goings with great interest. Sometimes they would involve me when they intended to put their trolley on the line to carry some materials up to a particular site. A partly laden trolley would play havoc with the Track Circuits, causing them to pick up and drop out unpredictably, but it was just a question of teamwork and co-operation when a Ganger needed to get out on the main line with a trolley. Light when unladen, they could be lifted off at a moment's notice, but not so easy when carrying any sort of load.

Having described Fred Humphries, I come now to the other member of the triumvirate, F. J. Trathan, another Fred who also lived in Braunston. In build and character he was not unlike 'Foggy' Dewhurst of *Last of the Summer Wine* fame but without the spectacles. Fred rode to work on an ancient lady's sit-up-and-beg bike, which he always pedalled along the main A45 highway at tremendous speed. I often watched his approach from the window of the box, a hedge separating the main road from the field. The bicycle and Fred's furiously pedalling legs were hidden from view – all that could be seen was his truncated body above the waist seemingly proceeding along the top of the hedge. As Fred held himself very upright, the sight was made even more amusing. Of the three, Fred Humphries was the oldest, Fred Trathan somewhere between, with myself as the youngster. FJT was last heard of working alongside Leo Rippin at Rugby Station prior to its closure.

Having introduced so many names in the catalogue of signalmen working the boxes in the vicinity of Braunston & Willoughby, maybe it would be a good idea to list them at their places of work and on their respective shifts circa 1951:

Rugby Station: Leo Rippin, George Wilson, Bert Windley
Braunston & Willoughby: Fred Humphries, myself, Fred Trathan
Staverton Road: Doug Henty, Percy Warr, Bill Solomons

Working with us from time to time would be various relief signalmen; some were Woodford-based while others would come from faraway Leicester. Some of the names I recall, the main ones being:

From Woodford: Colin Lambie, Paddy Crotty, George Huntley
From Leicester: Arthur Marriot, Doug Burge

There were others and I apologise for not being able to include them all, but the years take their toll!

9
Working Braunston & Willoughby box

The signal box would not be so called without the means of operating the various apparatus, and perhaps now would be an opportune time to describe in some detail the workings of the box at Braunston & Willoughby.

As already mentioned, each train had a Reporting Number, which simplified their identification. Up trains were (mostly) odd numbers, while Down trains were allocated even numbers. I say 'mostly' because I seem to remember the Up fish trains from Hull carrying the numbers 1272 and 1276. The Grimsby fish was 601. Up freight trains were given numbers in the range 30XX, down freight trains 35XX. For instance, there were three freight trains that followed closely behind each other between 9pm and 10pm – George Wilson always referred to them as Faith, Hope and Charity. Their reporting numbers were 3089, 3091 and 3095 – for some reason there was no 3093. The Up 'Master

Braunston & Willoughby signal box. *M. Mitchell*

BRAUNSTON & WILLOUGHBY LOCAL INFORMATION

Clearance points	Up line	Opposite disc 21, outlet from Up siding
	Down line	Opposite disc 27, outlet from Down siding
Fog marker	Down Home Signal 7	
Siding capacity	Up Refuge	=63 wagons
	Down Refuge	=65 wagons
Catch points	Up line	757 yards in rear of signal 32

Distances from signal box

Staverton Road box	3 miles 547 yards
Barby box	1 mile 1,635 yards
Rugby Station box	4 miles 1,215 yards
Up IB Signal (32)	1 mile 960 yards

Running times

Class F freight	to Staverton Road	approx 8 minutes
	to Rugby Station	approx 10 minutes

Calculating margins
Allow: 2 minutes to stop
3 minutes to start
3 minutes to set back
Add these times to running times as appropriate. For example, Up freight: time to Staverton Road to shunt, 8 + 2 + 3 = 13 minutes

Cutler' was 105, the Down train 46, while the 'South Yorkshireman' was 36. There are so many numbers that I cannot remember now, so it is better that I leave them lost in the mists of time instead of guessing and producing misleading facts. Besides the Class F freights there were a considerable number and variety of Class Cs and Class Ds, not to mention the daily quota of fast passengers interspersed with stopping passenger trains, the 'ords'. And one must not forget the two pick-up freights calling each day, six days a week.

When I first took over as signalman at Braunston & Willoughby there were still several original Great Central signals, which lasted until the early 1950s with their pitch pine posts and cedarwood arms, lower-quadrant of course. Some of the original wooden posts had been replaced by concrete much earlier when wood became scarce after the 1914-18 war, and these also had the arms superseded by upper-quadrants as they became life-expired.

The main running signals were as follows:

No 6 Down Distant: Original lower-quadrant GCR signal with pine post, eventually became two-aspect colour light.

No 7 First Down Home*: Concrete post with upper-quadrant arm.

No 8 Second Down Home*: Pitch pine post and lower-quadrant cedarwood arm, removed after signal became defective as described in text.

No 9 Down Starter: Original wooden post upper-quadrant signal replaced by new signal 100 yards further from box in 1953 to avoid trains having to pass it at danger when requiring to shunt.

* These two Down Home signals, placed quite close together, were described as First and Second Homes, and were a GCR way of protecting a trailing crossover and station as separate items. In reality there was no need for the Second Home, which was why it was not replaced. First and Second Home signals are also mentioned at Rugby Station in Chapter 4.

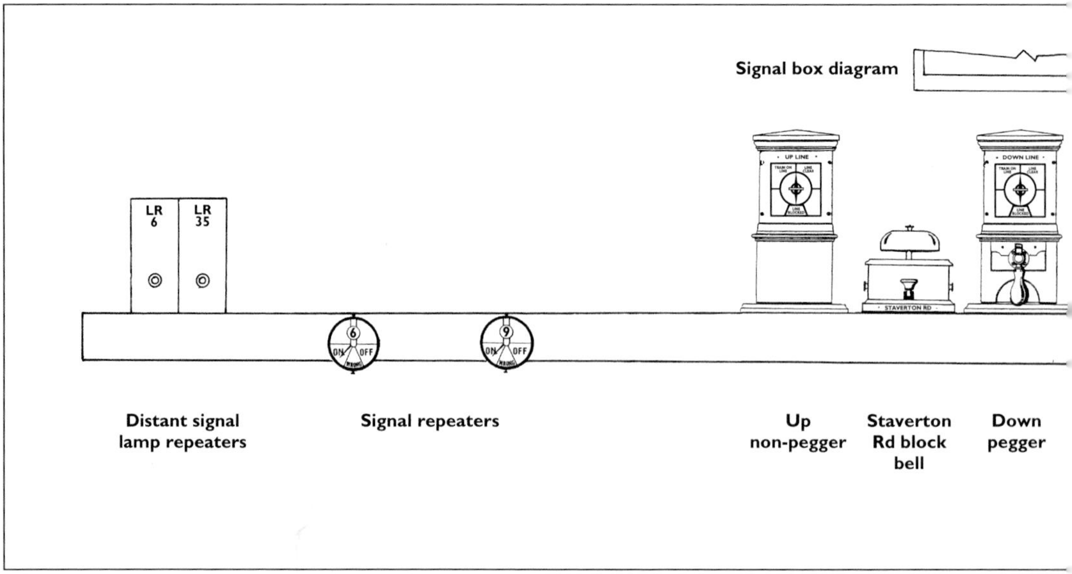

Above The block shelf at Braunston & Willoughby. *PJW*

Right Braunston & Willoughby Table of Interlocking (Railway Signal Co frame with 5½in centres)

No 32 Up IB Home signal: Two-aspect 'searchlight' IB signal 2 miles 800 yards from signal box. Prior to 1941 lever 32 worked a lower-quadrant Advanced Starting signal a short distance on the London side of No 20 points.

No 33 Up Starting: Three-aspect 'searchlight' Starting signal with IB Distant. Prior to 1941 lever 33 worked a lower-quadrant Starting signal adjacent to end of Up platform.

No 34 Up Home: Concrete post with upper-quadrant arm sited perilously close to top of embankment and A45 road bridge.

No 35 Up Distant: Upper-quadrant arm carried on wooden Doll on right-handed bracket supported on concrete post.

Some Ground signals were GCR pattern with revolving heads, but they were replaced by standard LNER Ground signals at times I cannot recall. No 29 disc was placed on the parapet of the A45 road bridge to aid sighting, and had its own short ladder for access and maintenance.

Interlocking

By studying the accompanying Table of Interlocking, and taking two or three examples, the following moves can be described.

After pulling lever 34 (Up Home), points 16, 20 and 25 are locked and cannot be operated. Conversely, if any one of those three sets of points is operated, No 34 signal will be locked and so will the other two point levers – study of the table should make this clear.

The Distant signal levers 6 and 35 cannot be pulled until their respective Stop signals have been cleared: 6 requires 7 and 9, 35 requires 34 and 33. After the Distant levers have been pulled, the Stop signal levers are locked reversed and cannot be replaced.

Lever 9 (Down Starter) locks points 28 *both ways*, ie 28 normal and 28 reverse. This is because signal 9 is within a train's length of the trailing exit points from the sidings, and the locking prevents the points being reversed or moved while the signal is 'off'.

'Simple' wire adjusters for signals 7, 9 and 34 were provided in the frame and were adjacent to the lever concerned, while Distant signals 6 and 35 were equipped with cog-and-worm adjusters with removable handles. Distant signal 6 was converted to a colour light in the mid-1950s.

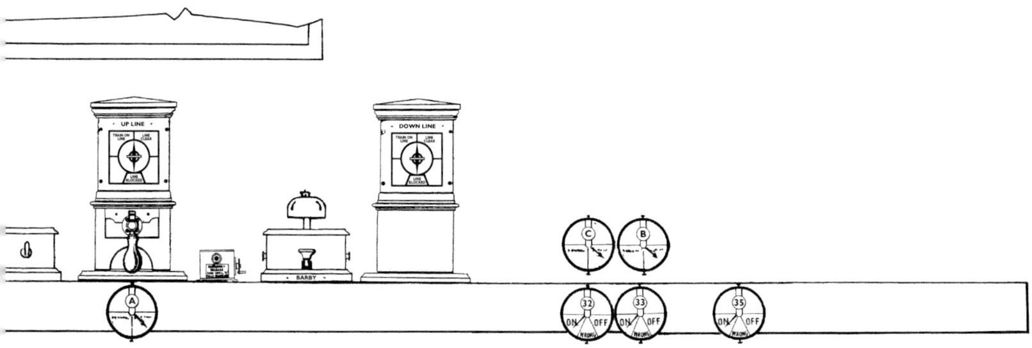

Lever No.	Work.	Released by.	Locking.
1 - 5	Spaces.		
6	Down Distant.	7.9.	
7	Down Home.		16. 23. 25. 28.
8	Spare.		
9	Down Starting.		23.(23).25.(25).28.(28).
10 - 13	Spaces.		
14	Disc: Up Main to Up Siding. or No. 15 Disc.	20. 15.	21.
15	Disc: Up Main to Down Main. or Down Sidings.	16. 16.18.	17. 19.
16	Main Crossover (South).		7. 20. 23. 25. 28. 34.
17	Disc: Down Main to Up Main.	16.	15. 18.
18	Points: Down Sidings to Up Main.	16.	17.
19	Disc: Down Sidings to Up Main.	16.18.	15.
20	Points: Up main to Up Siding.		16. 25. 34.
21	Disc: Up Siding to Up Main.	20.	14
22	Disc: Down Siding to Down Main.	23.	
23	Points: Down Sidings to Down Main.		7. 16. 25. 28.
24	Disc: Up Main to Down Main.	25.	26.
25	Main Crossover (North).		7. 16. 20. 23. 28. 34.
26	Disc: Down Main to Up Main.	25.	24.
27	Disc: Down Siding to Down Main.	28.	29.
28	Points: Down Siding to Down Main.		7. 16. 23. 25.
29	Disc: Down Main to Down Siding.	28.	27.
30 - 31	Spaces.		
32	Up Intermediate Block Home Signal		
33.	Up Starting.		
34	Up Home.		16. 20. 25.
35	Up Distant.	34.33.	
36 - 40	Spaces.		

IM 4/95.

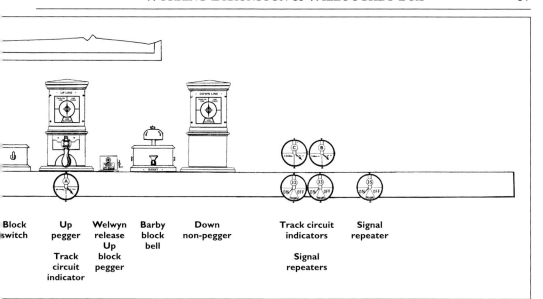

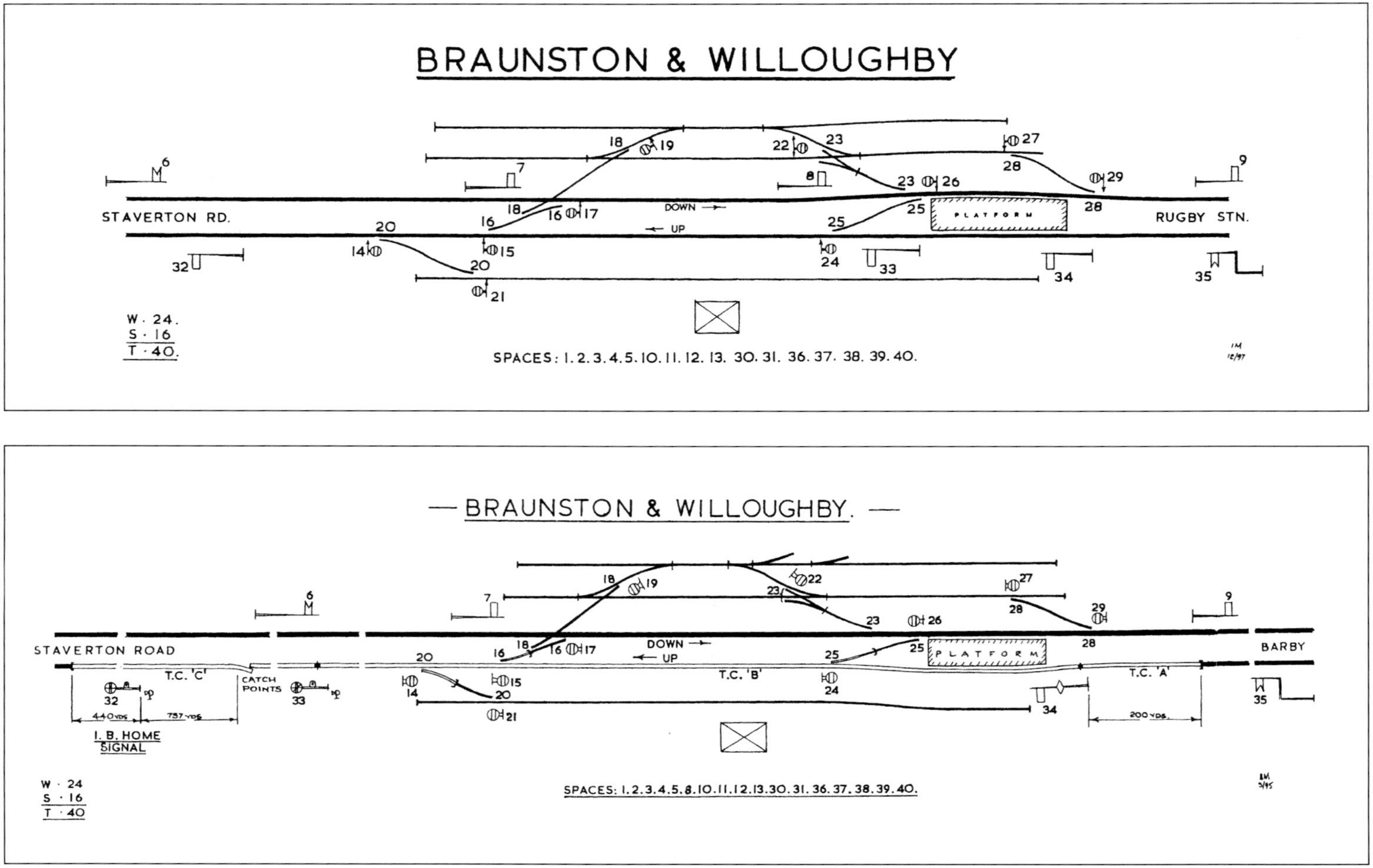

Signal box diagrams for Braunston & Willoughby before and after the installation of the Up line track circuits and IB signals.

Apparatus.	Requires.	
Signal 32.	'Line Clear' from box ahead.	Over-run alarm operates when T.C.'C' clears with 32 normal.
Signal 33.	T.C.'C' clear. Lever 32 normal.	T.C.'C' occ'd restores red asp't*
Signal 34.	T.C.'B' clear. Lever 33 normal.	
Up Block Instrument.	Line Clear: T.C.'A' operated and clear. Levers 34 and 35 normal. Signal arms 34 & 35 'ON'.	T.C.'A' Occupied places Block indicator to 'Train on Line'.

* When box switched out T.C.'C' clears restores signal to green.

Table of electrical controls

Detonator placers were operated by 'stirrups' provided in the frame between levers 7 and 8, and 34 and 33.

Electrical controls

The signal box was equipped with a non-illuminated diagram. There were no electrical controls on Down line signals.

Signals 6, 9, 32, 33 and 35 were repeated.

Signals 6 and 35 had 'lamp burning' indicators in a combined unit on the block shelf.

Welwyn Control

In 1935 a serious collision occurred at Welwyn Garden City when a second train was permitted to enter an already occupied section. In order to prevent future accidents of this sort a system was devised whereby a Track Circuit had to be occupied and cleared and all relevant signals replaced to danger before a second 'Line Clear' could be given. A Track Circuit of 200 yards was provided in rear of the Home signal and this provided the basis upon which the Welwyn Control operated: the Home and Distant signal arms had to be 'on' and the Track Circuit clear before a 'Line Clear' could be given. However, in the event of a train being cancelled after it had been accepted, an Emergency Release was provided adjacent to the Block Instrument. This took the form of a small box with a handle on its right-hand side. The handle had to be turned some 100 times in order to obtain a second 'Line Clear', which would take probably a minute; the theory was that any train already in the section would travel a mile at 60mph during that minute! At Braunston & Willoughby this applied to Track Circuit 'A' on the Up line.

10
LIFE AT BRAUNSTON & WILLOUGHBY

Every other Thursday saw the arrival of the S&T Linesmen (they were not Technicians in those days) from Leicester on the 8.10 'ord' – Len Robinson was accompanied by his two henchmen, Frank and Harry, and their task was to check and maintain the signalling equipment in the area. I was honoured to receive them every sixth week, when it would be my privilege to relinquish the use of my stove, kettle, frying-pan and two lockers in order that they might undertake their first priority of preparing breakfast. This was never an ordinary breakfast of cereals and toast – oh no, any self-respecting weight-watcher would have thrown up their hands in horror at the gastronomic orgy that was prepared on those Thursday mornings. The delightful aromas of cooking were meals in themselves and were in direct competition with Tubby's Cafe nearby – but with no chips! And so, the host would hover hopefully for any tit-bit that would fall from their table – the S&T culinary abilities far outshone those of yours truly. With the ritual of breakfast over, the washing-up done and the remnants cleared away, the trio would go to their various tasks below decks and to all of the battery cupboards and apparatus cases in the locality. Batteries were checked and the cells topped up with distilled water; cranks pulleys and spindles were oiled, signal arms and 'dolly' faces cleaned, and spectacles polished in a frenzy of activity until, by midday, everything was spick and span. They would then catch the 2.20pm 572 bus service to Rugby, and that would be it for another fortnight. As their tour of inspection and maintenance involved both Distant signals and the IB signal, they certainly did a fair amount of walking at each visit. They needed their breakfast!

While on the subject of signal maintenance, the story of signal No 8, the Second Down Home, must be told. It is customary for signalmen to observe signals as they are operated to ensure that they respond to the pull on the lever. Rule 65 devotes a full three paragraphs to the subject. Accordingly I was amazed to watch the arm of No 8 come off, literally, as I worked the lever. The lower-quadrant arm sagged and finally left the spectacle plate to which it had been attached since the birth of the line 50-odd years before and lay a forlorn relic in the cess, its signalling days gone for ever. Len Pen had to be told and the S&T were informed. The signal was never replaced and the lever was painted white.

Signal lamps were trimmed and filled each week on Friday, and this was the responsibility of the station staff, in this case 'Irish' Peggie. Peggie was related in some way to our beloved leader down at the station house, together with his wife and 'Barby Bill' (of whom more later). Peggie spoke with the most wonderful Irish accent of which I am constantly reminded when I hear Frank Carson on the TV. She also had a typical Irish sense of humour and would follow her jokes with a great guffaw, throwing back her head with her mouth wide open. This was always funnier than her joke as her upper dentures were never quite secure and they would drop down with a click, ending her merriment abruptly. Peggie was a dab hand at spotting mushrooms when in season from her elevated position up the signal posts, and she would often bring back a sizeable collection after her visit to the Down Distant. Most of them went to the 'big house', but I was often favoured by being offered a few. Her Irish upbringing also gave her the skill of spotting the winners from the sporting pages. I was never tempted, as anything I back has a nasty habit of coming last! I've never won anything in my entire life, but that's nothing to do with this narrative. As a consequence of this amazing ability, which was never known to fail (well, hardly ever), she was extremely popular with the Permanent Way gangs. How they were able to place their bets from the remoteness of the place is a mystery, particularly as betting shops were a few years away in the future.

As the station staff were responsible for the lamping, I always made a point after signing on for night duty to make sure that all the lamps were burning properly before the station closed at 10.30pm. It happened one night that the lamp in the Up Home was out, and I rang the office to report the matter. Napoleon answered and I told him that the Up Home signal had no light.

'Right, I'll go and look.'

After a few seconds he was back on the telephone.

'It's showing a good light.'

'I tell you, it's out from where I'm standing.'

The receiver goes down with a clatter, then shortly he's back again.

'No – there's a good light in that signal. You must be mistaken.'

'Which signal are you looking at?' I ask with rising impatience.

'The one behind Tubby's Cafe,' comes the reply.

'That's the Down Starter! There's no light in the *Up Home*.'

'Oh, sorry. I'll get Peggie out to look at it.'

I was thankful that the matter was being attended to as the signal concerned stood immediately on the bridge over the A45 and I am terrified of heights!

Friday afternoons were spent partly with the weekly point-oiling session with the Platelayers; armed with 'dosh' pots full of thick black oil, scrapers and long-handled brushes, they would clean and oil the slide chairs of the switches (the moving blades of the points). They had to be done both ways, and this sometimes meant lengthy waits when there were trains about, which was most of the time. Each and every slide chair was scraped to clear the accumulated 'gunge', then oiled with the long-handled brush. Then a wave would request the points to be reversed for the other sides of the slide chairs to be similarly treated. I often attempted to catch the brush by putting the points back suddenly, but the gang were up to all of those sort of tricks.

In those days all the points were used regularly; the Up and Down pick-ups called each day and the 'top' points into the Refuge Sidings were in frequent use for setting back (waylaying) 'runners' for more important traffic. The North Crossover (25) was always used for single-line working as it was a) nearer the box, and b) did not have a slip point, which would have complicated the clipping arrangements. No 25 points were also an easier turnout, which suited passenger rolling-stock better. Point-oiling was a duty that took place in the three-weekly timetable among window-cleaning, lever-burnishing, and floor-scrubbing. Braunston & Willoughby wasn't the cleanest box on the line (that honour went to Lutterworth), but it was always clean and tidy. However, Napoleon didn't think so on one of his visits to sign the book. It was an accepted thing that the box was swept at the end of each shift, and when I refused to break into the morning's work to do his bidding I was told that the matter would be reported to Mr Probert, the District Operating Superintendent at Nottingham Victoria. I learned later through the grapevine that the scheme had misfired and Napoleon had been instructed *not* to interfere with the signalmen in the course of their duties unless it was a *serious* matter.

The 'competent person' acting as Pilotman during single-line working for Sunday engineering work was often a Relief signalman, while on weekday emergencies it was left to the local Station Masters to don the red armband. I was always much relieved when the Pilotman on these occasions was anyone other than our own Station Master. Poor old Nappie never seemed able to get his act together, and although he was always strutting about looking very important, he was invariably being guided by others with more experience. He actually came up to the box one day to introduce single-line working. He had appointed the Flagman armed with point clips and everything was set up except for one thing – the single-line working was between *Barby* and Rugby. The operation was delayed while he redeployed his troops.

Then there was the day when emergency single-line working between Rugby and Braunston over the Up line was instituted as a result of a serious engine failure, the engine being totally disabled at Barby. When the problem had been solved and the obstruction removed, George Wilson at Rugby informed me that the next train on the Up would be the last train over the single line – all very straightforward, but things didn't quite work out that way! The train, an Up 'runner', approached the Up Home signal where I brought it 'quite or nearly to a stand'. I then pulled off 34, 33 and 32 ('Line Clear' having been received from Staverton Road earlier). As the engine passed the box I gave the driver the 'OK' and he opened the regulator to take a run at the bank. I remained at the window to convey the same message to the guard when I became aware of a portly gentleman waving his arms furiously from the brake-van. Napoleon, no less, was heading south at an alarming speed. I rang Percy at Staverton and made him aware of the situation, to which he replied,

'___ Napoleon! I've pulled off and I never put back except in an emergency, and this isn't an emergency.'

And so it was that our fat friend took an unexpected trip to Woodford when he should have been hard at work in his office.

I was severely reprimanded the next day when he marched up to the box in a state of great indignation. Standing me to attention, he rebuked me in no uncertain terms. Why hadn't I given him time to alight from the train? Why hadn't I stopped the train at the platform to facilitate his disembarkation? (He was never at ease when getting on or off the footplate of engines in view of his corpulent stature.) Why ... why ... why? To which I eventually replied:

'I *did* bring the train to a stand at the Home signal. From there the driver could have moved forward to deposit you on the platform. According to *my* Rule Book, however, it states that the Pilotman must travel on the *footplate of the engine*, and be clearly visible to all personnel at the lineside. As you were in the brake-van...'

End of diplomatic relations for several weeks.

Rules 189-192

WORKING TRAFFIC OF A DOUBLE LINE OVER A SINGLE LINE OF RAILS DURING REPAIRS OR OBSTRUCTION.

189. When the traffic of a double line has to be worked over a single line of rails during repairs or owing to an obstruction, the following precautions must be adopted.

Limit of single line working. **190.** Single line working should be confined to the shortest length practicable and, whenever possible, between crossover roads where there are fixed signals, but in the event of a crossover road not protected by fixed signals being used the provisions of Rule 199 must be observed.

Appointment of Pilotman. Pilotman's armlet. **191.** A competent person must be appointed as Pilotman, who must wear round his left arm above the elbow, a red armlet with the word " Pilotman " shown thereon in white letters, thus :—

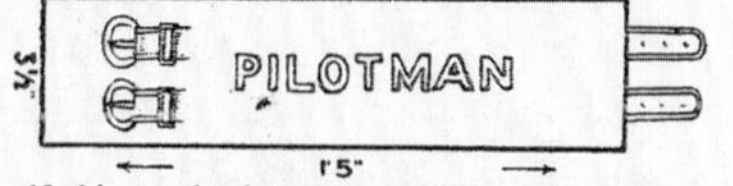

If this armlet is not immediately available the Pilotman must wear a red flag in the position indicated until the proper armlet is obtained.

Pilotman to be present. **192.** (*a*) Except as provided in clause (*b*) of this Rule and also in Rule 200, clause (*f*), and Rule 206, no train must be allowed to enter upon or foul any portion of the single line without the Pilotman being present and riding upon the engine, except when a train is to be followed by

200

Beauty is in the eye of the beholder – there is something to commend most places in Britain – and I was able to sit at the window and admire the changing seasons as they occurred in Northamptonshire. I could see the spire of Braunston Church and the hills to the east through which the Grand Union Canal had a tunnel. On the Down side of the line Willoughby village was much closer: the Four Crosses Inn was just visible beyond the weighbridge at the goods yard gate. Looking south, the railway ran in a straight line towards Staverton Road; an overbridge at Wolfhampcote crossed the line just beyond No 33 signal, and at about this point the railway crossed the Oxford Canal and also the Weedon to Leamington branch of the LMS. Northwards, the view of the line was more restricted as the platform buildings stood in the way; the line curved away to the left just beyond the Down Starting signal, No 9, beyond which was the overbridge carrying the road to Barby at Navigation Inn. Behind the signal box was a field that at one time had been cultivated as allotment gardens (Sammy Russell had one of them in years past). During the month of June there appeared the most wonderful crop of Sweet Williams (Dianthus barbatus), which had naturalised after the gardens had been abandoned. It was to these flowers, as I thought, that a group of women were attracted one day when a coach stopped on the adjacent A45 road. The matronly figures made their way into the field, there to disperse to discreet locations to answer an urgent call of nature. And a Peeping Tom barely 100 yards away! Why do people always assume that railway premises are unoccupied?

I have mentioned earlier the Platelayers' cabin that was situated in the goods yard immediately opposite the signal box. This provided an ideal dormitory when I found myself with a 'double back' turn on Saturday night/Sunday morning. To arrive home after 11pm only to return to work by 6am was pointless, and to have to cycle 7 road miles was an added burden, so I kipped down in Bill Homan's hut, which could be made very cosy with a banked-up fire and the big black kettle bubbling away on the hob. The cabin was constructed of stout timbers and draught-proofed using (I think) a material somewhat similar to wagon tarpaulins. Most of these huts were lean-to styles, while some were built with pitched roofs. They were usually divided in two, one end being devoted to storage of tools and equipment while the other provided accommodation for the gang with suitable seating around the walls. The fireplace and chimney were of brick, providing a facility for generous fires (there was never any shortage of coal). Having experienced the comforts provided by these simple huts, I am left to wonder how the workers on the Permanent

The platelayers' cabin can be clearly seen opposite the signal box as 'B1' No 61041 re-starts the Saturday 10.14am Hastings-Sheffield train after a signal check on 26 August 1961. *M. Mitchell*

BRITISH RAILWAYS
THE RAILWAY EXECUTIVE

YOUR REF.
DATED

LM. REGION

OUR REF. S. 4391
DATE 5.11 53.

E.R.O. 11

TO Dist. Operating Supt.,
Nottingham Vic. (Centre No.)

FROM S.M.O.
RUGBY Central (Centre No.)
Extn............

No. 3099 Up "H". 8-25 pm. Annesley to Woodford 4.11.53.
Divided at Lutterworth.

"Train Divided" Signal was received at Shawell from Lutterworth for the above train at 11-43 pm. The first portion of the train arrived at Shawell at 11-53 pm and consisted of engine No.63773 - Driver Townsend - and 9 wagons. On examination it was found that the last wagon was complete with drawbar and coupling.

Guard Field arrived back at Lutterworth Box and reported the Down Line clear. Shawell signalman was so informed and that engine No. 61206 would enter the section at Lutterworth under Regulation 14 and propel the second portion of the train to Shawell. This was done at 12-28 am. arriving at Shawell at 1-0am. When the train was re-coupled and proceed to Rugby at caution for the two wagons involved, Nos. 243366 & 40929 to be detached for examination by the C & W Dept.

No. 54 Down "A" arrived at Shawell at 12-40am and was held there until the arrival of the rear portion of No. 3099 at that point at 1-0am.

Shawell signalman's report and extract attached.

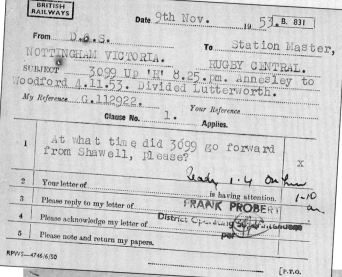

BRITISH RAILWAYS

Date 9th Nov. 1953. B. 831

From D.O.S. NOTTINGHAM VICTORIA.

To Station Master, RUGBY CENTRAL.

SUBJECT 3099 Up 'H' 8.25.pm. Annesley to Woodford 4.11.53. Divided Lutterworth.

My Reference G.112922. Your Reference

Clause No. 1. Applies.

1	At what time did 3099 go forward from Shawell, please?	X
2	Your letter of .... is having attention.	
3	Please reply to my letter of	
4	Please acknowledge my letter of	
5	Please note and return my papers.	

Ready 1.4 On line 1-10 am

FRANK PROBERT
District Operating Superintendent
per

RPWS—4746/6/50 [P.T.O.

G.112922
9.11.53.

S. 4371
10.11.53.

D. O. S.
Nottingham Vic.

xxxxxxxxxxxxx SMO.
RUGBY Central

3099 Up. "H" 8-25pm Annesley to Woodford 4.11.53.
Divided at Lutterworth.

3099 was accepted by Rugby at 1-4am. and sent into section at 1.10am.

All incidents had to be reported and generated considerable paperwork and correspondence with Frank Probert's office at Nottingham. This is part of a sequence of notes between Rugby Station Master Ernie Potts and the District Operating Superintendent relating to an Up Class H goods train becoming divided late at night on 4 November 1953 between Lutterwoth and Shawell signal box. It is unlikely to have inconvenienced passengers at that time of night!

Way of the Southern Railway fared in their mass-produced and somewhat too functional concrete huts.

Catesby Tunnel was 3,000 yards long on a rising gradient of 1 in 176 in the Up direction at the summit of the long 6½-mile climb from Braunston & Willoughby. It was a feature that could have been avoided had the owner of nearby Catesby House been a little more tolerant to the coming of the railway. A deep cutting was all that was needed at that location, but the line had to be hidden from the view of the aristocracy. I seem to remember some facts from my history lessons that involved Catesby House with the abortive attempt by Guido Fawkes to blow up the Houses of Parliament. Incidentally, G. Fawkes Esq and his fellow conspirators used a house at Ashby St Ledgers to plot their misguided scheme, and that house was close to Kilsby Tunnel on the LMS line.

Catesby Tunnel was the cause of total chaos one summer Saturday afternoon when I had the misfortune to be on late turn. The driver of an Up train stopped at Charwelton and reported hearing a 'loud bang' as he went through the tunnel. Everything, but everything, stops when a tunnel is involved in an emergency of that sort. Two 'competent persons' were duly appointed to walk through the tunnel to find out the cause of the reported 'loud bang'; the persons concerned were the Station Master and the porter from Charwelton station; they equipped themselves with Tilley lamps and set about the long walk to examine the tunnel. The effect on the traffic was catastrophic. There were trains to Ramsgate, Margate and Bournemouth. There were the usual 'runners' queuing for a path to Woodford. Napoleon was in his element, as I had brought the Nottingham to Margate holidaymakers' train to a stand at the platform, and he was explaining to the long-suffering passengers the cause of the hold-up. Although officially off duty, the sight of an express train detained at *his* platform was too big an opportunity to miss, and he was doing his job by keeping the travelling public informed – it was the cap in hand bit that didn't quite ring true.

On that afternoon there was a train at each and every signal, with two at Staverton, three with me at Willoughby, and goodness knows what the situation was like at Rugby and points north. My three were at signal 32, signal 33, and one standing *inside* signal 34 – I had deliberately flagged him inside the Home signal as I felt safer that way. Eventually the examination was completed, nothing was found, and trains were allowed to proceed through the tunnel as normal after the first one had been cautioned to proceed at reduced speed – just in case. The cause of the loud bang was to remain unsolved for a little while longer, until Monday morning in fact, when a Platelayer working in the tunnel asked one of his mates, 'Hey, Jack, have you seen my wheelbarrow?' Close examination discovered fragments of the missing implement scattered at intervals along the sleeper ends.

Incidents of this sort were few and far between. It was always an acute embarrassment to me to have trains standing about when they should have been on the move. Passengers always looked so accusingly at me when their trains were delayed, as if I was doing it out of sheer vindictiveness. Although it was the signalman's duty to ensure the safe movement of trains, it was essential that the wheels were kept moving as any delays, however slight, would involve a lot of written explanations to the 'powers that be' following receipt of their 'Please explain…' memos. Movement was always of paramount importance in railway work, that very movement in itself producing a pleasing sound as the wheels passed over the rail joints.

In these days of mass motoring, it seems difficult to manage even the shortest journey without the assistance of the motor car; in fact, I think the word 'walk' is bracketed with other four-letter words and should not be referred to! To come to the point, I sometimes walked home from Braunston to Rugby when I was finishing an early turn and the weather was fine. It was all open track and the 4 miles presented no real hazards. The concrete lids of the cess drains provided an excellent footpath in cuttings, and progress could be fairly rapid. This way I was able to visit 'Barby Bill', and I must admit that his behaviour as quoted in the next chapter never occurred while I was with him.

11
Barby Sidings

'Barby Bill' was another from the ménage at the Station House, and he was the signalman at Barby, the small wartime-constructed box between Braunston and Rugby. It served the Ministry of Supply depot and was opened between 8am and 4pm each weekday. Bill (I never learned his surname) was an American, and he always spoke with an American accent, most of which was put on to impress us natives. The cosmopolitan nature of the residents at the Station House was always a subject of conjecture – Irish, American, Napoleonic... But I digress. I remember an occasion when I had thumbed a lift on a Down 'runner' and was told by the engine crew to 'take cover' as we approached Barby box. There, on the top step of the box, was 'Barby Bill' armed with a broom, which he pointed menacingly at the engine as it drew near – the Sheriff, armed with a Winchester repeater, was having no truck with those critters on the railroad. What made the scene even more ridiculous was to see the driver and fireman, both grown men, hiding behind the cab side sheets and firing back using hand guns as is the wont of small boys the world over. Cowboys and Indians in the wilds of darkest Northamptonshire!

Barby Sidings was a wartime addition to the Great Central and was thus a typical utility style of building. It was more of an elaborate ground frame than a signal box, built of brick with metal casement windows; it had a flat roof and the frame was at the back of the box. It had all 'mod cons' including electric lighting and running water at the tap and a sink. The frame was a Westinghouse, and an Illuminated Track Diagram was provided above the Block Shelf whereon stood the traditional Fazak Block Instruments. Both Up and Down pick-up freights called at Barby on weekdays. The box was closed on Sundays unless required for engineering work. Naturally, as it was a modern layout, the Distant signals were both automatic three-aspect colour lights. The Up Home signal was a three-aspect 'searchlight'-type colour light displaying a green aspect when the mechanical Starting signal arm was 'proved' off. Similarly, on the Down the Home signal had below it an Accelerating Distant (usually referred to as an Inner Distant), which allowed the Main Distant to show double yellow when the Starter was 'on'. Again, the arm of the latter *and* the operating of the Inner Distant put a green aspect in the Automatic Distant. This arrangement sometimes presented problems on warm summer days since, unless the mechanical arms were carefully adjusted to cater for the temperature changes, the Auto Distant would show a double yellow when any of the other arms had a tendency to droop when they were supposedly 'off'. The Up Home signal mentioned earlier became Rugby Station's Up Intermediate Block Home signal when Barby was switched out. There was no prescribed fog marking point as both of the Distants were colour lights, obviating the need for Fogsignalmen. The clearance points were also electrical functions in the form of Track

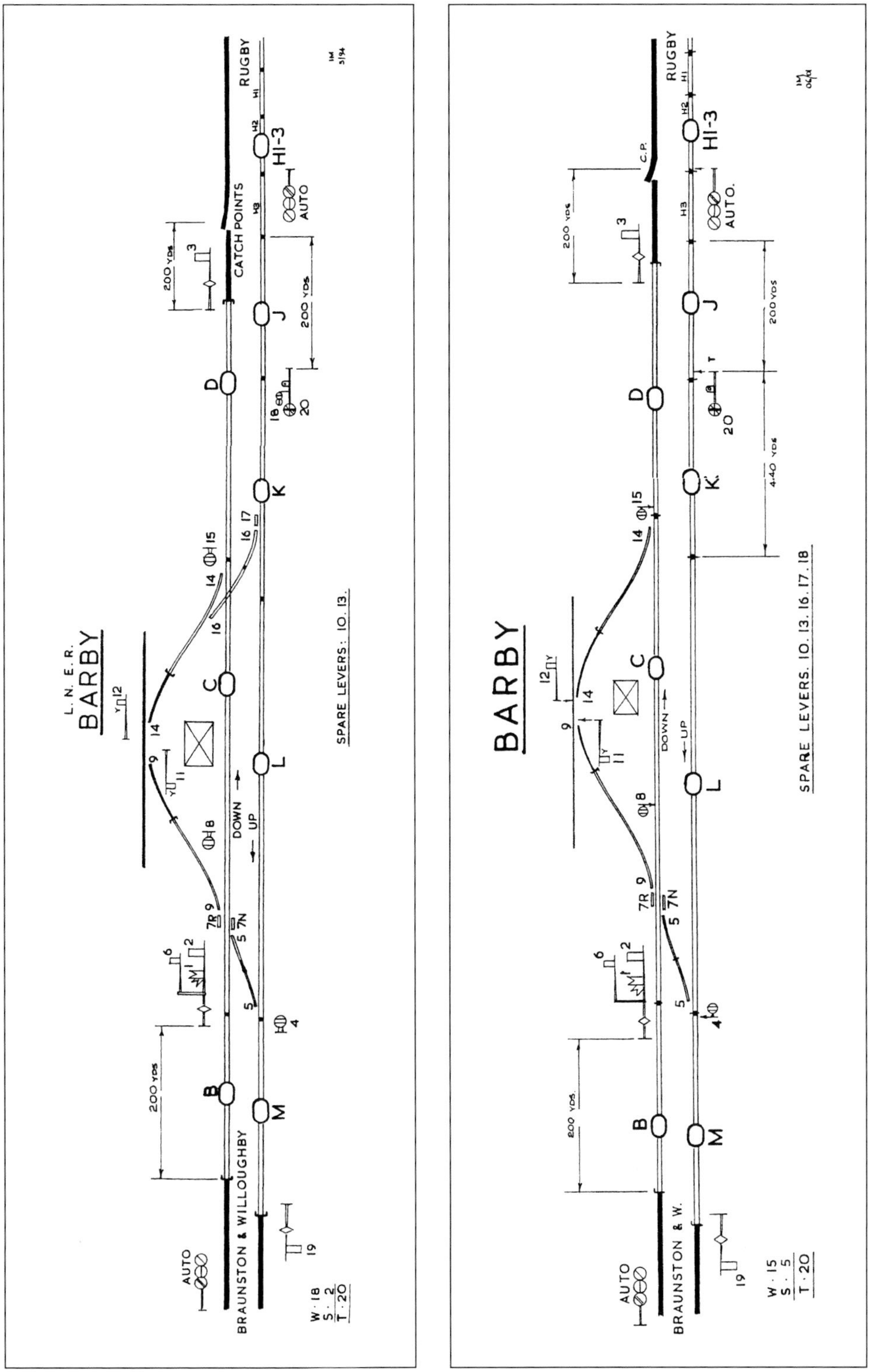

Signal box diagrams at Barby before and after the facing connection from the Up main to the sidings was removed.

Circuits, which prevented the signalman 'pegging' 'Line Clear' until either 'C' on the Down or 'K' on the Up were clear. Catch points were provided 200 yards beyond the Starting signal on the Down main.

Barby was the subject of gradual disintegration. Firstly the facing connection from the Up Main to the sidings was removed in the early 1950s, resulting in levers 16, 17 and 18 being painted white. In September 1955 the box was abolished and all connections removed except points 14, which were released by new lever No 10 at Braunston; a ground frame operated by the guard of the train was installed at Barby. As the crossover had also been removed, Up trains requiring to call at Barby shunted the consignment at B&W, to be taken on the next day by the Down service. While the box at Barby was fully operational and Switched In during the day, it shortened the rather hefty section between B&W and Rugby on the Down; there was always the IB Section on the Up main. The additional time required to allow 'runners' to reach Rugby was a problem, but it seldom presented any real difficulties. I was often puzzled by the development of facilities such as Running Loops and Intermediate Block sections on the Up, while the Down line was very much the poor relation. After leaving Woodford on the Down the first Running Loop was at Ashby Magna – the tedious process of running forward and setting back into Refuge Sidings was required elsewhere.

The long rising gradient of 1 in 176 on the Down line from Barby to Rugby was laid upon high embankments providing vast views to both east and west. This particular earthwork passed very close to the ancient village of Onley, which disappeared in the Middle Ages; some think it was the Plague that caused its extinction. The church was removed stone by stone and became part of the church at Barby. A similar fate affected the village of Wolfhampcote, where the church remains intact, a lonely monument standing alongside another relic of the past, the Weedon to Leamington railway line. The M45 motorway now passes beneath the remains of the Great Central between Barby and Rugby. There was hope that trains bound for the Channel Tunnel would use that high embankment again, but perhaps not.

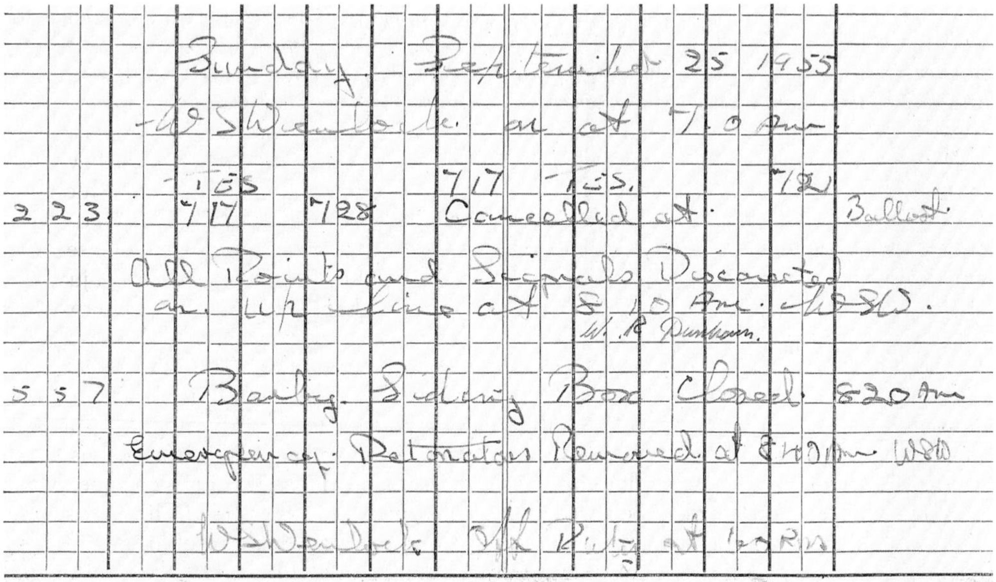
Sunday September 25 1955
W S Wardle on at 7.0 Am.
TES 7 17 TES. 7 [illegible]
2 2 3 7 17 7 28 Cancelled at Ballast
All Points and Signals Disconnected on Up line at 8 10 Am. WSW.
W. R Dunham.
5 5 7 Barby Siding Box Closed 8 20 Am
Emergency Detonators Removed at 8 40 Am WSW
W S Wardle off Duty at [illegible]

The end of Barby Sidings signal box: its closure at 8.20am on Sunday 25 September 1955 recorded in the last Train Register Book.

12
Braunston & Willoughby: Night-time, Fog and Phones

Gremlins always tended to reserve their ill-disposed spite until the unfortunate recipient was on night duty. Each and every occasion when something of a serious nature happened it was on nights – the six 'hot boxes' mentioned earlier was a prime example. Not very serious, perhaps, but something that could only happen during the hours of darkness was the occasional 'tail lamps on but out' situation. This meant that the tail lamp was on the train but the lamp was out. On one occasion 9 bells from Percy at Staverton Road told me that the London Mail had passed without a tail lamp, but this time Percy had not seen the actual lamp. I stopped the train and requested the driver to 'draw forward' so that I could inform the guard of the circumstances. After having a word with the man concerned, I felt that my share of the responsibility was done and I returned to my cup of tea. Minutes later there was still no movement from the train, but the tiny figure of the guard arrived at the box complaining that he couldn't reach the offending lamp! The station staff at Marylebone had put it on the top bracket. Being somewhat taller, I felt it my duty to clamber up on to the buffer stocks to reach down the lamp for relighting so that the long-delayed train could proceed.

A much more serious incident occurred one night when the guard of an Up 'runner', which was over time in section, came on to the IB telephone to report a serious landslip effecting the Up Main line. It was a case of 6 bells to Staverton Road – Obstruction Danger to the uninitiated – and the 'block on'. Track Circuit 'C' had been showing occupied for a considerable period, and it meant either a Track Circuit failure or a train occupying the track for some reason. As it happened it was the latter. The train had been brought to a stand with the brake-van a matter of yards from the end of the track, and a mini drama was being enacted by the train crew.

'I wasn't happy with the bit of track back there, there were too many extra pitches for my liking. You'd better go back and have a word with our guard. Have him walk back and take a look. Go with him if you like to save him having to come up to the engine to let us know if he's found anything.'

So the fireman walked back to convey the message to the guard and together they set off along the sleepers of the track over which they had just travelled. They had walked only a very short distance when they realised that the fears of the driver had been fully justified, as the embankment under the Permanent Way had slipped away, leaving the Up line suspended in mid-air. They placed detonators on the Down line at a suitable distance and then phoned in. The IB telephone was only yards away and it was by that means that I received the dire news of the collapse, which subsequently closed the Up line for several weeks so that repairs could be effected. Thankfully the instinct of the engine crew had averted what could have been a very serious accident. Locomen become accustomed to the rolling and pitching of their engines, being able to tell, even in the dark, their whereabouts by the reactions of the locomotive to the small irregularities in the track. This particular bank-slip caused a facing crossover to be installed at Willoughby to ease the single-line working that was to be very much part of our lives for several weeks. Flag signalmen were on permanent duty to flag and clip at the crossover during that time.

There is only one thing worse than working at night, with its all-embracing darkness, and that is working at night when visibility is further reduced by fog! We are no longer subjected to the 'pea-soupers' that were common in the middle years of the last century when it was difficult to actually see more than a few feet, let alone yards. My narrative turns to an incident that could have been very tragic – the only real tragedy that ensued was that it began my addiction to tobacco, which proved difficult to shed in later years.

It was just after midnight, the dreaded hour, and a light mist was developing into something a little more sinister as the night wore on. Trains were already running out of their correct 'paths' due to more serious conditions further south. The Down London Mail was running rather late, behind the Western Mail, which it normally preceded. I could still see my fog marker – but only just. The Western, with its 'Hall' Class engine, was detained at my Down Starting signal awaiting the Park Royal to Newcastle 'Beer' train to clear Rugby. As the weather was a bit doubtful, I had not cleared back to Staverton Road for the Western, but waited until I 'had the road' for the Western to Rugby. Having eventually got the 'clear', I cleared back to Staverton Road and accepted the London Mail. I was a bit surprised to receive 'be ready' followed fairly soon afterwards by 'on line', or 'Train Entering Section'. I had been under the impression that the express was still some distance away. Not so, as was soon to be revealed. All of my signals were 'on', at danger, but I could hear the London Mail coming down the bank from Staverton Road with steam on. I kept thinking, 'He'll shut off in a second! He must shut off in a second!' But he didn't. The train came out of the mist going like the proverbial bat out of hell. I did the only thing I could have done in the circumstances – I reached for the emergency detonator placer and prayed. A flash, a bang, then a firework display to end them all – every wheel on the train must have locked solid in that brake application as the train literally slid

which is closed, the Driver must proceed cautiously and report the circumstance to the Signalman at the next signal box.

It will not be necessary for a Driver to inform the Signalman of a defect if previously advised by notice or by the Signalman at the box in rear.

Electrical locking, &c., not to be released.

83. Electrical locking or controlling devices in connection with signals, points, or block apparatus must not, in case of failure, or supposed failure, be released unless special instructions are issued to the contrary.

SIGNALLING DURING FOG OR FALLING SNOW.

Appointment of Fog-signalmen.

84. The Station Master must arrange beforehand with the Permanent-way Inspector the allocation of the Permanent-way men who are to act as Fogsignalmen at the various posts. If there are insufficient Permanent-way men for the purpose the Station Master must report accordingly to his superior officer.

A regular Fogsignalman, and where necessary a relief Fogsignalman, must be appointed for every fogging post and a list of the names and addresses of these men showing the post to which each man is assigned must be exhibited in a conspicuous position in the Station Master's office and signal box.

The Ganger or other person referred to in Rule 221 must not be assigned a fixed post, but must be left free to examine the line in accordance with that Rule. He may, however, when no other competent man is available, be employed to call Fogsignalmen, to visit them at their posts, and distribute detonators as required.

82

Supply of detonators, hand lamps and flags to be kept.

85. A sufficient supply of detonators, hand lamps, and flags for the use of the Fogsignalmen must be kept at stations and signal boxes in connection with which the men are employed.

Station Master to satisfy himself that Fogsignalmen are at posts.

86. During fog or falling snow the Station Master must satisfy himself that the Fogsignalmen have proceeded to the posts where their services are required.

Calling and reporting of Fog-signalmen.

87. (*a*) When a fog or snowstorm occurs during the normal working hours of the men appointed to act as Fogsignalmen they must at once report to the Signalman and take his instructions. The Signalman must advise the Station Master if any Fogsignalman fails to report for duty.

When it is necessary to employ Fogsignalmen outside their normal working hours the Station Master or Signalman must, unless the men have been previously notified, arrange to have them called and sent to their respective posts, but any Fogsignalman who becomes aware that his services are required must report for duty without waiting to be called.

(*b*) If a Fogsignalman, proceeding to the signal box to report for duty, has to pass the signal to which he is appointed, he must, if that signal is at Danger, or Caution in the case of a distant signal, place one detonator on the rail of the line to which the signal applies and then proceed to the signal box, getting back to his post as promptly as possible. He must keep a few detonators in his possession for the purpose of this Rule.

(*c*) When a Fogsignalman has to pass a signal box on his way to take up duty at a signal worked from another box, he must inform the Signalman that he is going to commence fogsignalling at such signal, and the Signal-

83

into the gloom. It was several minutes before a handlamp came bobbing along the track from the direction of the now stopped train. A very white-faced driver, in spite of his grime, came into the box.

'What have we done, Bobby?'

'Nothing, but you would have done something if you'd gone much further. The Western Mail had only just left when you came down the bank.'

'I didn't see your signals – they were all "off" at Staverton and I assumed... Are you going to report it?'

By this time he had offered me a Woodbine to calm my nerves and we sat smoking.

'No, there's no real harm done except my exploded dets. Square your guard and be on your way. The Western has just cleared Rugby.'

He gave me the remainder of the packet of 'coffin nails' and went off into the night.

It took me 30 years to rid myself of the addiction to the wretched weed – the trouble was, I found it did help to calm the nerves in times of crisis.

There is a sequel to this near disaster that happened a matter of days afterwards. I was dusting around the frame and had pulled the Up line detonator 'stirrup' up in order to sweep the frame properly. I was 'all off' for a 'runner' on the Up and Napoleon was walking along the cess in my direction. Then the telephone rang! I went to answer it and watched the train approaching – then I also saw, out of the corner of my eye, the 'stirrup'! I leapt across the box, but too late – the engine reached the detonators before I had a chance to replace the handle. But not a sound. Not as much as a splutter. At that precise moment Napoleon entered.

'Good morning, signalman.'

'Good morning, boss – did you hear those detonators go off?'

'What detonators?'

'The detonators that that train has just passed over, and your ears only yards away!'

'Great Scot! Do you mean they were duds?' (This sounds like a Victorian melodrama, but it was something like that.)

'Precisely.'

It was a chance in several hundred million that two defective detonators were together in that machine on that day. Had they been on the Down line a few days earlier... The entire stock of emergency detonators was returned to the stores for replacement, but I still came out in a cold sweat when I thought of what might have been.

Telephones ringing at inopportune times could be a nuisance. Napoleon, on the other hand, had little else to do other than answer 'the blower'. The 'omnibus' telephone, with its Morse-code-type call codes, presented problems one day when the engineers came to renew a canal bridge further up the line. The jib of their crane occasionally made contact with the overhead wires, thus causing the telephone bell to ring. By listening on the instrument one heard something like this:

'Willoughby. Willoughby station. Who's ringing?'

Silence.

After a short pause it rang again.

'Willoughby. Who's ringing? This is Willoughby station.'

This sort of thing went on until poor old Napoleon could stand it no longer. He was told that the problem was caused by the engineers' crane and off he went to do battle with said crane. I watched him set off in high dudgeon to walk the three-quarters of a mile to the site of work. It was a sunny afternoon, just right for a walk, and Napoleon set off in his shirt sleeves to get to the root of the problem. Unfortunately, a short but heavy shower came on while he was sorting out the engineers' crane, and he came back in a little while looking as if he had taken a dip in the canal. He was not a happy man, and he went straight down to the Station House to change out of his sodden clothes. End of story, you might think, but there was more to come. Peggie confided in me a day or so later that the boss had left his clothes to dry in front of the fire, but when Mrs Boss had come home she found the room full of smoke and a large hole scorched in the seat of his trousers.

The 'omnibus' telephone circuit was open to all who cared to lift the receiver – it was certainly not a system to encourage privacy. Explained briefly, the circuit that served Braunston & Willoughby linked Woodford No

4 and Rugby Station, and all signal boxes and stations in between. There were very few quiet periods where traffic was concerned, but when they did occur there would be some intellectual conversations to be heard on the 'omnibus' telephone. One night I heard Harold Carpenter at Woodford No 1 complaining bitterly about his mate on the earlier turn:

'He's disgusting, I tell you!'

'What's he done, then?' asked Colin at No 2.

'I wanted to throw up when I came to use it.'

'It must be bad to make you want to do that!'

'He's a real dirty beggar and no mistake,' continued Harold.

'I only wish you'd tell us what his dirty habits are!' joined in Percy at Staverton Road.

'He makes cocoa in my teapot!'

Another such conversation was overheard between Jack Lambie and Joe Godfrey, both at Woodford boxes:

'You know those allotments on the Eydon Road?'

'Yes.'

'Funny thing – I saw a herd of cows in there eating their way through a crop of cabbages!'

'Bloody hell, that's *my* allotment!'

Jack Lambie was the subject of another problem that is worth the telling. He worked at Woodford No 4 and the sliding window at the London end of the box had a tendency to stick because of a faulty casement. He was in the habit of putting his head out of the window to shout instructions to the shunters outside and, before withdrawing his head, would begin the difficult process of sliding the window closed. One day the chippies came and fixed the window. Jack, on nights following the repair, did his usual trick of sticking his head out of the window, but it closed very much more rapidly when he started to pull it, resulting in his head becoming suddenly jammed between casement and frame, causing much profanity and damning all carpenters to hellfire.

One final story on this somewhat light-hearted topic concerns George Huntley and Bill Millership at Charwelton. George was Relief signalman and had many contacts on local farms, so was the recipient of various perks from their good-natured workers. It was Christmas and George had been presented with a duck for his Yuletide dinner. He was on nights and took the opportunity of plucking the bird while he was at work. Carefully placing the down into a parcel contained in a newspaper, he then placed it on the shelf over the door of the box. Six o'clock came, and with it Bill Millership, dressed in his best suit as he intended going to stay with his son immediately after finishing duty. Greetings were exchanged and George went off with his duck. Bill, sitting there drinking his cup of tea, looked up and saw the mysterious parcel, which he'd not seen before. Taking his chair, he reached up for the strange package but the newspaper opened when touched, covering Mr Nosey Millership in a cloud of duck down. Duck down sticks to serge like something or other to a blanket, and it was reported later that the unfortunate man joined his train later that day looking like the inside of a feather pillow.

We had a spot of bother with ASLEF in the 1950s when the train services were drastically reduced. Everyone seemed to be bloody-minded during these disputes, and even friend bit the hand of friend. As the trains were few and far between, I took the opportunity to give the floor of the box a good scrubbing. I removed all the furniture that wasn't fixed down and set about the task. When I had almost finished and was watching the approach of a Down express, I realised that he was stopping. Strange – I was 'all off' for him. I went to the window as the engine drew to a stand opposite.

'What's wrong, mate?' I asked.

'You tell me,' he said. 'You've a red signal outside the box.'

I looked around in bewilderment and could see no red hand signal.

'The fire buckets!' shouted the driver. 'On the balcony!' And he pointed to the three red fire buckets that I had placed outside the window while I scrubbed the floor. I was flabbergasted. To add insult to injury, I received a severe reprimand for delaying a train without due cause a few weeks later!

I had to delay an express passenger train again some time later. A Down 'runner', driven by the stuttering Jack Collins from Annesley, came to a stop outside the box and the driver came up to talk to me.

'S-s-signalm-m-man, th-th-there's a sh-sheet of c-c-corrugated iron on th-the up l-line b-b-by th-the t-t-top s-s-signal.' (He meant the IB.)

Having got the gist of the message, I put my Up signals back in front of the Manchester-Marylebone, which had just left Rugby. When it arrived I warned the driver, who set off at a much reduced speed. The train eventually arrived at Staverton Road, where the driver came on the telephone.

'That sheet of corrugated iron,' he said, 'was nothing more than a large sheet of cardboard from a box the size of a piano.'

Oops. Another 'Please explain...'

Jack Collins was involved in another incident when he stopped his train, again on the Down line, clambered down from the footplate and commenced hammering away at something underneath his engine. After a period of banging and thumping, he rejoined the engine and drove off without a word of explanation.

Another locomotive that stopped for no apparent reason, when I was on early turn, was a 'Hall' Class engine that had (unusually) failed at Leicester on the Down Western Mail the night before. The engine drew to a halt and the crew, both driver and fireman, came up to the box with their brew can.

'Got the kettle on, Bobby?' the senior man asked.

'If you want a brew, move your steed off the main line,' was my reply.

'Oh sorry, are we in the way?'

Having shunted their engine into the Up Refuge, they stayed on and enjoyed a tea break with me. Not often I was able to entertain Western men. They seemed quite human, really. I was amazed by their casual attitude in thinking that they were the only thing moving that morning.

I suppose the Great Western suffered as many engine failures as we did, the difference being that you never heard about them. I had a Class 'O1' drop a side-rod as it approached the Up Home signal one afternoon, and it ground to a halt with the engine on the south crossover. A crankpin had fractured and the engine was a failure. The brake-van was about 50 yards inside the Home signal – and in the platform. This brought our nosey friend out of his lair to give us the benefit of his two-pen'orth.

'What are we doing?'

'I'm waiting for the ballast train, which was working at Barby, to come and render assistance.'

'I see. And what do we intend to do with the train when the ballast arrives?'

'I'll re-marshal the train, put the cripple in the siding, and the ballast engine can work the train to Woodford.'

'Good. Here's the ballast now – aren't you going to pull off for him?'

I couldn't believe my ears.

'No, but you can do it if you like.' I handed him the lever cloth and he marched over to lever 34 with grim determination. He tried pulling it but found it locked. He turned to me for enlightenment.

'This is how you do it,' I informed him.

Going to the window, I gave the driver a green flag held steadily, there was a 'pip' on the whistle from the engineman, and the show was on the road.

Another breakdown in diplomatic relations.

A tremendous storm broke over the area one night – it just had to be on nights. I watched the lightning get closer and closer as it came up from the south-west, great jagged flashes of forked lightning that lit up the entire sky. Rain came down in torrents and was beating like drums on the window panes. Then the storm was immediately overhead and a great flash of lightning struck the pole at the back of the box. There was a bang as all the fuses in the relay cabinet blew, and the Block Bells and telephone bells all rang at the same instant. I then realised that all electrical equipment had suffered a major blow-out, and I had a total Block Failure on my hands. No telephones or Block Instruments. No Track Circuits, which effectively locked all the Up line signals at danger. Oh what fun! I couldn't even ring Len Pen to summon assistance. I was able to convey written notes by way of the first train, which approached cautiously some time afterwards. It was great fun while it lasted, and a thank you to Ernie Brown for the training he had given to cover such an eventuality.

13
REQUIEM TO THE GREAT CENTRAL RAILWAY

Sadly I was due to leave Braunston & Willoughby and move to a new vacancy at Rugby Midland; the London Midland Region had taken over the Great Central and vacancies were available on the 'other line'. I therefore moved from the box that had provided me with so much pleasure, some anxiety, and a considerable amount of valuable experience. The greatest sadness of all was the eventual closing of 'my' railway, and a feeling of contempt, even today, for the perpetrators of that heinous act. To give expression to that true feeling of grief, the following few lines say it all for me.

Gone, but not completely – the Lower Hillmorton Road bridge just north of Rugby Station. Some bridges still stand, although it may be difficult for the modern traveller to realise their function or history. At least the GCR Plc and MLST at Loughborough and the Leicestershire Records Office website mean that the Great Central Railway has not quite Gone Completely... *D. Caplan*

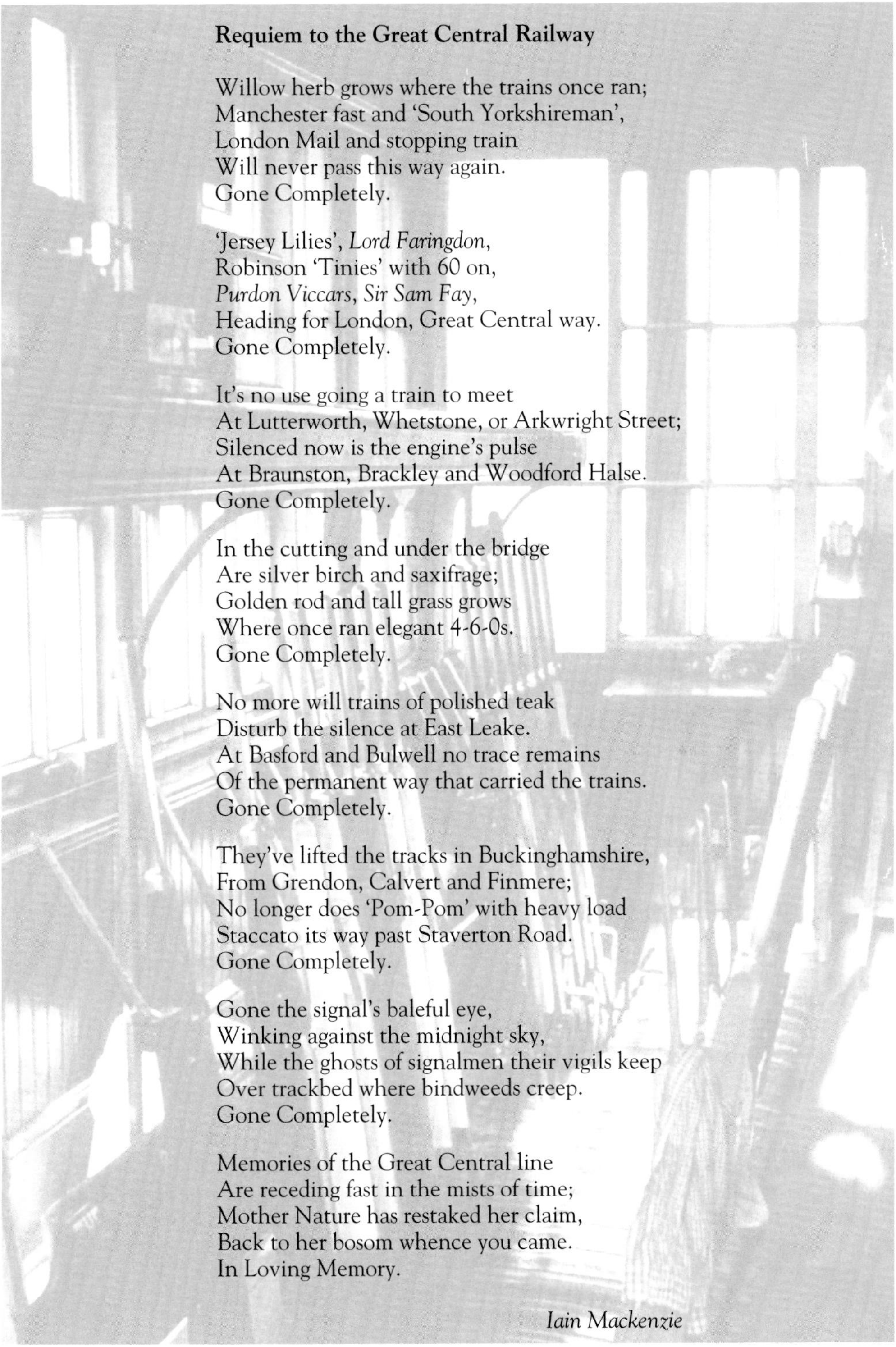

Requiem to the Great Central Railway

Willow herb grows where the trains once ran;
Manchester fast and 'South Yorkshireman',
London Mail and stopping train
Will never pass this way again.
Gone Completely.

'Jersey Lilies', *Lord Faringdon*,
Robinson 'Tinies' with 60 on,
Purdon Viccars, *Sir Sam Fay*,
Heading for London, Great Central way.
Gone Completely.

It's no use going a train to meet
At Lutterworth, Whetstone, or Arkwright Street;
Silenced now is the engine's pulse
At Braunston, Brackley and Woodford Halse.
Gone Completely.

In the cutting and under the bridge
Are silver birch and saxifrage;
Golden rod and tall grass grows
Where once ran elegant 4-6-0s.
Gone Completely.

No more will trains of polished teak
Disturb the silence at East Leake.
At Basford and Bulwell no trace remains
Of the permanent way that carried the trains.
Gone Completely.

They've lifted the tracks in Buckinghamshire,
From Grendon, Calvert and Finmere;
No longer does 'Pom-Pom' with heavy load
Staccato its way past Staverton Road.
Gone Completely.

Gone the signal's baleful eye,
Winking against the midnight sky,
While the ghosts of signalmen their vigils keep
Over trackbed where bindweeds creep.
Gone Completely.

Memories of the Great Central line
Are receding fast in the mists of time;
Mother Nature has restaked her claim,
Back to her bosom whence you came.
In Loving Memory.

Iain Mackenzie

14
THE GREAT CENTRAL: NOTES AND JOTTINGS

Wages

In 1952 a Class 4 signalman was paid 96 shillings per 48-hour week. (In the 1950s 96 shillings was £4 16s 0d, or £4.80 in decimal currency.) The wages for a Class 1 signalman were 123 shillings (£6 3s 0d, or £6.15). A Special Class signalman was paid 154 shillings (£7 14s 0d, or £7.70).

Classification of signalmen

Signalmen were paid in accordance with a marks system, which was calculated according to the amount of work done in a shift. Each lever movement was awarded a number of points, as were all the other duties carried out in the operation of the signal box(answering telephones, entries in the Train Register, etc). At the end of 24 hours the total number of marks accumulated would decide the rate of pay for that particular box. The lowest was Class 5 Porter Signalman, and the highest Special Class, which applied to the very large boxes.

Rugby Nos 5 and 7 were Special Class, but No 1 was Special Plus in view of the extra amount of work involved. The majority of boxes were Class 4: Braunston & Willoughby, Staverton Road and Charwelton are examples from a very long list. Rugby Station and Rugby No 2 were Class 3. Any dispute regarding the rates of pay at any box would be settled by an adjudicator taking the marks over a period of 24 hours on a normal working day. Signalmen having the marks taken would often hope that the day would produce some little out-of-the-ordinary occurrence that would enhance their final total.

Water

As a youth, I had cycled many miles in the pursuit of my unusual hobby. I had also shared many cups of tea with the friendly signalmen whom I had met during those travels. Tea cannot be brewed without water, and water was a commodity that was not 'on tap' in many signal boxes. This was understandable in the more remote rural situations, but piped water supplies even in urban cabins was not always available. I have known some signalmen take bottles of water with their sandwiches with which to charge the ubiquitous kettle.

Shawell, mentioned in Chapter 4, was fortunate in having a never-ending natural supply from a nearby spring. Staverton Road, on the other hand, relied entirely on a can of water supplied via the pick-up goods train from Braunston & Willoughby on a daily basis. In later years sinks with piped water began to appear in many signal boxes, but Staverton Road was far too remote to enjoy this facility.

Lighting

Lighting was another item that nowadays we take for granted – the touch of a switch and darkness is banished. Before electric illumination, gas lighting was the luxury of the day. If gas wasn't available, you had to use oil or paraffin lamps.

A signal box gas lamp in the preserved box at Rothley on the GCR. *P. J. Wortley, courtesy of MLST and GCR Plc*

Rugby Station signal box was gas-lit. The gas was town gas, as opposed to the North Sea variety that is common today. Town gas was produced at the town gas works by heating coal in such a way as to drive off the gases without combusting them. The gas was collected in tanks and piped to the consumer. A bi-product of the process was coke, which was used as a fuel in stoves for heating. The gas was burned in the lamp through a mantle, which gave quite a bright light, as can be seen from the accompanying illustration. The light was controlled by the chains on either side, which operated a gas valve via the lever.

Braunston & Willoughby, being situated in a village, had no gas supply, so the signal box was illuminated by paraffin-fuelled Tilley lamps. Paraffin lighting was still heavily relied upon even in the 1960s. The Tilley lamps were cleaned and filled by the early turn man to be ready for use after dark. From having been such a common item, a Tilley lamp is a difficult thing to find these days, even in a photograph.

Shift patterns, or turns

My calendar was inscribed with initials 'L', 'E' or 'N' alongside each week – this was to remind me of the shift patterns I was required to work. Late was 2pm to 10pm, Early 6am to 2pm, and Nights 10pm to 6am. This arrangement provided a long weekend every third week, when Early turn ended at 2pm on Saturday with a return to Nights at 10pm on Monday. Early turn on Mondays (after the box had been switched out for Sunday) commenced at 4am.

Of the three I think Late was my least favourite. The morning would be idly spent until I caught the 572 Midland Red Daventry bus service at 1.15pm from Rugby, which was nicely timed for my 2pm start. Early turn meant catching the 5.15am bus, but the 2pm finish allowed ample free time in the afternoon and evening. Nights required the 9.15pm bus, and a lonely shift spent in splendid isolation. In those days there was little traffic on the A45 road and the darkness was absolute. There were no lights to be seen (except my signal lamps) and the loneliness was almost palpable. I must admit to locking the door, especially after something stumbled into the signal wires and point rodding. Probably a fox – but you never knew! I remember being shown a truncheon that had been issued to signalmen in the very early years. Signalmen were then known as policemen, hence the term 'Bobby' by which signalmen were known for many years. The truncheon was part of the equipment at Brandon & Wolston, on the original Birmingham line from Rugby.

Getting to work

Many things have changed since those days in the late 1940s and early '50s. There were few motor cars and Relief signalmen used bicycles and motorbikes to reach their places of work. Those relying on pedal cycles used a combination of train services and pedal power when this was convenient, which was fine until ASLEF created problems with their strike in the 1950s. It was then that Relief signalman Arthur Marriot from Leicester cycled to and from Braunston & Willoughby, some 28 miles each way. This was not unusual, as some of the remote signal boxes were pretty inaccessible. Relief signalman George Huntley drove a very up-market Douglas 500cc twin motorbike, while others used BSA Bantams and Francis Barnets.

Routine duties

It was essential that the lamps were trimmed and filled each day, and at the end of each shift the box was swept, the fire in the stove attended to, the ash-pan emptied, and the coal bucket filled from the bunker

Other routine tasks were invariably the responsibility of the early turn man. A notice under the clock was a reminder that it was to be wound on Mondays. There was also a daily time check at 10am when a series of short rings on the 'omnibus' telephone circuit would give the correct time. Details of corrections (if any) and the winding would be noted in the Train Register Book (see page 23).

Detonators in the trackside machines were changed on the first Monday of each month. Detonators were colour coded to indicate the year of manufacture and had a 'use before' date. Upon expiring, unused items were returned to the stores.

Lever cleaning was a time-consuming task and involved burnishing the steel handles with emery cloth. I was in possession of a chain-mail-type of burnisher, which military personnel used to polish their bayonets. No doubt Corporal Jones would approve of this, as anyone who got it 'up 'em' would be in danger of catching tetanus from a dirty bayonet! Lever cloths were always used when handling the levers as sweat from the hands soon left rust marks on the steel tops. It was also a way of preventing roughening of the hands and calluses, which always occurred when handling roughened and rusting levers.

Windows were cleaned inside as and when it became necessary. Cleaning outside was more difficult, as it entailed climbing out on to the narrow platform provided for the purpose and could therefore be done only when a lengthy interval between trains permitted – usually on Sundays.

The floor was linoleum-covered and was scrubbed occasionally, but was given a polish at other times. Brasses were non-existent other than the GCR whistle and the bezel of the clock, so we were spared that time-consuming duty.

Lever movements, 'on', 'off' and 'reverse'

Signal levers in the signal box were normally in the 'on' position. This meant that the Stop signals were showing 'stop' and the Distant signals were showing 'caution'. When the signalman pulled the signal lever he moved it to the 'off' position, so both a Stop and Distant signal would then be showing 'clear'. Thus 'I pulled off for him' meant that all the signals for that train were clear so that it could proceed.

Point levers, when in the normal position, allowed trains to run 'normally' along the line. To change from normal running to put a train 'inside' (into a loop, or into a refuge siding, etc), the point lever was pulled by the signalman to the 'reverse' position, thus moving the point. After the manoeuvre was completed, it was returned to 'normal'.

Lever collars

A small but vital piece of apparatus was the lever collar, a typical example measuring 6 inches long by 2 inches or so wide. It was placed over the lever to remind the signalman of some hazard should the lever be operated – maybe the equipment was disconnected, or out of order. Other reasons were that the line or siding was occupied either temporarily or semi-permanently. Sometimes a train would be stabled or awaiting dispatch at a later time, and the point lever would have a collar placed on it to remind the operator of the circumstances. They also made excellent egg cups.

Wire breakage

Signal wires were regularly checked for defects in the wire runs between box and signal, but there were occasions when a wire would break suddenly. This could have serious results to the unfortunate signalman, especially when a Distant signal wire fractured. The tail of the

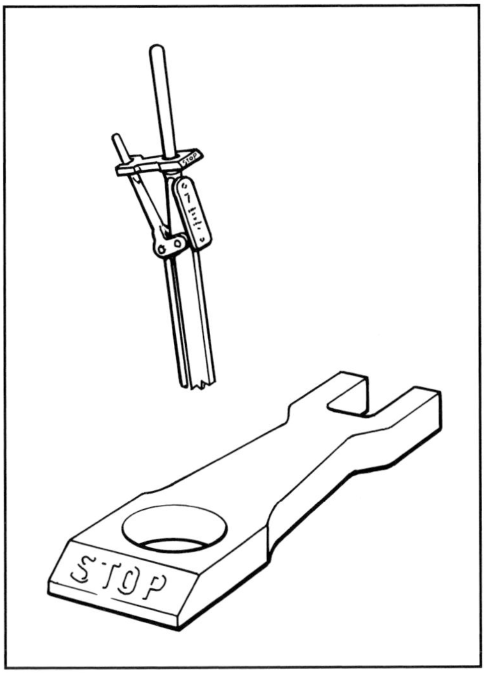

The collar shown here is typical of those used on the Railway Signal Company frames on the GCR's London Extension as at Braunston & Willoughby and Rugby. Note how it fits on the lever, and the shape and position of the lever description plate (BR days). *P. J. Wortley*

lever was provided with a weight of 40lb to assist in the operation, and this would be suddenly weighted against the pull; the lever might strike the operator a heavy blow in the abdomen and he could finish in a heap at the back of the box!

'During fog or falling snow...'

'During fog or falling snow' – into the cabin we must go! But our worthy Platelayers would be unable to enjoy their cosy refuge for long, as snow, particularly prolonged snowfall, would mean keeping points and signal wires free by the application of copious doses of salt around pointwork and the signalman working the points to keep them free. Only points vital to the safe working of the line would be so treated – to do all turnouts was unnecessary.

Before the advent of colour light Distant signals, a member of the Permanent Way gang would be appointed to sit guard at a mechanical Distant when fog or snowfall prevailed. He was provided with a hut (not unlike a sentry box), which was placed within sight of the signal concerned. There was also a brazier and a supply of coal. He would be supplied with at least 36 detonators, red, green and yellow flags and a lighted handlamp. At all times when the signal was at 'Caution' one detonator was placed on the running rail, and a yellow hand signal shown to the driver of a train. When the signal was 'off', the detonator was removed and a green hand signal shown to the driver. The detonator was replaced immediately after the passing of a train. It was a cold and thankless job, but a vital one if trains were to be kept moving.

Should a Fogsignalman *not* be on duty at a Distant signal, what was known as Double Block Working was operated. For instance, if there was no Fogsignalman at Braunston & Willoughby's No 6 Down Distant, the line would have to be clear all the way from Staverton Road to Rugby Station before a train could be accepted from Staverton.

In order to determine when Fogsignalmen were required, the No 7 Down Home signal was the fog marker: when it was obscured, fog or snow regulations were enforced.

The Southern Railway had a penchant for concrete, and many items were constructed of this indestructible material. Footbridges, fences, lamp posts, Platelayers' huts and Fogsignalmen's huts all appeared from the Exmouth Junction Works. Even today, long after the end of mechanical signalling, concrete Fogsignalmen's huts can still be seen on the Southern as forlorn relics guarding the site of a long vanished Distant signal. No doubt some archaeologist will unearth one in, say, 500 years and speculation will be rife as to its purpose.

Lengthmen/Platelayers/Permanent Way gangs

Unlike the railways of the 21st century, with forests of vegetation growing in great profusion at the lineside, the Permanent Way gangs in the days prior to dieselisation kept the banks clear of undergrowth. They were entirely responsible for the upkeep of hedges, fences and drains, in addition to their prime involvement with the Permanent Way. Scythes were used to keep the grass short – a tool and a skill that seems to have disappeared completely from the husbandry of today. Trackside maintenance was vital to prevent fires created by sparks from passing locomotives, especially when they were working hard, causing untold damage to nearby crops. Compensation for such damage was expensive and also caused ill-feeling towards the railway from landowners. Fire and smoke at the lineside could also disrupt timings.

The first duty of the day for the Ganger was to walk his 'length', the section of the railway for which he and his gang were responsible. The duty was performed every day and involved a visual examination of the track, hammering home any wooden keys that had become loose in the chairs carrying what was then mostly bullhead rail. He would also note any other items that might need attention by the gang. While he was thus employed, the gang would be setting about some task, in charge of a Sub-ganger. The actual length of the distance involved would vary, but I seem to remember Bill Homan taking about an hour to inspect his patch.

Platelayers, or Lengthmen to give them their correct title, were paid £5 10s 6d a week in their first year, rising to £5 14s 6d after two years service. In 1952 the ganger earned £6 7s 6d.

During fog or falling snow they were on call for other duties, including fog signalling and clearing snow from points and crossings when there was a surfeit of the white stuff (see above). Sundays usually provided them with welcome overtime payments when they could be seconded to other gangs to assist with track renewals.

Other duties might involve them in unusual one-off tasks, such as the one that occurred at Braunston & Willoughby one morning. A horse-box had arrived the previous day and had been left in the cattle dock. It was to be loaded and attached to the

A point clip being fitted to prevent movement of a point when a train is moving over it. *P. J. Wortley, courtesy of MLST and GCR Plc*

8 10am Nottingham-Marylebone 'ord', which involved me as signalman. All points had to be 'clipped' for a passenger-carrying train to enter the goods yard, and the entire gang were provided with point clips to perform this duty. That particular time in the morning was normally very busy with freights on the Down line, and these had to be 'refused' from Staverton Road until the 'ord' had been restored to the Up line.

Out of Gauge Loads

Abnormal loads are often encountered on our motorways, always presenting problems for the regular traffic. They were occasionally also to be seen on the railways, but there they were known as Out of Gauge Loads. I recall one Out of Gauge Load, which was an enormous stator on a special wagon. It overhung the wagon on both sides and during the course of its journey it had to be manoeuvred off-centre to clear obstructions such as station platforms, bridge abutments and signals; a team of men travelled with the consist to undertake these tasks. Small items such as ground signals were removed and replaced after the train had passed. Out of Gauge Loads travelled only on Sundays to avoid disrupting the normal traffic and naturally moved at a very slow pace. One such load was stabled in the Up siding at Braunston & Willoughby for a week before commencing the next slow leg of its journey. A resident team of men was on hand to supervise its slow progress and they were accommodated in a coach on the train. I seem to remember enjoying several well-prepared meals from the galley of this train. Apparently the first choice of stabling had been Staverton Road's Refuge Siding, but upon examination the ground under the siding was so riddled with rabbit runs that the idea was abandoned because of the enormous weight involved.

Colin Lambie and his skill

Colin Lambie possessed the skill of mimicry and this ability, when used on the telephone, would cause amusement and, in some cases anger. Percy Warr at Staverton Road was the butt of Colin's humour on several occasions. Percy received a telephone call from 'staff office at Nottingham Vic' to say that his preferred holiday dates had been refused. Percy was on the point of cancelling his holiday when he learned the truth! Another incident occurred when Colin was relieving next door at Charwelton. Unfortunately, Inspector Williamson appeared at Charwelton suddenly and without warning. Normally the presence of the District Inspector caused no problems, as a means could usually be found of warning the signalmen on each side of his presence. This was impossible in this case, and poor Percy fell foul of the failure. A minor irregularity in the use of block bells took place and Inspector Williamson rang Staverton Road on the telephone to rebuke the miscreant. The inevitable happened. Percy said, 'Muck off, Colin – you don't catch me again!' The next Down train delivered the genuine article to administer justice to a suitably chastened Signalman Warr. Relationships remained cool from then on!

Telephone conversations

It was the telephone that provided a much needed lifeline on nights. The 'omnibus' circuit could always be relied upon to produce the latest scandals, political opinions or gardening tips interspersed with the usual latest jokes. There was never any neglect of responsibility, as the person holding forth would announce, 'Just a minute...', then the receiver would be banged down followed by sounds of levers and block bells, a pause while the Train Register was attended to, then, 'Yes, as I was saying...'

Rugby Station signal box

In LNER days the diagram was suspended above the Block Shelf from the signal box ceiling by two steel straps. When the Illuminated Track Diagram came in 1940 it too was ceiling-mounted, but was about 6 feet long and in a heavy wooden frame. The Block Shelf contained the Block Instruments, with Signal Repeaters on the front face over the lever concerned. When the dreaded LMR stamped their mark on the place, the Block Instruments were replaced by the awful black bakelite specimens and the Derby-style diagram was positioned on the Block Shelf. Ugh!

The Railway Signal Company levers in the 40-lever frame were about 4 feet tall, give or take, and each was provided with a white description tablet mounted just below the polished handle. This gave a description of the function each lever performed and any releases that were required to operate that particular lever. There were variations in the number of working levers over the years, but there were never any spare (white-painted) levers. For many years when I knew the box and spent many hours there, there was always a space for 8 and 16, spaces for 26 to 31, and 36 to 40. Later a red lever was installed as No 16, and much, much later a shortened red lever appeared as No 31. Nos 5 and 10 were short levers, ie they had the top part of the handle reduced by half to signify that they worked electrical apparatus and did not require a 10-ton heave! With the final closure of Rugby Cattle Sidings, No 32 (Down Starter) lost its top; this had been retained despite working a colour light, because it continued to work the 'slot' with levers 33 (Rugby Station Inner Home) and 3 (Rugby Cattle Sidings Outer Distant, on the same post).

In the corner of the cabin at the London end was 'The Mangle'. This was a hand-operated generator used to power No 5 points in the event of a power failure. I would guess it measured 2ft by 2ft by 1ft high and stood on four legs. The handle was on the right-hand side nearest the end window. George Wilson let me wind over the points occasionally to keep the thing in working order.

In the same corner were the hand flags – red, yellow and green – tucked up in a home-made wire clip vertical to the corner post.

On the left-hand side of the door, held by a nail, were three emergency detonators, ready to hand just in case. These were in addition to the emergency detonators worked by the 'stirrups' between levers 33 and 32, and between space 8 and lever 9.

To finish these notes on Rugby Station box, some colour details. The interior in LNER days was cream and brown, and in BR days it was cream and maroon. Outside in LNER days the door, corner posts and barge boards were LNER green, in BR days maroon. The window frames were off-white. When the war intervened, everything became an overall economy grey. I was at Braunston & Willoughby when the painters came to put a lick of paint on the box after the war. I am convinced it was maroon even in Eastern Region days, before the transfer to the London Midland Region. [I found a piece of cast-iron guttering from the front of Rugby Station box and the colours remaining on it were a red oxide undercoat, LNER green, a light grey, and two differing shades of maroon – PJW] The Running-in Boards on the platforms in LNER days were a black ground with white frame and letters; under the Eastern Region they were blue with white letters, and under the LMR maroon. The signal box boards were black with white letters. The top panes of glass in the four large window frames at the front of the box were painted white.

Uniforms

Signalmen, unlike station staff, were rarely in the public eye, but were still expected to wear the standard-issue uniform, which consisted of black trousers, sleeved waistcoat and jacket. They were also issued with either a heavy overcoat or a raincoat and a peaked cap bearing the company badge or initials. I still possess the LNER lozenge-shaped logo that was issued with the cap. Unlike other sectors on the railway, there was never a cap badge displaying 'Signalman'. I have mentioned earlier that signalmen did not wear the caps as issued but preferred ordinary peaked caps if they wore any headgear at all. All uniforms bore the brass or nickel-plated buttons, which, with the coat of arms or initials of the company, were rather like military insignia. These have become collectors' items in recent years and are now increasingly rare.

To digress slightly at this point, I recall being given a railway uniform consisting of jacket and waistcoat, which, in a flush of enthusiasm, I was foolish enough to wear in the town of Rugby one evening. Now in those days the rules of the Lawrence Sheriff School were very strict regarding school uniform, which included wearing a cap at all times in public places. Fate decreed that I should have the misfortune to come face to face with a senior prefect who, naturally, challenged my choice of attire. I was duly reported and appeared before the Headmaster, Colonel C. Wheeler, who expressed his acute displeasure with such phrases as 'letting the School down', 'where will this sort of disregard for authority lead?' and so on. I was given 2 hours' stone-picking on the next Saturday afternoon on the recently acquired playing-field in Lower Hillmorton Road; the area had been devoted to agriculture and was unfit for games until its stony surface had been cleansed.

In the 1940s and '50s school caps were an emblem of the school that the individual attended. The boys of Rugby School, with their very distinctive caps, were forbidden absolutely to speak to anyone other than their own.

The black railway uniform and the school cap have both vanished into history.

Loco-spotting

Harping back to those times when loco-spotting was much in vogue, particularly in the war years, there were several spots in Rugby favoured for number-taking. The obvious place was the at 'The Girder' (or 'The Birdcage'), another was quite close by on a fence opposite the end of South Street and adjacent to Mr Eales's small-holding with its pig sties. This was a handy refuge when skirmishes with the LMS-ites became too hot to handle. It was also an ideal place in the days prior to D-Day when American troops on troop trains would throw chocolate bars and chewing gum to us who were starved of such delicacies in the era of wartime rationing. The third place was on the embankment behind Rugby Station box mentioned in Chapter 4.

The 'Yankee Tank'

This third spot was closer to home and I remember a strange little tank engine arriving on the Down line one Saturday afternoon, the footplate crammed with khaki-clad figures who disembarked on to the platform. After crossing to the Up line the strange little engine vanished the way it had come. It was, in fact, the 'Yankee Tank' that was employed at the newly opened Ordnance Depot at Barby, and its mission was to deliver soldiers for a weekend spree in Rugby away from the confines of the military discipline at the camp. These Saturday afternoon expeditions ceased abruptly and it was several years later that George Wilson explained why. Apparently, for some obscure reason, the 'Yankee Tank' failed to operate Track Circuits, and as this was vital for safe working its forays on to the main line were banned.

Sleep

Night shifts held the inevitable hazard of sleep overtaking the worker. It was so easy to sit in the warmth of the signal box and fall asleep, especially at about 4am. It happened to me – to my regret, as it spoiled an unblemished record – when I was at Rugby No 2. The fireman of a through 'runner' for which I had not 'pulled off' awakened me and, of course, it had to be reported!

An event on the Southern that involved a friend of mine in the later days of steam is worth recounting. He was a signalman at Tisbury, between Salisbury and Gillingham (Dorset), and was 'all off' for a Down parcels train when he suddenly realised he had nodded off to sleep. There was no way of telling if the train had passed or not, and he dare not ask the signalman at Gillingham if it had arrived without giving away his guilty secret. He paced the box in nail-biting anxiety, not knowing the best course of action, when he heard the sound of boots on the ballast. He was relieved to find the fireman of the train coming into the box to report his engine a failure!

It was so easy to fall asleep, just for a few seconds, and not be aware of the fact. It was even possible to sleep when the noise of trains passing the box failed to rescue the poor victim from the arms of Morpheus.

15
POSTSCRIPT:
AN ABIDING PASSION

In fiction, the final chapter sees the happy couple living happily ever after, and in whodunits the least suspected person is led away in handcuffs, but not so within our manuscript. The railways aren't quite the super transport system they ought to be, and we all know who has been responsible for its destruction, don't we? Unlike the whodunit, they aren't being led away in handcuffs.

To provide a modern railway a considerable amount of investment is required. New techniques are essential for the efficient and safe operation of the network, but new techniques are of little value if the people responsible for its working do it purely for the pay packet at the end of the month. There is also the involvement of the Health & Safety Executive, which decrees that tasks can only be performed by staff who are suitably qualified. This ruling alone would certainly have stopped the job in the days mostly remembered in this volume. In the event of a points failure in those distant days, a member of the station staff could have been called upon to help out until qualified persons arrived. Trains would have continued to run, albeit under caution, but at least the wheels would have been turning. Not so today. Everything *stops* until the authorised technician for the company arrives on the scene. He has to be notified and may have to travel miles to the site of the problem, but nothing moves until he arrives.

The replacing of signal boxes and block working with electric signalling centres has made the supervision of many miles of railway routes very much simpler and safer. Main lines are track circuited throughout, signals in remote areas are automatic and are three- or four-aspect colour light signals according to the intensity of traffic and/or the line speed limitation. In spite of these improvements the number of trains on some routes is considerably less than in the 'good old days', when passenger trains *and* freight trains were running.

The normal weekday timetable for the Great Central listed some 120 freight trains, together with express passenger trains and the 'ords'. The Train Register for 1960 in Chapter 2 is from a time when the line was being run down, a shadow of its former self, yet the number of trains in the 24 hours was still 123, and yes, they did run throughout the 24 hours. On Saturdays during the summer there was a considerable number of additional seasonal trains from the North serving seaside resorts on the South Coast, and Southern and Western trains for the northern holiday centres at Blackpool and Butlins on the East Coast, as well as trains to and from Newcastle-upon-Tyne. All of these extras were part of the job and made life a little more difficult for the men involved, particularly the signalmen, but it also provided the challenge to keep everything moving.

Time-keeping was paramount, and the slightest delay to a passenger train brought a 'Please explain...' from the Superintendent's office. Some drivers accepted a delay as a

The last train of timber into Travis & Arnold's timber yard at Rugby in April 1964. Imagine, if you will, all this timber on lorries, on the roads from the dock to here! What else needs be said – what better illustration can there be? *A. Franklin*

chance to have a go at catching up time with some really fast running. This was not always welcomed by the poor fireman, who was responsible for providing the steam for that extra effort, but here again footplate crews were a team and one would always back the other as it was often a question of pride in the job.

Catching up lost time is seldom attempted by the drivers of trains today as the use of computers and advanced technology fixes the speed of the train in the timetable to the speed of the route. Any attempt to exceed that route speed can be identified and the driver admonished. The system is similar to the tacho in coaches and lorries.

Fast running during fog or falling snow was not encouraged where semaphore signals were involved, but with their replacement with colour light signals providing high-intensity beams in difficult weather conditions the problem was considerably reduced. But even colour lights failed to prevent serious accidents such as St Johns, Lewisham, in 1957 when 90 people lost their lives.

With so many freight trains occupying the line between Annesley and Woodford, it was vital that time-keeping was maintained as closely as possible. They were booked to take water at specific places and stopping out of sequence by crews was definitely discouraged. The pecking order of traffic made certain that passenger trains took priority, with fish and other perishable traffic next, and the 'runners' would be shunted to give the faster traffic the road; at certain times during the evening a 'runner' would sit in the Up Loop at Rugby for two fish trains and a Manchester-Marylebone express to pass.

Another situation that arises nowadays would never have been contemplated in former times. A problem occurs, the line is closed, and buses are brought in to replace the trains. Single-line working was an accepted method of keeping a reasonable service going. In the past it could be done as the track layout at most stations included at least one crossover, as the diagrams show, with local control from the signal box and station staff. It was tedious with trains setting back over crossovers to enter the single line, but at least the passengers weren't inconvenienced any more than was absolutely necessary, and possibly time could be made up over the remainder of the journey when the single-line working had been cleared. Sunday engineering work was taken as part of the job. It was all planned well beforehand with the appointment of a Pilotman for the engine crew, staff to clip and flag at the various crossovers, and of course there was that welcome bit of overtime on a Sunday, thank you very much. On days such as those it was not possible for the signalman to attend to this extra work and keep the signal box floor clean; there were hob-nail boots and other sources of mud and muck from the constant comings and goings of those visiting the box for instructions, etc. This would never happen in a modern signalling centre, as it is impossible to see the trains from many of them!

With the introduction of modern signalling methods, colour lights replaced the mechanical signals that had been so prominent a part of the railway scene for so long. Signals and the signal cabins that controlled them were as recognisable as the locomotives and coaching stock of the owning company. Each company had its own style. The North Eastern Railway seemed to provide a signal for every possible move likely to be made, which meant forests of gantries at places like York and Newcastle. The Great Northern adopted the unique and surprisingly long-lasting 'somersault' type. The LNWR provided signals that were strictly functional and had little to commend them for elegance. I'm not a staunch supporter of Swindon, but the GWR's signals were both elegant and provided very clear indications with their steeply sloping arms when in the 'off' position. Signal boxes were distinctive too, and each company had its preferences. The Midland Railway's signal boxes were unmistakable, and Airfix produced an OO gauge plastic model of Oakham, which has been in production for many years.

All of these distinctive features, semaphore signals and signal boxes in the distinctive company style, have or are being swept away. Even though some are still in evidence on some main lines and country routes, sad to say there is not much Great Central still extant. But we are left with equipment that is safer in so many ways. The baleful eye of the colour light penetrates difficult weather conditions in a way that no paraffin lamp could in semaphore signalling days. Ah well.

The Great Central was the last main line to be built in this country and to many it was considered to be a total waste of money and effort. Be that as it may, the Great Central produced a number of excellent ideas that would become standard practise in later years, and its method of working fast freight trains would never be equalled. Some examples might be in order. In 1911 the Locomotive Engineer, J. G. Robinson, produced the Class 'K' 2-8-0 freight locomotive. It was chosen by the Ministry of Munitions to be built in large numbers as the standard ROD freight engine for use in Britain and Europe during the First World War. These engines went on to prove their worth up until the end of steam in the 1960s, and were more widespread than any other class of locomotive.

The Great Central's Signal Engineer from 1906 until 1922 was A. F. Bound, and during that time he introduced Intermediate Block signals in 1911 between Whetstone and Ashby Magna. He adopted pneumatic systems in Lincolnshire, which are fully described in A. A. Maclean's excellent treatise on LNER Signalling, which also dwells in great detail on the automatic system in the London area in the 1920s. It is interesting to note that A. F. Bound is credited with first describing the GCR-funded signal gantry on the LNWR lines at Rugby as the 'Rugby Bedstead'.

The Great Central, then, was not the non-entity that some would have us believe it to be. The passenger trains were well patronised and punctual. The men who worked the line were extremely proud of their railway and this manifested itself in the working of the line in every department.

Other than the replacement of Distant signals with colour lights, the Great Central remained entirely mechanically operated throughout. In spite of this the line boasted the fastest freight trains in the country. They were governed by strict rules regarding water stops, calling either at Leicester or Rugby in the Up direction; I do not remember a 'runner' stopping for water on the Down. At certain times of the day the Up Loop at Rugby provided refuge for a 'runner' to allow more important traffic to overtake. There was invariably a 'runner' in the loop at about 6pm to allow an 'ord' to pass and Grimsby and Hull fish trains, which were always in a hurry. They also left a distinctive aroma, leaving no doubts as to their contents.

Freight trains on the former LMS were never in quite so much of a hurry. I recall in the 1940s and '50s Up goods trains queuing engine-to-brake-van in the goods loops between Rugby No 1 and Hillmorton. There were loops on both the Up Northampton and the Up London sides that could accommodate several goods trains under Permissive Block regulations. The double-track sections on both routes beyond Hillmorton created a serious bottleneck, and the slow-moving freights had to wait their turn, giving way to express trains.

On the GC things could be far more hectic on a Saturday in summer when extra services would be provided to serve the popular holiday resorts on the South Coast. There were also specials during the football season when supporters travelled by train to reach the stadium where their teams were playing. For the spotter these trains always provided some rare engines from faraway places. Take a Newcastle United game against Portsmouth, for instance: two or three specials hauled by 'Pacifics' based at Gateshead would result in great cheers of joy from the crowds of enthusiasts for the 'one on the top'.

And this, of course, is where we came in.

Appendix 1
Local whistle codes

Whistle to be given at		Whistle
Woodford		
No 4 Box	Up Goods Independent and LMS line	1 short, 3 long
	Up Sidings and Shunting Neck	1 short, 2 long
No 3 Box	Up and Down Goods Independents	2 short
	Middle Siding and Up Main	1 short, 1 long
	Down Goods Independent and Middle Siding	1 long, 3 short
	Middle Siding and Down Main	1 short, 2 long
	Down Goods Independent to Down Passenger Independent	2 short, pause, 2 short
No 2 Box	Up and Down Goods Independent	2 short
	Coal Stage Road	1 long, 3 short
	Wagon Shops Siding	1 long, 4 short
	Set back on Up Goods Independent to No 2 Box	2 short,1 long
Ashby Magna		
Station Box	To indicate that train is clear in siding	2 short
Leicester		
Goods South Box	Goods Yard and No 1 Shunting Neck	1 short, 3 long
	Goods Yard and No 2 Shunting Neck	1 short, 2 long
	Shunting Neck No 2 and Down Goods Independent	2 short, 1 long
	Up Goods and No 1 Shunting Neck	1 short, 1 long
	Loco Yard and Goods Yard	1 long, 3 short
	Down Main and Goods Yard	1 long, 4 short
	Goods Yard and Up Main	4 short, 1 long
	Goods Yard to Loco Yard, via Slip Road	3 short, 1 crow*
	No 1 Shunting Neck to Down Goods Independent	2 short, 2 long

* A 'crow' is sounded on the whistle like a cockerel's crow – 'cock-a-doodle-doo'.

Passenger South Box	Down Main and No 3 Bay	1 long, 3 short
	Down Main and No 4 Bay	1 long, 4 short
	No 3 Bay and Up Main	3 short, 1 long
	No 4 Bay and Up Main	4 short, 1 long
	No 3 Bay and No 4 Bay	2 crows
	Turntable Siding and Up Main	1 short, 1 long
Passenger North Box	Up Main and No 1 Bay	1 short, 1 long
	Up Main and No 2 Bay	1 short, 2 long
	No 1 Bay and Down Main	2 short, 1 long
	No 2 Bay and Down Main	2 short, 2 long
	No 1 Bay and No 2 Bay	2 crows
Woodford		
No 4 Box	For Banbury Branch, *on passing*	3 short
Charwelton		
Station box	For Up Goods Independent Line at Woodford, *on passing*	1 long, 2 short
	For LMS line at Woodford, *on passing*	3 short
	Trains for Banbury Branch not stopping at Woodford, *on passing*	2 long
Braunston & Willoughby		
Staverton Road box	Down Freight trains requiring to stop at Rugby for water, *on passing*	1 crow
Lutterworth		
Station box	Trains requiring examination at Leicester and not having wagons to detach, *on passing*	1 crow
Ashby Magna		
Station box	Down Freight trains not stopping at Leicester, *on passing*	1 crow
	Up Freight trains requiring water at Rugby, *on passing*	2 crows
Whetstone		
Station box	For Down Goods Independent at Leicester, *on passing*	1 long, 2 short
	Down Freight trains requiring water at Leicester, *on passing*	1 crow

APPENDIX 2
SOME SIGNALLING BASICS

This appendix is an explanation of the terms and technicalities used throughout this narrative. For some it will be purely of interest only, but for others it will be a useful explanation of the text and diagrams. Either way, it is now a part of our heritage, the old tools of an old trade that has nearly disappeared. The national track authority is busy installing electrical control centres and doing away with signal boxes and all that that entails. Thank goodness for preserved railways where most, but not all, of the equipment mentioned can still be seen actually in use.

Fixed signals (see also page 16)
The signalman is provided with 'fixed signals' by which he conveys his instructions to drivers; they are so called in view of their permanent location at the trackside. Hand signals with flags/lamps are used at other times. Under this heading come 'running' or main-line signals, which are covered here, while shunting signals and secondary signals will be covered later in this Appendix. Some consideration must be given to why and when signals are positioned where they are.

Distant signals
Distant signals provide a warning of the indications of the Stop signals ahead, and are therefore placed a comfortable stopping distance from the first Stop signal, usually 1,000 yards. The description 'comfortable' means that the speed of the train can be brought under control in order to bring it to a stand at the Stop signal without the risk of breaking all the china in the restaurant car. There are certain conditions that dictate the actual positioning of the Distant signal; for example, on falling gradients there needs to be a greater distance than on the level or on a rising incline.

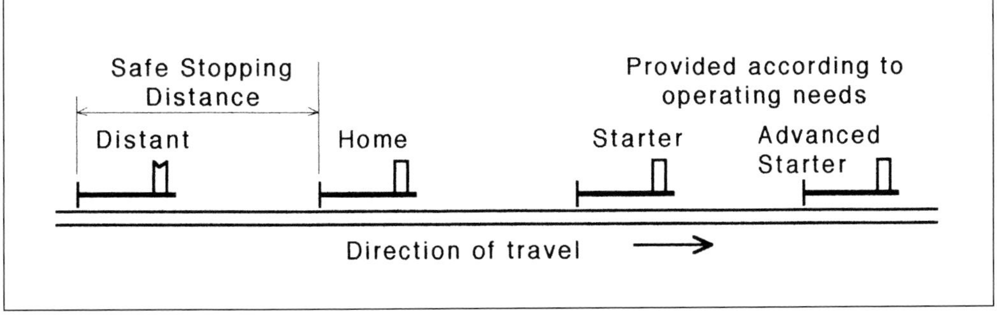

The basic arrangement for fixed 'running' signals

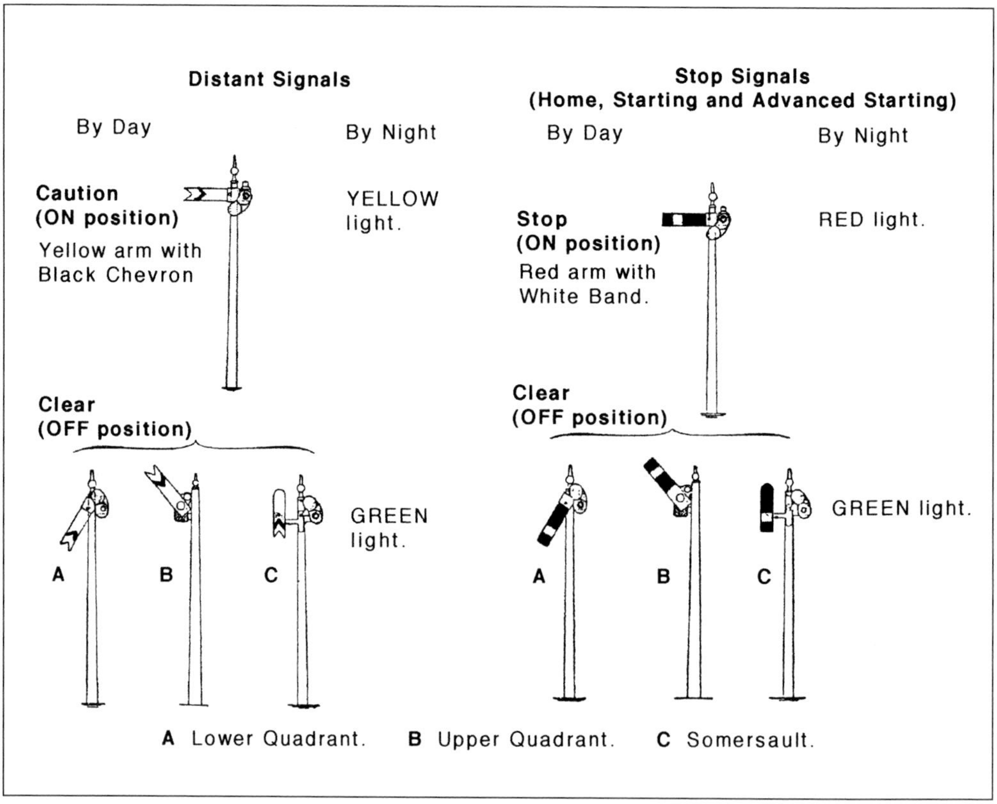

Types of fixed signals

Stop signals

Stop signals provide protection at places where there are obstructions or where conflicting movements are possible, and they are placed well clear of any such obstruction. The provision of Stop signals is governed by certain rules and regulations and they are also given titles that can create problems in understanding for the uninitiated.

The Stop signal immediately before the obstruction is referred to as the **Home signal**, while an **Outer Home signal** gives extra protection at places where regular conflicting movements are being made ahead of the Home signal, which is given the name of **Inner Home signal** in such instances. According to Signalling Regulation 4, before a train can be accepted there *must* be a quarter-mile clearance ahead of the Home signal, therefore an Outer Home, when present, allows free acceptance of trains at places such as junctions. Culworth Junction is an excellent example where Outer Home Signals were vital.

Starting signals, as their name implies, give authority to leave the station limits and proceed into the section ahead. Where additional connections (points, etc) exist beyond the Starting signal, or Starter, an Advanced Starting signal is provided. The Down Main signals at Lutterworth give an example of the situation where an Advanced Starting signal is needed. All signals that allow entry into the forward section are referred to as **Section signals**, whether they be Home, Starter or Advance Starter.

Junction signals

Junction signals are arranged as in the accompanying illustrations. The first shows the more usual bracketed signal with Dolls of varying height to indicate the geographical

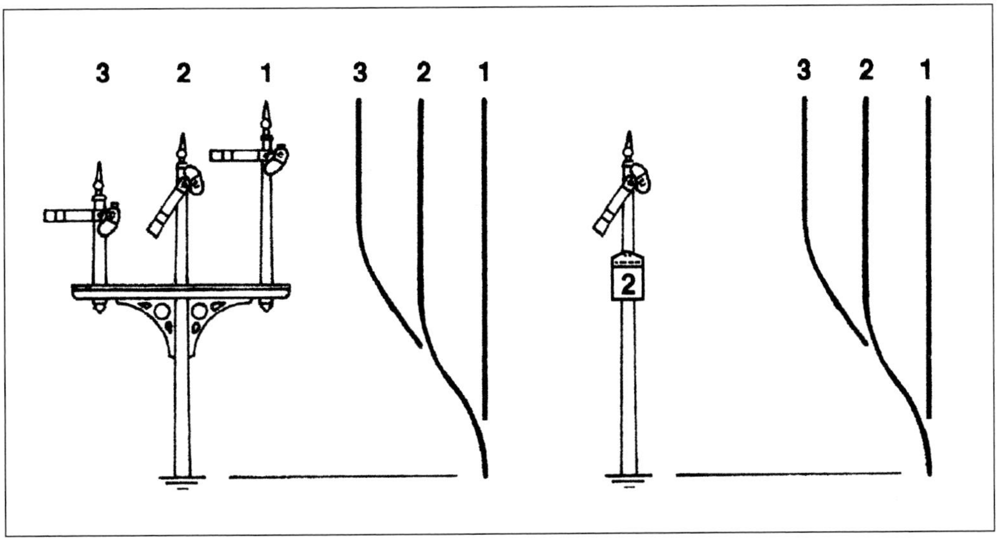

Typical junction signals

layout, the tallest referring to the main route. The second illustration shows a junction signal employed where running speeds are low, at the approach to a terminus for example, with an indicator showing the line selected.

There are many variations of junction signal in the signalling diagrams in this book, but the ordering and the height of the arms is as explained here.

The Block system

The primary purpose of railway signalling is to secure an adequate interval of space between following trains. The object of the Absolute Block system is *to prevent more than one train being in a Block Section on the same line at the same time.*

In order to do this a main line of double track is divided into what are known as Block Sections with a signal box at each end to control entrance into and exit from each section. The length of the sections governs the number of trains that can use the route.

The object of the Permissive Block system is *to allow more than one train to be in a Block Section on the same line at the same time.* It is authorised on goods lines when *no passenger trains* are involved, and in large stations for

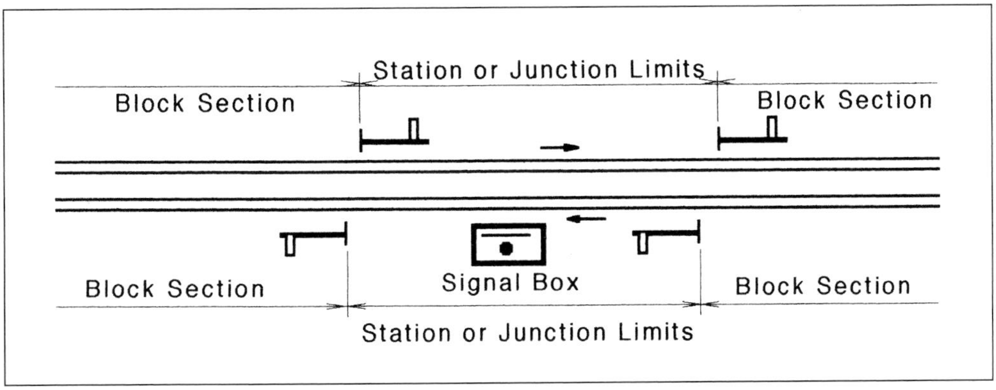

Block sections

passenger trains when *no goods trains* are involved.

Track Circuit Block

So far no mention has been made of automatic signals and the Track Circuit Block. There were two sections operated on this principle on the GC, between Bulwell North Junction and Hucknall Central on the Down line, and between Whetstone and Ashby Magna on the Up (the diagrams for these two boxes are shown in Chapter 4). The lines involved were track circuited throughout between the last Stop signal (Starter or Advanced Starter) of the box in rear and the first Stop signal (Home or Outer Home) at the box in advance, as described above. In Absolute Block signalling areas this was known as an Automatic Section.

The signalman at Whetstone was able to 'pull off' his Up Starting signal, provided that the Track Circuit was 'Clear', without the need to ask Ashby Magna for acceptance; an electric lock on the lever only allowed this movement if the Track Circuit was 'Clear'. The signalman would send a special 'Train Entering Section' on the bell to Ashby Magna with a description of the train. The train itself would work the colour light signals as it proceeded along the track by way of a Track Circuit linked to each signal. The signal immediately behind the train would automatically be at red, the previous signal before that would show yellow and the third green. As the train progressed from one Track Circuit to the next, the signals behind it changed accordingly, allowing further traffic to proceed along the same line without the need for signalmen.

The short sections of Track Circuit Block introduced on the GC were a very small part of what was to become the signalling of the future on British Rail.

Intermediate Block (IB) signals

The length of the block sections governed the number of trains that could use a railway route. Many signal boxes were provided merely as Block Posts, separators to shorten sections, as more sections meant more trains, faster times and more revenue. However, the employment of sufficient signalmen to man these boxes made it expensive to retain them. Consequently a system was devised whereby these small Block Posts, some containing only two signals on each running line, could be

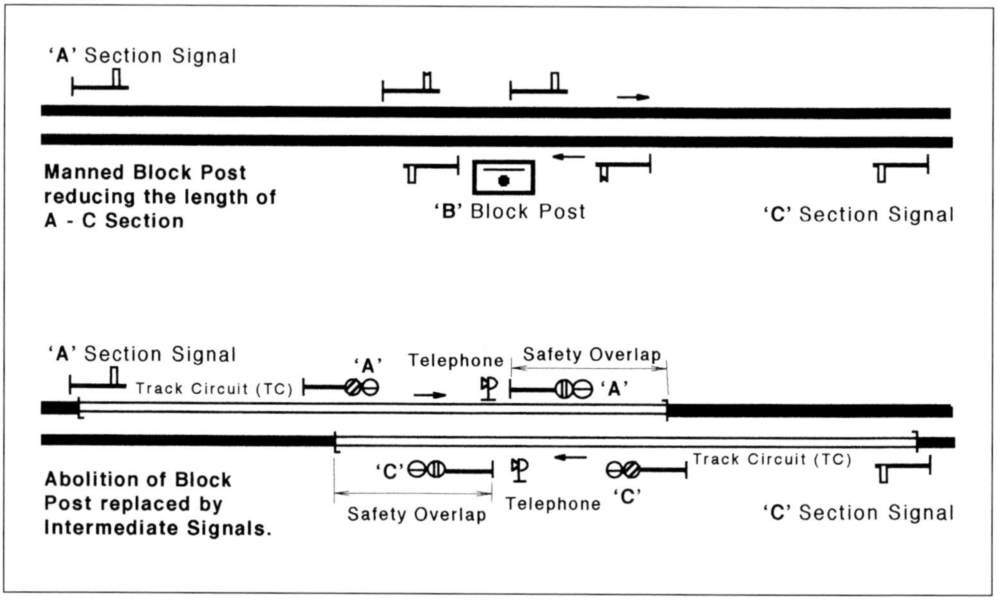

Replacement of a block post by IB signals

made redundant and the signalmen more usefully employed; the cost of installing IB signals was soon recovered in the savings of the signalmen's wages. The signals were replaced by colour lights, which were controlled by one additional lever in the box in the rear. Track Circuits were provided from the rear box's Section signal up to the colour lights replacing the redundant mechanical signals, plus a safety overlap. Telephones were provided to enable train crews to contact the controlling signalman.

When a train passed the IB signal a bell or buzzer sounded to remind the signalman that the IB section was now clear. In the event of a train passing the signal at Stop (a modern day 'SPAD' – 'signal passed at danger'), a much more strident bell announced the fact so that the signalman could take immediate appropriate action.

Method of Block working

This example involves an Up local passenger train passing through Block Sections A-B and B-C. Before the train can be allowed to proceed, 'Train Out Of Section' must have been received for the previous train and the Block Instrument must show 'Normal' ('Line Blocked').

1 The signalman at A sends the 'Call Attention', 1 beat on the bell, and the signalman at B answers with 1 beat.

Signalman A now asks B 'Is Line Clear for a Local Passenger Train', 3 pause 1.

If the line is clear at B and the signalman there is able to accept the train he will reply with 3 pause 1. If he cannot accept the train he does not send back the code.

Having accepted the train, signalman B places his 'pegger' (Block Instrument with an operating handle) to 'Line Clear'. The 'non-pegger' (repeating Block Instrument without an operating handle) at A now also shows 'Line Clear' as proof of B's acceptance. A can now clear his signals for the train to proceed into the Block Section A-B.

2 When the train passes A and is about to enter the section, signalman A sends 'Train Entering Section', 2 beats. Signalman B

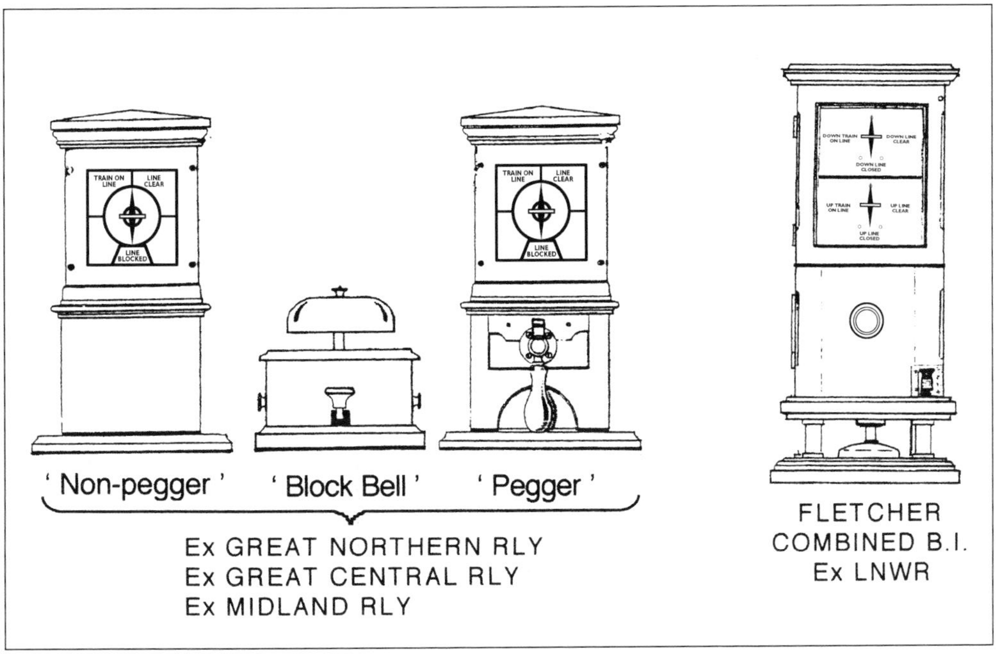

Some typical block instruments. Other railway companies favoured other styles, but the principle was the same.

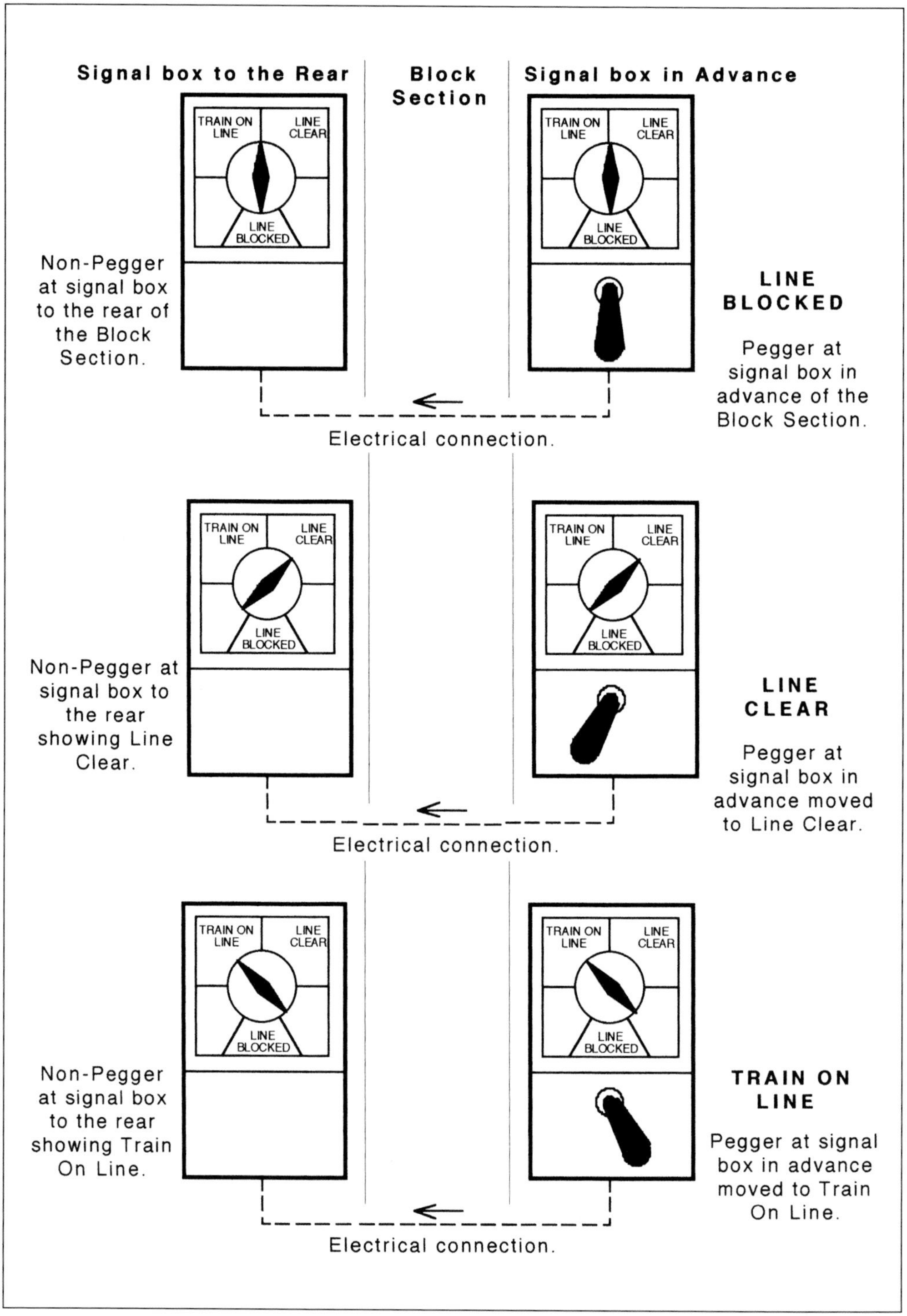

Block instrument displays

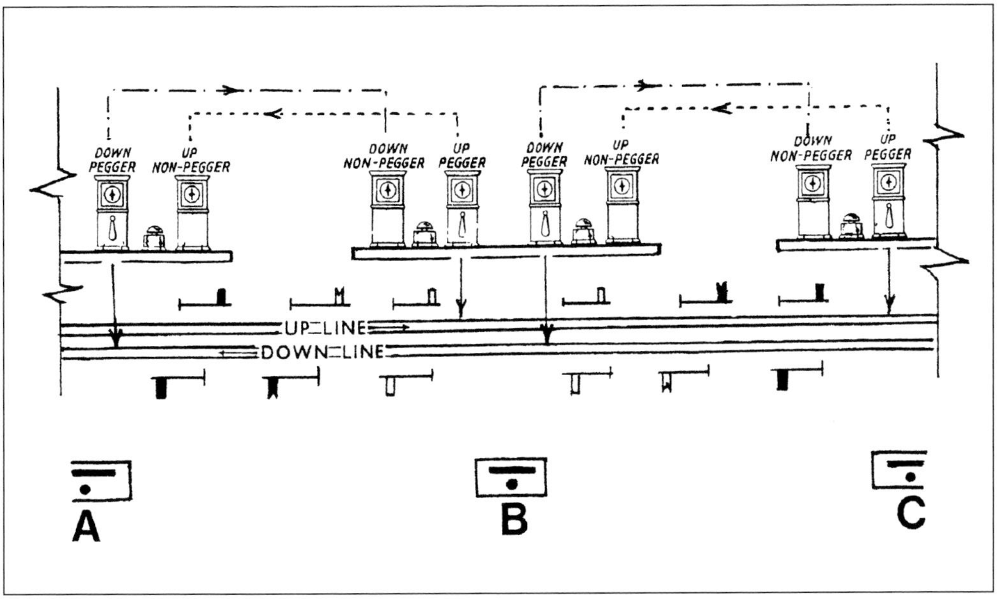

Method of block signalling

acknowledges by repeating 2 beats and turns the handle on his 'pegger' to show 'Train on Line', which also shows on the 'non-pegger' at A. The signalman at A now puts his signals back to Stop, thereby protecting the rear of the train.

3 B now offers the train to C using the same procedure. Once the Block Instruments in both C and B show 'Line Clear', B can pull his signals 'off' to show 'Clear to Proceed'.

4 The train passes B into the Block Section B-C and 2 beats are sent to C, who answers and places his 'pegger' to 'Train on Line'. Signalman B makes sure that there is a tail lamp on the rear of the train before he calls the attention of A with 1 beat. When A replies with 1 beat, B gives 'Train Out of Section', 2 pause 1, to A, who repeats the code. B then 'unpegs' his Block Instrument to show 'Line Blocked' for the Block Section A-B. He has also replaced his signals to Stop behind the train.

5 This same process is used when the train passes C.

Every train on either the Up or Down lines must be worked by this same basic procedure (for simplicity some details have been omitted).

Bell codes

The bell codes used are explained on the following pages. The 'Is Line Clear for...' codes show the Train Classification in a column alongside. This distinguishes one type of train from another and allocates the priority/speed appointed to it.

Head lamp codes

In order that types of train can be recognised and worked appropriately by a signalman, the locomotive at the head of the train carries lamps displayed according to the Train Classification. Head lamp codes for the 1950s period are shown in the table on page 132; there were many company variations of train classification and headcodes before this period. Also the codes changed with regard to the goods, or freight, trains as the wagon braking systems altered. The Southern Railway, and Great Eastern Railway in London, used headcodes to show the train route, not the type or class of train, but that is beyond the scope of this book.

Regulations for train signalling on double lines by the absolute block system—*continued*

BELL SIGNALS

See Regulation	Class of Train	Description	Code
APPLICABLE TO ALL REGIONS			
	—	Call Attention	1
APPLICABLE TO ALL REGIONS EXCEPT SOUTHERN			
1 and 4		**Is line clear for:—**	
	A	Express passenger train, newspaper train, breakdown van train or snow plough going to clear the line, or light engine going to assist disabled train Officers' Special train not requiring to stop in section	4 consecutively
		Electric express passenger train	4–2
	B	Ordinary passenger train, mixed train, or breakdown van train NOT going to clear line	3–1
		Electric ordinary passenger train	3–1–2
		Branch passenger train (Where authorised)	1–3
	C	Parcels, fish, fruit, horse, livestock, meat, milk, pigeon or perishable train composed entirely of vehicles conforming to coaching stock requirements	1–3–1
		Express freight, livestock, perishable or ballast train, pipe fitted throughout with the automatic brake operative on not less than half of the vehicles	3–1–1
		Empty coaching stock train (not specially authorised to carry "A" headcode)	2–2–1
		Electric empty coaching stock train	2–2–1–2
	D	Express freight, livestock, perishable or ballast train, partly fitted, with the automatic brake operative on not less than one third of the vehicles	5 consecutively

Regulations for train signalling on double lines by the absolute block system—*continued*

Bell Signals—*continued*

See Regulation	Class of Train	Description	Code
1 and 4	E	**Is line clear for:—** Express freight, livestock, perishable or ballast train, partly fitted, with not less than four braked vehicles next to the engine and connected by the automatic brake pipe Express freight, livestock, perishable or ballast train, with a limited load of vehicles NOT fitted with the automatic brake	1–2–2
	F	Express freight, livestock, perishable or ballast train, NOT fitted with the automatic brake	3–2
	G	Light engine or light engines coupled (See Regulation 3) Engine with not more than two brake vans	2–3 1–1–3
	H	Through freight or ballast train, not running under class "C", "D", "E" or "F" headcode	1–4
	J	Mineral or empty wagon train	4–1
	K	Freight, mineral or ballast train, stopping at intermediate stations Branch freight train (Where authorised)	3 consecutively 1–2
1, 5 and 8	K	Freight, ballast or Officers' Special train, requiring to stop in section	2–2–3
1, 5 and 9	—	Trolley requiring to go into or pass through tunnel	2–1–2
1	—	Train entering section	2 consecutively

Regulations for train signalling on double lines by the absolute block system—*continued*

Bell Signals—*continued*

See Regulation	Description	Code
10	ENGINE ASSISTING IN REAR OF TRAIN	1–4–1
	ENGINE WITH ONE OR TWO BRAKE VANS ASSISTING IN REAR OF TRAIN	1–5–1
APPLICABLE TO ALL REGIONS		
1 and 4 (Also Out-of-Gauge Instructions)	Train which can pass an out-of-gauge or exceptional load similarly signalled on the opposite or an adjoining line	2–6–1
	Train which cannot be allowed to pass an out-of-gauge load of any description on the opposite or an adjoining line between specified points	2–6–2
	Train which requires the opposite or an adjoining line to be blocked between specified points	2–6–3
	Opposite line, or an adjoining line used in the same or opposite direction, to be blocked for passage of train conveying out-of-gauge load	1–2–6
1	Train approaching (where authorised)	1–2–1
2	Cancelling	3–5
	Last train signalled incorrectly described	5–3
5	Warning Acceptance	3–5–5
	Line now clear in accordance with Regulation 4 for train to approach	3–3–5
6 and 12	Train out of section, or Obstruction Removed	2–1
7	Blocking back inside home signal	2–4
	Blocking back outside home signal	3–3
	Train or vehicles at a stand	3–3–4
APPLICABLE TO ALL REGIONS EXCEPT SOUTHERN		
10	Engine assisting in rear of train	2–2
	Engine with one or two brake vans assisting in rear of train	2–3–1

Regulations for train signalling on double lines by the absolute block system—*continued*

Bell Signals—*continued*

See Regulation	Description	Code
APPLICABLE TO ALL REGIONS		
11	Engine arrived	2–1–3
	Train drawn back clear of section	3–2–3
12	Obstruction Danger	6 consecutively
16	Train an unusually long time in section	6–2
17 and 20	Stop and examine train	7 consecutively
19	Train passed without tail lamp	9 consecutively to box in advance; 4–5 to box in rear
20	Train divided	5–5
21	Shunt train for following train to pass	1–5–5
22	Train or vehicles running away in wrong direction	2–5–5
23	Train or vehicles running away in right direction	4–5–5
24	Opening of signal box	5–5–5
	Closing of signal box	7–5–5
	Closing of signal box where section signal is locked by the block	5–5–7
26	Testing block indicators and bells	16 consecutively
31	Shunting into forward section	3–3–2
	Shunt withdrawn	8 consecutively
32	Working in wrong direction	2–3–3
	Train clear of section	5–2
	Train withdrawn	2–5
Signalmen's General Instructions	Distant signal defective	8–2
	Home signal defective	2–8

			Bell Code
Class A		-Express passenger train, newspaper train, breakdown van train going to clear the line, or light engine going to assist disabled train. -Officer's Special train not requiring to stop in section.	4 consecutively
Class B	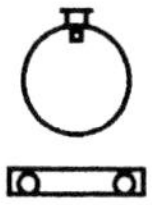	Ordinary passenger train, mixed train, or breakdown van train NOT going to clear the line.	3 - 1
Class C		-Parcels, fish, fruit, horse, livestock, meat, milk, pigeon,or perishable train composed entirely of vehicles conforming to coaching stock requirements. -Express freight, livestock, perishable or ballast train, pipe fitted throughout with the automatic brake operative on not less than half of the vehicles. -Empty coaching stock train (not specially authorised to carry "A" headcode)	1 - 3 - 1 3 - 1 - 1 2 - 2 - 1
Class D	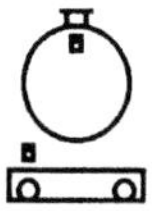	Express freight, livestock, perishable or ballast train, partly fitted, with the automatic brake operative on not less than one third of the vehicles.	5 consecutively
Class E		-Express freight, livestock, perishable or ballast train, partly fitted, with not less than four braked vehicles next to the engine and connected by the automatic brake pipe. -Express freight, livestock, perishable or ballast train, with a limited load of vehicles NOT fitted with the automatic brake.	1 - 2 - 2
Class F	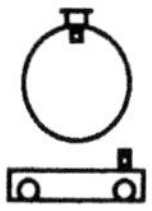	Express freight, livestock, perishable or ballast train, NOT fitted with the automatic brake.	3 - 2
Class G	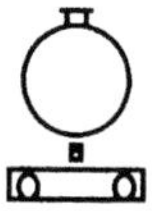	-Light engine or light engines coupled. -Engine with not more than two brake vans.	2 - 3 1 - 1 - 3
Class H	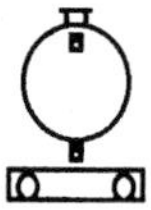	Through freight or ballast train, not running under class "C", "D", "E", or "F" headcode.	1 - 4
Class J	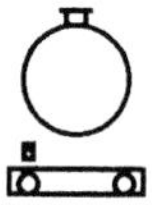	Mineral or empty wagon train.	4 - 1
Class K	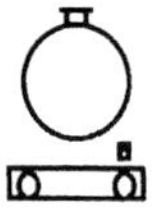	-Freight, mineral or ballast train, stopping at intermediate stations. -Branch freight train (Where authorised) -Freight, ballast or Officer's Special train, requiring to stop in section.	3 consecutively 1 - 2 2 - 2 - 3

Left Locomotive head lamp codes. The headcode for the Royal Train was four lamps on the front, and two red lamps on the rear.

Whistle codes

The signalman also had to listen for train whistles, for which again there was a code. A list of standard whistle codes is shown here, with special whistles for our part of the Great Central listed in Appendix 1.

Colour light and 'searchlight' signals

Multiple aspect colour light signals are now the accepted standard and have been installed during all resignalling projects since the 1960s, replacing the semaphore signal. As mentioned in the previous chapters, such resignalling began in 1939 on the LMS, and in the 1940s on the LNER. Therefore mention is made of them throughout this book.

Standard three- and four-aspect colour light signals contain separate lamps housed one above the other, each of which shows through a lens of appropriate colour according to the indication intended. There was a fear in some signalling departments that stray light from outside the signal might be reflected by the mirror behind the bulb through the coloured lens and hence give an incorrect indication. There are certain times of the day, early morning and late evening, when the rays of the sun shining directly into the lens can create this dangerous situation.

The LNER opted for 'searchlight'-type

STANDARD CODE OF ENGINE WHISTLES

The following code of engine whistles applies at all Stations, Junctions and Sidings not otherwise specially provided for in the list of Special Routing Whistles or the Local Code of Engine Whistles shown in the following tables.

In order to avoid annoyance to passengers at Stations and residents in the neighbourhood of the Railway, Drivers are requested not to make more frequent use of the engine whistles than is absolutely necessary to ensure safe and efficient working in compliance with the Rules and Regulations:—

Description	Whistles
Main or Fast lines	1 long.
Passenger Independent No. 1.	2 long.
Passenger Independent No. 2.	3 long.
Goods Independent No. 1.	2 long, 1 short.
Goods Independent No. 2.	2 long, 2 short.
Note—The above codes of whistles to be given when approaching signals at Danger or when necessary to indicate when ready to proceed on same line.	
Approaching Junction on Main Line and intending to proceed beyond the Junction:—	
If leading to the Left	1 long, 1 short
If leading to the right	1 long, 2 short.
To or from Passenger or Goods Independent or Loop and Main Line	5 short.
To cross from Main to Main	4 short.
Down Main, Passenger or Goods Independent or Loop to Down Sidings	1 crow.
Down Main, Passenger or Goods Independent or Loop to Up Sidings	2 short, pause, 3 short.
Up Main, Passenger or Goods Independent or Loop to Up Sidings ...	2 crows.
Up Main, Passenger or Goods Independent or Loop to Down Sidings	3 short, pause, 2 short.
Up Sidings to Down Sidings and *vice versa*	3 short, pause, 3 short.
To indicate whole of train is clear in Siding	1 short, 1 crow.
Train ready to leave Sidings	2 short, pause, 1 short.
Shunt from Sidings to Main Line	2 short, pause, 2 short.
Shunting movement in Shunting Yards or Sidings	1 short, pause, 1 short.
To or from Loco.	3 short.
Express Trains requiring a fresh engine at next stopping place or Depot	3 crows.
*Fire on Lineside	1 crow, 1 long, 1 crow.

* To be repeated when passing next Permanent Way men, Station, Signal Box, or Crossing Keeper's Hut.

Standard whistle codes

colour signals, which only had one light source and were introduced by the GCR in 1923 at Marylebone. The operating principle of the 'searchlight' signal is a mechanical device that has a roundel of coloured glasses between a plain-glass lens and the lamp, the roundel being moved by an electrical relay. Mirrors behind the bulb concentrate the light in the same way as in multiple-aspect signals, but the danger as described earlier is avoided, as the only indication to be seen will be the one selected. The mechanical roundel moved by the relay is designed to drop back to the red indication in the event of a fault or failure. A double-yellow indication by a 'searchlight' signal is achieved by providing an additional single lamp unit above the main head.

My favourite signal at Rugby Station was replaced by such a 'searchlight' signal (see the photograph on page 15).

Subsidiary signals

Subsidiary signals are miniature arms located below the main Stop arms. At night they show either a small white light or no light, according to the operating preferences of the railway employing them. A letter indicates the actual purpose of the signal when it is in the 'off' position, but has no significance when 'on'.

The **Calling On signal** (C) indicates, when 'off', that the line ahead is occupied by a train or vehicles, so the driver must proceed at caution only as far as the line is clear.

The **Shunt Ahead signal** (S) allows the Stop signal to be passed for shunting purposes only, usually to provide access to a siding ahead of the main signal.

The **Warning signal** (W) is used in conjunction with Regulation 5 when the line is clear only to the Home signal of the box ahead, and the mandatory clearance point beyond that signal (440 yards) is obstructed.

Shunting or Ground signals

These signals are located at ground level close to the points to which they refer. When 'off' they allow movement only as far as the line is clear. Shunting signals bearing a yellow arm or 'target' (disc), as opposed to the normal red, are provided where frequent access is required to sidings beyond the signal; it only needs to be cleared when exit to the main route is required.

Railwaymen refer to ground signals as 'dollies' or 'dummies', and they were essential items at points where they were used in conjunction with detectors to prove the lay of the points to which they applied.

Stacking of ground signals where there were several arms or discs placed one above the other was a guide to drivers to indicate which road was set for them. The uppermost signal indicated the line to the extreme left, and so on depending upon the number of routes involved. Examples of stacked ground signals can be found in the diagrams of the larger Rugby signal boxes.

A **Backing signal** is a shunting signal mounted on a post or gantry above the ground and facing the train. It is provided where it is impossible for the driver to see the 'dolly'

LNWR 'dummies' at Embsay in 1989, an example of stacking. The signals apply to the right-hand road: the top arm allows movement to the line on the extreme left, the middle one to the line on which the train is running, and the bottom one to the siding in front of the Midland signal box. *P. J. Wortley*

Two views of 'target' or disc Ground signals, the first indicating a diverging route. The lamp behind the lens can be seen, and the white plate, the 'back blinder', indicating the position of the target to the signalman in the signal box. The white diamond on the red bar indicates a track circuit. *P. J. Wortley*

concerned. One was installed at Rugby Station on the Down line.

Banner Repeater signals

A Banner repeater is provided to repeat the indication of a signal obstructed by line curvature or buildings. It is a black semaphore arm centrally pivoted within a circular glass-fronted case with a lamp behind. It is mounted on a signal post.

Slotted signals

When two signal boxes are situated close together, the Distant signal of the box in advance may be placed on the same post and underneath the Section signal of the box in rear. It is important that the Distant arm is prevented from showing a 'Clear' indication when the Stop arm above is at 'Stop'. An ingenious arrangement linking the balance weights of the two arms makes conflicting indications such as this impossible, and this system is known as 'slotting'.

On occasions an additional, or Outer, Distant provides an increased stopping distance for the box in advance, and this arm is controlled by a 'back slot'.

The Down line signals at Rugby provide an excellent example of this (see the diagram overleaf), with the Distant signals of Rugby Cattle Sidings, ③ and ④ , sharing the posts with Rugby Station Stop signals 33 and 32.

A Banner Repeater signal. *I. Mackenzie*

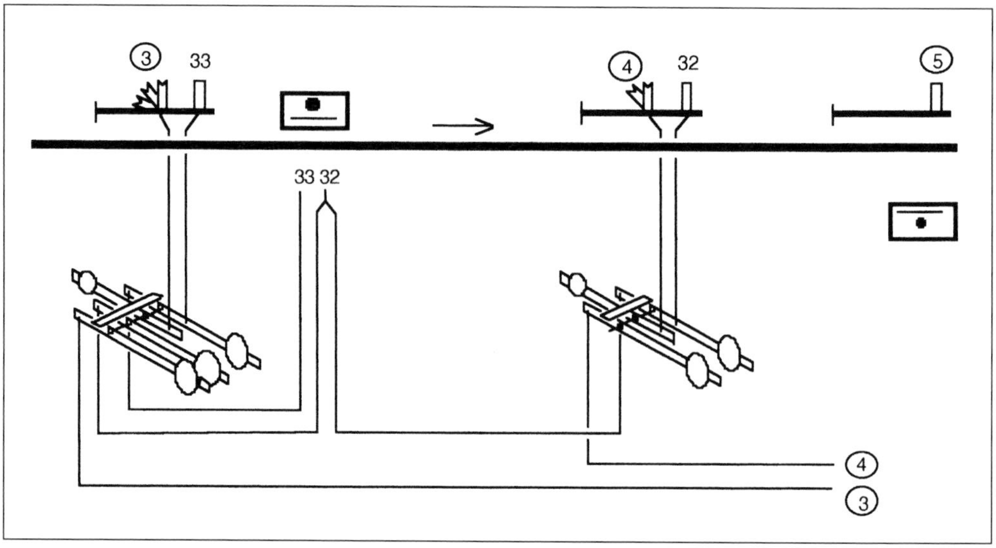

Schematic diagram to show the slot and back slot signals and their operation at Rugby. Note that the slotted signal is shown with two arms, and the back slot shows three arms. This notation will be seen on the diagrams where applicable.

Referring to the accompanying diagram, the Inner Home 33 has Outer Distant ③ below it, and the Starting signal 32 shares its post with Inner Distant ④ (note the method of identifying the two different box lever numbers). Here we are faced with an additional problem as the Cattle Sidings Outer Distant *must not* show 'Clear' when Starter 32 is at 'Stop', hence the need for the 'back slot'.

Approach-lit signals

In rural areas, where the supply of mains electricity presents a problem, colour light signals take their power from batteries. To avoid wasteful use of the battery power the signals were 'approach-lit' on the GC, the lamp illuminated only when required at the approach of a train by the use of Track Circuits.

Signal indication

Signals facing the signalman could be seen to change indication by the red or green lights at night, whereas signals with their backs to the box would have a 'back blinder'. A small white light at the back of the lamp housing

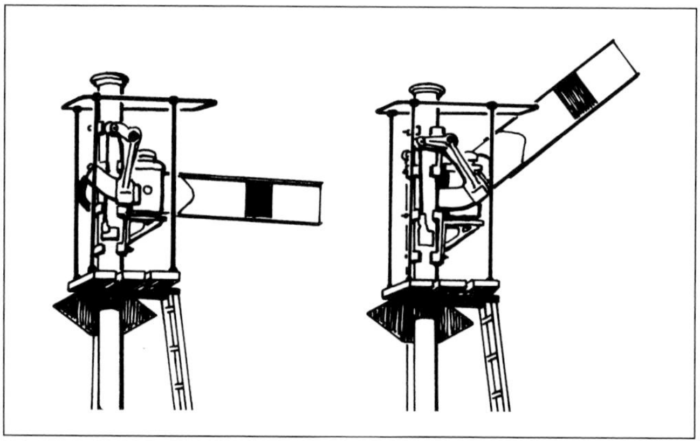

Operation of a back blinder. *PJW*

could be seen by the signalman at night when the signal arm was 'On' and also to show that the lamp was alight, but this would be obscured by the blinder when the signal arm was 'Off'. As we have seen earlier, Ground signals were similarly equipped.

Signal repeaters

Signal repeaters were provided when a signal could not be seen from the signal box, and showed 'ON', 'WRONG' or 'OFF'. Normally a signal arm would respond correctly to the operation of the lever, but hotter weather caused the wire to expand and the arm consequently to droop, when the repeater would show 'WRONG' and corrective action would need to be taken by using the appropriate signal wire adjuster.

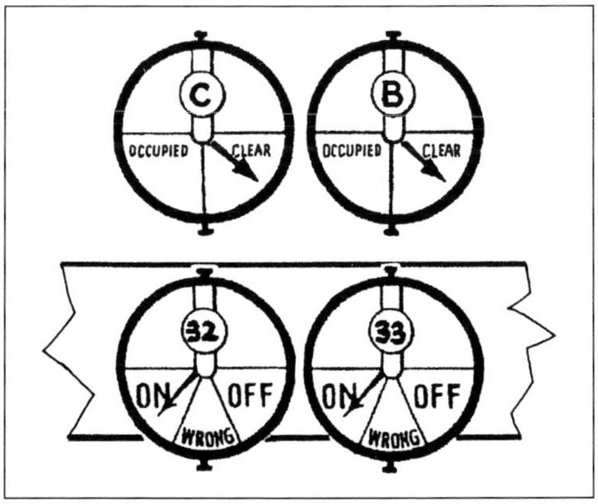

Indicators and repeaters: Track Circuit Indicators (above) and Signal Repeaters (below). These examples are as they appeared on the block shelf at Braunston & Willoughby (see Chapter 9). The drawing shows how the Track Circuit Indicators were positioned relative to the signals.

Track Circuit Indicators

Track Circuit Indicators were very similar to signal repeaters but were inscribed 'OCCUPIED' or 'CLEAR'. They were used in the majority of boxes when illuminated track diagrams were not installed. Also, most railways favoured letters for the identification of track circuits, 'A', 'B', 'C', etc. The LMS had a system of numbering, which is illustrated in the various track diagrams in this volume.

Signal wire adjusters

A drooping signal arm due to hot weather expanding the signal wire was corrected by use of the signal wire adjuster. A few turns on the appropriate adjuster would take the slack out of the wire and the problem was easily solved. Conversely, correction had to be reversed when the weather cooled and the wire became over-tightened; this would be made only too obvious when the lever was hard to pull.

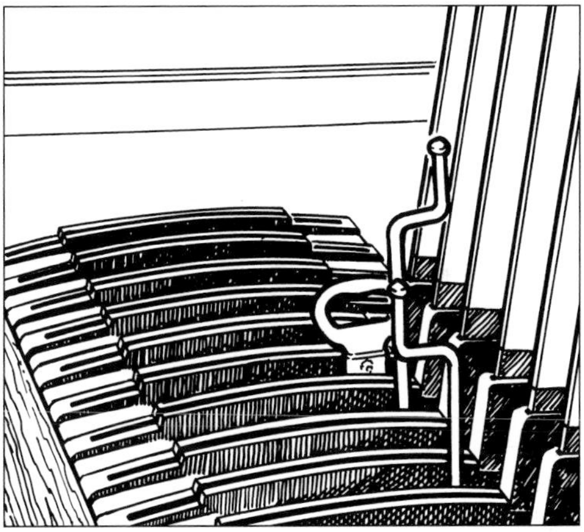

Two Stop signal wire adjusters are seen here, together with a detonator 'stirrup'. Distant signals had a much more substantial ratchet-type adjuster, or a cog-and-worm adjuster, with a removable handle situated behind, or close to, the appropriate lever.

Interlocking

Interlocking is a device that prevents conflicting moves being made. Mechanical interlocking is built into the lever frame and is usually housed in the space below the floor of the signal box. The same basic principles apply at all boxes from the very small to the enormous frames that could be found on British railways in the mechanical signalling age. Today's modern signalling relies upon electrical interlocking – the same basic principles, but operated by electrical apparatus.

Two or three examples and the Table of Interlocking at Braunston & Willoughby are described in Chapter 9.

There were different designs of interlocking mechanism. The tall signal boxes at Rugby Midland had a vertical interlocking frame

Above A rarely seen view of a signal box locking room. In the foreground can be seen the installation of electric controls and locks connected to the lever tails, while above are the mechanical interlocking trays on the lever frame beneath the floor joists, awaiting connection to the lever tails. *P. J. Wortley, courtesy of the Main Line Steam Trust*

Below A GWR tappet locking frame, shown by way of a comparison. *I. Mackenzie collection*

made up of many vertical bars and horizontal interlocking bars, hence their height. The Great Central used trays to contain the mechanism, as shown in the accompanying photographs.

Clearance Bars

As with many things, once commonplace items of railway equipment are rendered redundant and disappear from the scene as they fall victim to the march of progress. Clearance Bars and mechanical Facing Point Locks come into this category. They were once commonplace and of vital importance, although their function was not particularly obvious. Clearance Bars were as much a part of Facing Point apparatus as the Locking Plunger itself. The change came with the introduction of Track Circuits, the purpose of both being to prevent the points being 'unbolted', and so able to be moved, while a train or vehicle was in close proximity. The Track Circuit operates an electric lock on the lever concerned, while the Clearance Bar served the same purpose but was, as its name implies, mechanically operated.

The **Mechanical Clearance Bar** (MCB) was (usually) a 40-foot-long T-iron suspended by short levers that worked on cast iron clips fitted on the inside of the running rail immediately approaching a set of facing points. The length of 40 feet was, at the time, considered to be the longest distance between the wheels of any rolling-stock in use in this country. The top of the T-iron was positioned so as to lie just below the position where the flanges of the wheels would run. The Clearance Bar and the Facing Point Lock were both operated by the same lever.

As the bar was designed to move through an arc, raising it above the crown of the rail, before the point lock could be withdrawn, it *could not be moved* if a wheel was standing anywhere on the corresponding running rail. The illustration should make this clear.

Mechanical Clearance Bars were related to their facing point cousins but were installed at any location where it was essential that no conflicting move could be made when an obstruction was present. The situation at Woodford No 4 was an excellent example of

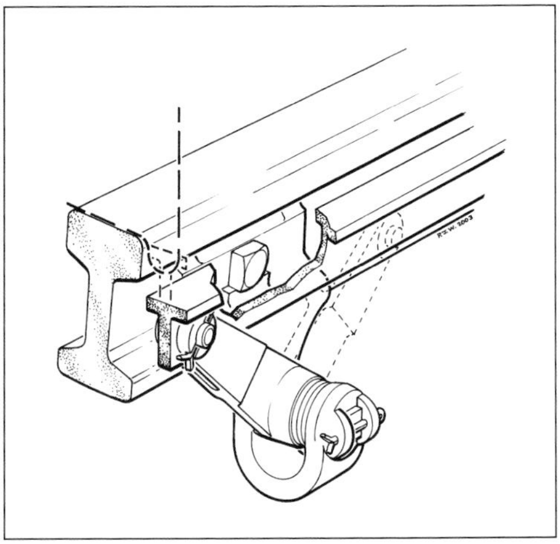

Above Operation of a Mechanical Clearance Bar. *PJW*

Below MCBs at Woodford No 4

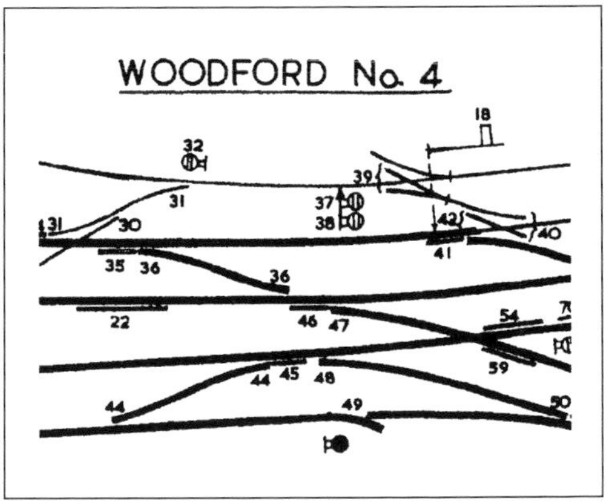

MCBs being used (22, 54 and 59 on the accompanying extract from the signal box diagram) before the introduction of Track Circuits caused their replacement in the fullness of time.

Electrical Clearance Bars were basically identical to MCBs, differing only in that they operated electrical contacts in much the same way as track circuits. They were employed mostly to prove clearances at the end of Reception Sidings in marshalling yards. ECBs were used in abundance in the yards at Woodford No 1 and No 2 ('R', 'Q', etc, on the accompanying extract from the diagram).

Facing Point Locks

Facing Points are those where a train is facing the diverging tracks (as opposed to 'trailing points' into a siding, for example, where the train has to reverse over them). Facing Point Locks have already been referred to, but the photograph overleaf may be of use to those too young to remember when everything was mechanically operated. Before electric operation using motors, switches and circuitry, mechanical means were employed to ensure the safety of a train moving over a Facing Point.

Detection

It is vital that points are proved to be 'fitting up', laying correctly before a move is made over them in the facing direction, ie when the vehicle *meets the blades first.* It is impossible to see the position of point blades from the signal

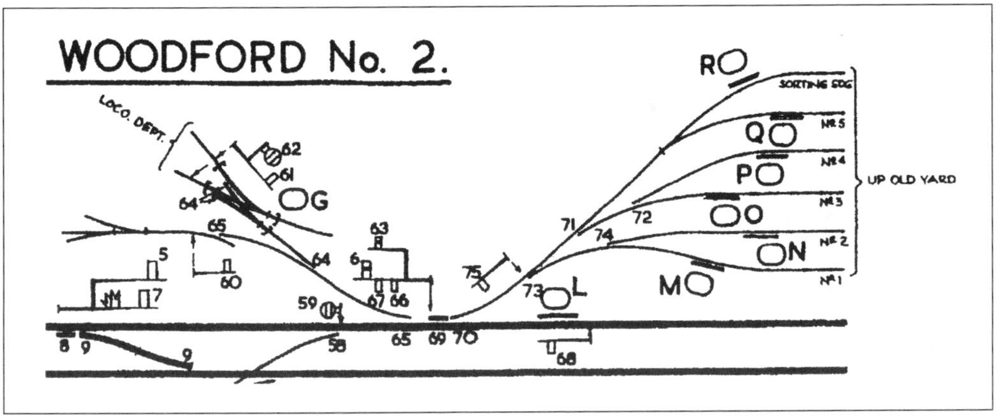

Electrical Clearance Bars at Woodford No 2

The Facing Point Lock can be clearly seen as the white box between the point blades. The Locking Plunger Bar within the box is operated by the linkage in the foreground and engages in one of two notches in the heavy Lock Stretcher Bar connecting the point blades, thus proving movement of the blades and locking them in either position. One of the notches can be seen to the right of the cover, and the nose of the Locking Plunger Bar can just be seen forward of the cover. The point operating rod can be seen to the right, while the three rods to the left are for the detector slides, one for each point blade and one to prove Lock Stretcher Bar engagement. The Clearance Bar is not shown, but would be behind the photographer. *I. Mackenzie*

box, and therefore a means of 'proving' the position of the blades after they have been operated is imperative. This can be done by either a mechanical detector or an electrical detector.

A mechanical detector consists of two slides, each with a notch in them. A slide is inserted in the wire run between the lever and the signal adjacent to and referring to the points. A similar slide, at right angles to the first, is attached to the tie bar of the points. Notches cut into the slides allow the signal to be cleared *only when the points are properly closed*, and the notches coincide, allowing a free pull on the signal lever.

Track Circuits

A Track Circuit is commonly employed to indicate to the signalman the presence of a train on a piece of track by operating a repeater or by illuminating a lamp on the signal box diagram. The track concerned must be insulated from the remainder of the rails and any operating mechanism such as at points, and Bond Wires must be fitted across all rail joints within the length to be track circuited to ensure electrical continuity. A low-voltage electrical current is then passed through one of the rails and, via a track relay, back through the other rail, completing the circuit. The metal wheels and axles of a train

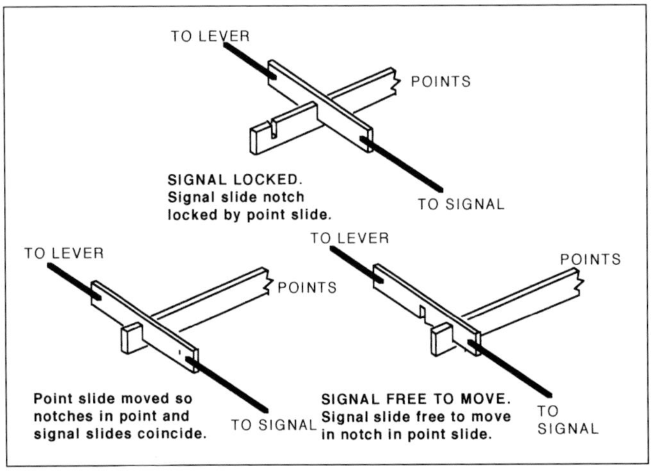

Mechanical detection

'short circuit' the current, de-energising the track relay and operating the repeater or lamp. The safe operation of the railway has always been important, and track circuits provide a way of maintaining that safety without the need for complex and expensive Mechanical Clearance Bars.

Flags and handlamps

Flags and a handlamp were provided for hand signalling as and when required. Red and green **signalling flags** were readily available close to the corner window of the signal box, and were normally used for communicating with 'outside personnel'. A yellow flag was also provided, but I cannot remember using it.

The paraffin **handlamp** was lit and kept alight during the hours of darkness ready for immediate use. It had three coloured glasses, red, yellow and green, and one clear. It was topped up with paraffin and the wick trimmed each morning. To be caught in an emergency in the dark without a lamp could be very serious, as an unfortunate signalman discovered when his negligence resulted in an accident that could have been avoided. He stood in the dock of the Criminal Court indicted as a result of his carelessness. The Prosecution offered evidence quoting the Rule Book's stipulation that 'a handlamp should always be lit after dark'. Council for the Defence countered with the assertion that 'daylight comes after dark'! This legal loophole caused all references in the Rule Book to 'after dark' to be revised to read 'after sunset'!

Detonators

Some signal boxes had levers as detonator placers. On the GC's London Extension 'stirrup' handles were more common, fitted between the quadrant plates of the frame adjacent to the Home signal lever and operating a detonator placer at the lineside (see the drawing on page 137).

The signalman also had detonators that could be placed by hand on the crown of the rail to give protection should it be needed; three would be placed 10 yards apart to the rear of an obstruction. They were flat discs, colour-coded and stored until used or time-expired. Usually there was an interlinked string of three on a nail by the door. The detonators in the lineside machines were replaced on the first Monday of each month at Braunston & Willoughby.

Above A detonator placer at the lineside, showing the prongs to which a detonator would be fitted, extended over the rail. *P. J. Wortley, courtesy of the Main Line Steam Trust*

Below A detonator clipped to the crown of the rail. *I. Mackenzie*

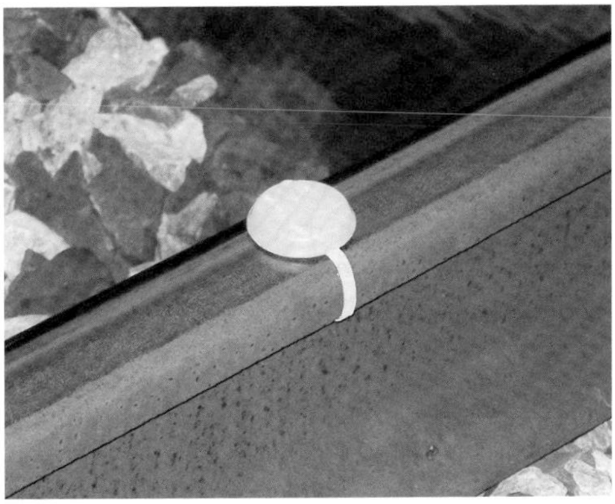

Tail lamps

It was the signalman's duty to visually check each train as it passed and ensure that all was in order and that the tail lamp was in place and alight. This all-important item was an indication that the train was complete. This may sound obvious, but it was not unknown for couplings to part, leaving a portion of the train somewhere on the line if the locomotive crew were unaware of the occurrence. Loose-coupled freight trains, those conveying goods vehicles with no direct brake control from the locomotive, carried two side lamps, one on each side of the guard's-van. These lamps also provided an indication to the crew of the engine, when they looked back, that the train was following intact.

Side lamps were fixed to the outside of the van, and were accessible from within by the guard. The red shades were removed from these lights and the tail lamps lifted off their brackets when the train was sidelined for more important traffic to pass; to have left them in place would have presented confusing signals to the driver of a train approaching on an adjoining line.

Paperwork

The Working Time Table gave the signalman the description of the trains and the times. This had to be adhered to, and was regularly renewed. Each week the Station Master would bring the 'orders' to the signalman; these included a timetable of Special Trains, and the Special Notices, which detailed any signal alterations, track work, single-line working or speed restrictions, etc, for the week to come.

Three books in the signal box had to be kept up to date as they were an integral part of the working of the box. Every piece of first aid equipment that was used had to be recorded in the **First Aid Book**, while the **Occurrence Book** was a record of minor happenings that were not included in the **Train Register Book**, which has already been covered with examples in Chapter 2.

Signal wires and point rods

It is worth mentioning the signal wires and point rods because they were once a prominent lineside feature. Without them the signalman could not operate any signals or points.

The signal wires are supported by pulleys attached to posts, as in the foreground. When a sharp change in direction is needed, the wire has a length of chain fitted, which runs around a pulley, often seen at the base of signals, for instance. The point rods are horizontal and are an inverted 'U' section running on rollers in 'A'-frames mounted on blocks at the edge of the ballast. The arrangement of links in the foreground is a compensator to allow for the expansion of the rods – once a common sight! *A. Franklin*

Index